COLT
MEMORABILIA
PRICE GUIDE

JOHN OGLE

All rights reserved. No portion of this publication may be reproduced or transmitted in any form or by any means, electronic or mechanical, including photocopy, recording, or any information storage and retrieval system, without permission in writing from the publisher, except by a reviewer who may quote brief passages in a critical article or review to be printed in a magazine or newspaper, or electronically transmitted on radio or television.

Published by

 **krause publications**

700 East State Street, Iola, WI 54990-0001

Please call or write for our free catalog. Our toll-free number to place an order or obtain a free catalog is 800-258-0929 or please use our regular business telephone 715-445-2214 for editorial comment and further information.

Library of Congress Catalog Number:
ISBN: 0-87341-514-0
Printed in the United States of America

The following are registered trademarks:

Boker	Colt Stones	National	Teleshot
Buck	Colt-ainer	NRA	Tobac-A-Dor
Camillus	Colt-ier	PaperMate	United Cutlery
Case	Coltrock	Parker	Wenger
Colt	Cross	Pilot	Zippo
Colt Jar	Forsome	Pipe-A-Dor	
	Hubley	Schrade	
	Jarette	Serv-Round	
	Kool-Pull	Some-Sette	

Dedicated to my father who gave me my first Colt.

TABLE OF CONTENTS

CHAPTER 1	INTRODUCTION	6
CHAPTER 2	THE EARLIEST ITEMS	11
CHAPTER 3	PLASTICS	20
CHAPTER 4	PATCHES	46
CHAPTER 5	DECALS	72
CHAPTER 6	BALL CAPS	83
CHAPTER 7	KNIVES	93
CHAPTER 8	BUCKLES	107
CHAPTER 9	JEWELRY	118
	LAPEL PINS	119
	PIN BACKS	139
	STICK PINS	140
	CUFF LINKS	140
	COLT INDUSTRIES	141
	TIE BARS	142
	BUTTONS	143
	BOLO TIES	145
CHAPTER 10	TIES	147
CHAPTER 11	KEY CHAINS	151
CHAPTER 12	BADGES	158
CHAPTER 13	BAGS	163
CHAPTER 14	SHOP SUPPLIES	168
CHAPTER 15	GLASSWARE	180
	COASTERS	181
	COFFEE MUGS	182
	BEER MUGS	187
	GLASSES	189
	PACIFIC INTERNATIONAL	195
	OTHER	196
CHAPTER 16	WATCHES & CLOCKS	198
CHAPTER 17	CARDS & DICE	203
CHAPTER 18	OFFICE SUPPLIES	207
	PENS & PENCILS	208
	POCKET PROTECTORS	212
	SAFETY AWARDS	213
	M16 RELATED	215
	OTHER ITEMS	218
CHAPTER 19	ASHTRAYS, LIGHTERS & ZIPPO	228
CHAPTER 20	STATUES	233
CHAPTER 21	TOYS	238
CHAPTER 22	BANNERS	246
CHAPTER 23	ARCHERY	249
CHAPTER 24	OTHER COLT COMPANIES	252

ACKNOWLEDGEMENTS

In the five years that I collected material and information for this book, I have met many fine individuals who contributed to its development. I had the privilege of personally meeting three grand gentlemen who worked for Colt and are responsible for preserving much of Colt's history —Johnny Hintlian, Ron Wagner and Marty Huber.

Mr. Johnnie Williams is also an important figure that I have yet to meet personally. Another one of the great gentlemen among the collectors of Colt is the late Keith Cocran who graciously shared his time and collections with me.

Albert Brichaux, Dan Chesiak, Bill Judd, John Kelley, Stan Newman, Mike Poulin and Tom Saady all allowed me to invade their homes and attics to photograph their collections. Tom Saady continued to supply me with photographs from his collection. Without their help this book would be much less than it is. Mr. Ron Lough and Norman Green carried parts of their collection to me, since I could never seem to get to them. Thanks. Dick Fraser, Will Johnson and Doc Palmer provided photographs of several items I could not obtain. Mr. Larry Genzel provided information on how to make patches. Mr. Dick Miranda contributed the information on pins and Mr. John Thomas explained how buckles are made. Mr. Donald Chiquet kindly furnished me with his research notes on knives. William Schmalz explained how the plastics were made. Dick Fraser reviewed a draft and provided the text on cartridges. Many of the items in this book were supplied by Mr. Jim Alaimo of NetMeg Sports. Mr. Ed Scott of Photos Your Way processed most of the film used in this book.

To the cadre of collectors who also helped either intentionally or not, I am grateful. Thanks to Dave Anderson, Wayne Becicka, Wallace Beinfeld, Charles Bentley, Bill Blankenship, Bob Bracken, Gurney Brown, Bob Cherry, Kevin Cherry, Ken Condre, Steve Corey, Lloyd Crede, Craig Clyburn, Al DeJohn, Chuck Durfee, Bill Dascher, Jackie Frascarelli, Gary French, Donald Foise, Norm Fladerman, Ed Faust, John Fischer, Herb Glass, Karen Green, John Guest, Sydna Guest, Bryson Gwinnell, Ted Hake, Robert Hanafee, Cherie Heard, William Hosley, Kathleen Hoyte, Bruce Johnson, Bob Kaminiski, Keith Mckenzie, Pat McKune, Gary Marino, Harry Mikolowski, Gerald MacNeish, Steve Messemer, Joe Miranda, Bob Morrison, Kimberly Murphy, Don Mitchell, Tom Motter, Wally Neys, Steve and Vicki Otto (the first Colt collectors I met), K.C. Owens, Mrs. George Opalenik, Les and Jan Quick, Al Poulson, Beverly Rhodes, C.J. Ruda, Michael Reissig, Ed Romanik, George Ryan, David Ridley, Debbie Randorff, Rob Roy, Lewis Sharp, Lynn Shea, Linda Schaff, Doug Sheldon, Ken Snider, Fred Sweeney, Karl Tunestan, John Thomas, Michael Warford, Richard Welch, Ron Whitaker, Don and Carol Wilkerson and R.L.Wilson.

Thanks to Krause for agreeing to put my passion to print, especially Ned Schwing who led me through the early phases and Tracy Schubert who put it all together.

I would like to thank the Colt Manufacturing Company for providing such a rich history—the legend lives on.

And lastly, I would like to state that this book was accomplished in spite of the almost constant ridicule and harassment by Casey Nicholson and Kathy Beaugez.

Chapter 1

INTRODUCTION

There are two types of people in the world, collectors and non-collectors. Collectors are of four basic types, investment, decorating, sentimental and serious. During inflationary times, investing in collectibles is often recommended as a hedge for one's money. However, collecting things and hoping they will increase in value is a risky business.

Those items one saves up as a momento of some occasion or place comprise a sentimental collection. Whether stored in a shoe box or a scrap book, that group of dissimilar items are in fact a collection. The rock picked up at the border of every state visited on a road trip is part of a sentimental collection. The rocks used for road fill probably do not originate from that site, and most likely have no geological value, but they are collected as a treasure.

More common, and often overlooked, are those similar items purchased for decorative purposes. In most cases, two similar items are a collection. Some people may decorate utilizing a unified style or theme. The bathroom accented with frogs, the kitchen having matching mushroom accessories, the herd of elephants or pride of cats in the living room or the owls watching over the bedroom are all collections.

Then there are serious collectors who may be either casual or complete collectors. Casual collectors simply pick up collectibles as they find them in the pursuit of their normal lives. Complete collectors must acquire a complete collection for their mental well-being. They are relentless in their pursuit of every last known item, no matter how useless, senseless or mundane that collectible may be. Complete collectors must categorize and list the items so they know when their collection is whole.

Anything is collectible. Glancing through a recent collectible magazine reveals collectors of everything from paper clips to canning labels. For the serious collector, rarity is prized but so is affordability. As few collectibles fit this description, most complete collectors have to specialize. This is certainly the case for Colt collectors.

Whether collecting Colt firearms or Colt memorabilia, the amount of material produced by the six separate companies over the past 160 years is almost impossible to collect in its entirety. However, that is one reason many feel compelled to try.

A second reason of the high collectibility of Colt is the historical significance of the man and his company. The Colt Peacemaker revolver has been well romanticized in this country's history. Lesser known, but of more importance, is the role of Sam Colt and his company in the nation's industrialization.

The concepts of interchangeable parts, mass production, vertical integration and diversification can all be attributed to Sam Colt in some degree. Sam Colt worked in conjunction with the likes of Eli Whitney and Samuel Morse. The Colt factory served as a technical school for machinists and engineers such as Charles Billings, Amos Whitney, Francis Pratt, Christopher Spencer, William Gleason and E.P. Bullard. In addition, a number of companies operated within the Colt factory producing adding machines, dishwashers, steam engines and sewing machines. Finally the recent hysteria over firearms and the specter of gun control has made anything with a Colt on it highly collectible.

Colt collectibles can be divided into the three broad categories of guns, paper and memorabilia. Colt memorabilia can be divided into the major categories of personal, internal, publicly distributed and commercialized. Those items owned by Sam Colt and his family comprise a collection of exclusive and singular items residing in the Wadsworth Atheneum of Hartford, and a small number of private collections. The catalog for the recent exhibition (September 8, 1996 to March 9, 1997) for Sam and Elizabeth Colt, at the Wadsworth Atheneum in Hartford, provides an excellent guide to those items.

Colt is a company that makes guns for a business. The paperwork and tools involved in making those guns, running a business and dealing with thousands of employees are ancillary to the making of guns. Documenting and saving those tools and that paperwork has not been a concern for the people at Colt. This makes those internal Colt items all the more collectible.

The most common, and therefore most collected, are the items that were publicly distributed in support of the selling of guns. Catalogs, price lists, promotional gifts and advertising items were produced at the Colt factory to be distributed to as many people as possible. Some people saved them. As people started saving the promotional items, Colt, like many other companies started merchandising items solely as collectibles of the company. Interestingly, the catalogs, price sheets and advertising publicly distributed to promote the sale of the collectibles are in themselves becoming collectible.

Excluding the personal possessions of Sam Colt, the first mass produced and publicly distributed collectible given away by Colt may have been a lapel pin. A lapel pin reportedly reproduced in the 1940s or 1950s is labeled on the back as having been given out as a gift from Sam Colt at the Crystal Palace Exposition in London during May 1851. An original has not been examined, but if the copy is a faithful reproduction, the original would be the first known Colt collectible. This pin might also be the first fantasy Colt collectible.

Company logo items that are the fantasy of some individual and have no association with the original company are known as fantasy items. The first authenticated collectable is a button. R.L. Wilson (The Rampant Colt, 1969, fig.30 page 27) reports that Steele and Johnson made buttons for the coachman serving Sam Colt in 1856. Other early items are as follows. A pin from the Colt bicycle club is dated from 1891. A Colt pin back exists from approximately 1910 (Hake and King, 1986, fig. 369-2-F, page 187). Sam Colt's 100th birthday was celebrated by the company with a medallion in 1914. The medallion was issued in gold, silver and bronze.

A Rampant Colt charm once owned by Arthur Ulrich is thought to date from the 1930s. The first pin sold by Colt was manufactured by the Robbins Co. (Attleboro, Mass.) in 1938. It represented the .45 automatic pistol. The first known emblem patch was probably distributed sometime during the 1930s. A cigar cutter and half a cuff link are also known from this period. Also company ID badges are known from World War II. A number of items including a patch, bolo ties and pins were offered for sale in a 1962 company publication (Colt Promotional Aids and Free Mat Service for Registered Dealers). The first publicly distributed catalog of accessory items was published in 1968.

The majority of Colt memorabilia on the market today is modern (post-WWII) with a couple of exceptions. In 1925, the company of Conner and Lattin was acquired by Colt and operated as the plastics division. A number of plastic wares were produced by that division until it was sold in 1955. The bakelite items are known of as ColtRock, while the urea formaldehyde based plastics are known simply as plastics. These items are among the most highly valued by Colt collectors. Some interest is also shown for some of the items manufactured by the electrical division or the Autosan commercial dishwasher division of Colt.

With the exception of the above mentioned memorabilia, there are very few early collectibles—especially prewar. Occasionally an item is found that was awarded to an individual for some special occasion. Such awards included guns, service pins, war bonds, TV sets and bicycles. Personal memorabilia was usually fabricated by placing an engraved plaque on some ordinary items such as a radio or clock. It is therefore, my current opinion that the lack of early memorabilia is due not to the loss of those items, but instead to a lack of manufacture. This is fortunate for today's collectors because it means that most of the Colt memorabilia is recent and therefore, still available.

Until recently, Colt was reluctant to put its name on merchandise. A concern over public perception of tee shirts or ball caps worn under circumstances that Colt could not control had prevented them from allowing such use of its logo. The first major use of logoed and distributed merchandise was the 1982 Colt Family Day open house.

However, in 1986 Colt put its name and logo on everything to celebrate the 150th anniversary of the Company. Logo merchandise has been used since 1986 as awards and gifts for employees, customers and friends of Colt. Safety awards, Family Day, management club, sales awards and show gifts account for the bulk of the internal Colt logoed merchandise.

However, any division of Colt that operated profitably could order logoed items for its employees or friends. Many of the fulfillment houses producing logoed merchandise on order would also produce samples or prototypes which were left at the factory. These very limited prototypes are finding their way onto the collectible market today. Those same companies can still manufacture the same items.

Collectors should be cautious and deal with reputable dealers. Unless an item is purchased from a dealer who can trace its ownership to the Colt factory or an ex-employee, it would be almost impossible to validate the authenticity of any item. Colt has in recent years aggressively attempted to curtail unauthorized use of its logo on what are called fantasy items. Unauthorized reproduction of original items is harder to control, especially if the same companies are making both items. In some cases it may be possible to distinguish the reproduction by comparison with a known original. For that reason, many non-factory released items are included here. Such items are labeled as non-factory. In addition, items of unknown origin are included and so labeled. If the value of an item is high enough it will be counterfeited or reproduced. In any case, the collector is urged to heed Sam Colt's own words of advice and "beware of counterfeits and patent infringements."

The most reliable source of memorabilia is, of course, the Colt company. They publish a yearly catalog of accessories in their Wears Catalog. These items are reasonably priced and readily available. Once items are discontinued by the company the price increases and they become scarce.

The second best source is probably the annual meeting and trade show of the Colt Collectors Association. They meet during the first weekend of October in a different city every year. There are over 2,000 members, and the membership list provides a wealth of sources of collectors and dealers. The association's secretary, Karen Green, may be reached at (408) 353-COLT.

Other sources are dealers, trade journals and auctions. Nutmeg Sports (Suite 145, 1131-0 Tolland Tnpk., Manchester, CT 06040) is the largest company dealing exclusively in Colt collectibles. The publication *Gun List*, available in many bookstores and by subscription from the publisher (Krause Publications) is another source of quality and usually authentic Colt memorabilia. Many of the collectors and dealers who publish periodic lists of items for sale can be found in *Gun List*.

Catalogs and auctions from cross collectible companies will occasionally yield a Colt treasure. For example, Hake's Americana and Collectibles (P.O. Box 1444, York, PA 17405), which publishes five auction catalogs yearly, has rewarded the author with several lapel pins and the Hubley Colt cap pistol. Less fruitful and reliable are local gun shows and gun stores. However, there is always a story about the box of treasures having been given away at a show or store that keeps us attending. It also gives us something to do between Colt shows.

Portrayed in this pictorial for your perusal and pleasure are some of those collectibles of the Colt companies and no, I don't own them all — yet. Represented are photographs from a number of collections. However, this is not the final word. Previously unknown items are constantly coming to light and additional items are currently being produced by Colt.

This volume should be considered just a beginning, since additions and corrections are welcomed. All photographs of items from outside collections are identified. In a few cases photographs were provided, which are also identified. I am grateful to those collectors who have loaned me items or allowed me to come into their homes and photograph their collections. I am even more grateful for the time many current and ex-Colt employees have shared with me providing information about Colt company collectibles.

A note about pricing, I didn't want to do it, the editor made me. All Colt memorabilia is overpriced. This was explained to me by an eight-year old. She grabbed up a Colt M16 marked calculator and to my horror started punching the buttons. Dismayed that it didn't work, she discovered the price tag and exclaimed "What you paid forty bucks for this piece of junk?" Well, yes, I did. Companies have their logo put on merchandise as inexpensively as possible in order to allow them to give it away or make a profit selling it. Lapel pins can be made with a company logo for less than a dollar. The pins given away at Shot Show by Colt will sell for as much as $30. Coffee mugs can be made for as little as $2 and will sell for as much as $100. Patches manufactured for as little as 30 cents will sell for as much as $250.

Over time, some items such as plastics have risen dramatically while others are just starting to appreciate. Prices listed here should be considered to be retail. In most cases, they represent what I paid for the item. Now everyone knows. In cases where a range is given, that range represents the lowest and highest price I know an item has sold for. Prices from dealers' lists and auctions were used when possible. In the rest of the cases I estimated the prices. In cases where an item has not been sold to establish a price, it is labeled as $NEP (no established price). *For questions about items contained in this book contact the author at the following address:* **John Ogle - P.O. Box 252, Ocean Springs, MS 39566**

Mr. Ron Wagner was born in 1904. He worked at Colt from 1918 until 1972. He was the Colt factory's historian from 1957 until 1972. He is still active in researching Colt history today.

Mr. Johnny Hintlian was born in 1911. He worked at Colt from 1929 until 1949. The persistence of Mr. Hintlian in pursuing and collecting Colt memorabilia over the past sixty years is largely responsible for the preservation of what we have and know today. Currently, he is still buying and selling memorabilia.

Mr. Marty Huber was born in 1913. He worked at Colt from 1936 until 1993. He was the Colt factory's historian from 1973 until 1993. Today he actively attends gun shows.

Chapter 2
THE EARLIEST ITEMS

Early collectibles of the Colt companies are rare. Sam Colt attended any and all of the trade shows of his time, where he was known to freely give his business card, brandy and cigars to anyone he thought would be of help to his business. Sam Colt also gave away a number of guns as samples or presentations.

Excluding guns and paper leaves little for the modern memorabilia collector. Therefore, collectors aspired to obtain memorabilia from the associated companies of Colt. The associated companies and their collectibles are of four basic types, non-gun companies owned by Sam Colt, independent companies who contracted with Colt to manufacture their products in the Colt factory, groups loosely or directly associated with the Colt factory and independent companies that happen to have the name Colt.

Other companies that Sam Colt started during his lifetime include The New York and Offing Electro-Magnetic Telegraph Company, The Submarine Battery Company, Colt's Willow Ware Manufacturing Company and Colt's Cartridge Works.

Colt encouraged his workmen to participate in leisure activities. He built the Charter Oak Hall and supported the formation of such groups as the Armory Band, The Armory Guard, Armory Glee Club, Armory Dramatic Association, South Meadows Division Sons of Temperance, a baseball team and a shooting club. Memorabilia from these groups is also prized by collectors of Colt.

A number of independent companies contracted with the Colt Patent Firearms Manufacturing Company to manufacture their products. The Colt factory contained the most modern manufacturing equipment of the time, some of it developed and patented by Colt machinists. The Colt factory also contained a highly trained manufacturing work force. The Colt factory was contracted to manufacture such things as sewing machines (Colt's Armory Sewing Machine Company, Morrison, Charter Oak and Wardwell), lawn mowers (Archimedean and Charter Oak), steam engines (Baxter and Colt's Disc), adding machines (Federal), printing presses (Colt Armory, Universal and John Thomson Press) and punches (Railway Alarm Registry Punch). These items are rarely found today, so most collectors attempt to gather a representative sample of the paper associated with those companies.

The fourth group of associated companies, those that are Colt in name only, are dealt with in another chapter. It is generally agreed that the early collectibles' scarcity is due to a production shortage of giveaway items rather than simple misplacement. Paper collectibles are the exception to that assertion.

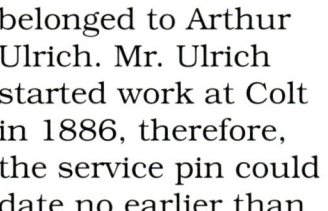

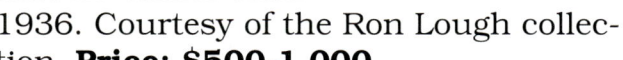

According to R.L. Wilson's book, *The Rampant Colt*, this button was made for the coat of Sam Colt's coachman in 1856. Courtesy of the Ron Lough collection. **Price: $1,000-1,500**

The rampant Colt pendent and fifty year service pendent are documented as having belonged to Arthur Ulrich. Mr. Ulrich started work at Colt in 1886, therefore, the service pin could date no earlier than 1936. Courtesy of the Ron Lough collection. **Price: $500-1,000**

The Colt bicycle club was organized with 30 members in 1890 and operated until 1897. This charm is dated from 1891. Courtesy of the Ron Lough collection. **Price: $1,000**

The watch fob celebrates the organization of the National Association of Power in 1882. However, it also celebrates Colt's ownership of Vulcabeston. Colt acquired the Vulcabeston product line with its acquisition of John's Pratt Company in 1923. This watch fob would therefore date from after 1923 and could not be 1882. Courtesy of the Wayne Becicka collection. **Price: $500**

This pin purported to have been given out at the Crystal Palace Exposition in London in 1851, is most likely a fantasy item made sometime in the 1940s or 1950s. **Price: $5-20**

The first mass produced item given out by Colt may have been this pin loosely dated by Ted Hake as from 1910. Photo Courtesy of Hake's Americana, York, PA.
Price: $800-1,200

The first authenticated collectible mass produced for distribution by the company was a medallion made to honor the 100th birthday of Sam Colt in 1914. Courtesy of the Dan Chesiak collection.
Price: $400-1,000

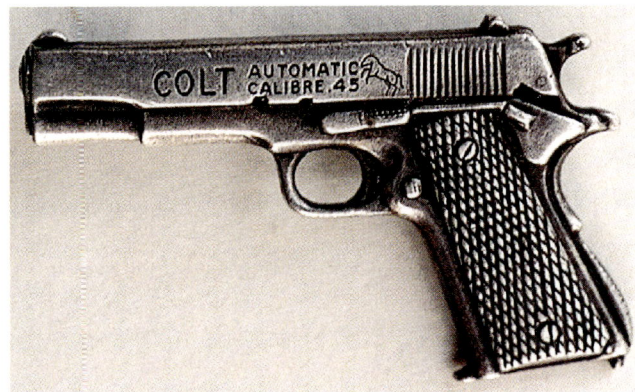

The best documented item that was sold by Colt is a pin made in 1938 by the Robbins Company. The pin sold for 25 cents. **Price: $50-70**

Sam Colt had a dozen lithophanes with his image made during the last visit to Europe. They were found in his safe when the company was sold in 1902. Colt used lithophanes freely throughout his home for decoration. Lithophanes were first made in 1827. A negative wax carving is used to make a positive plaster cast which in turn is used to make a negative porcelain copy. The porcelain copy is fired to produce the finished lithophane. When the lithophane is held up to a light a positive image is produced. Courtesy of the Tom Saady collection.
Price: $3,500-5,000

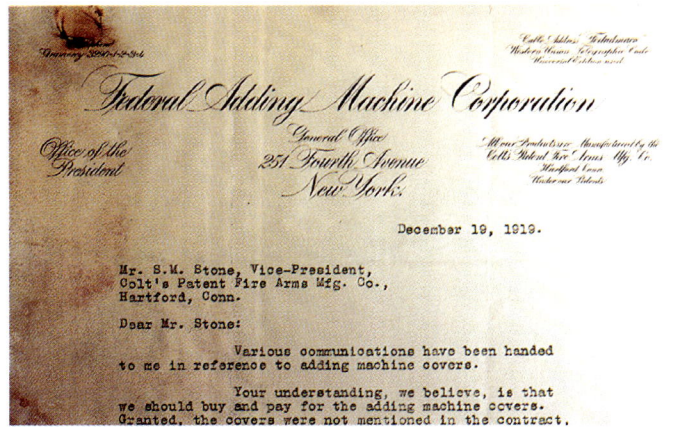

Price: $75-150

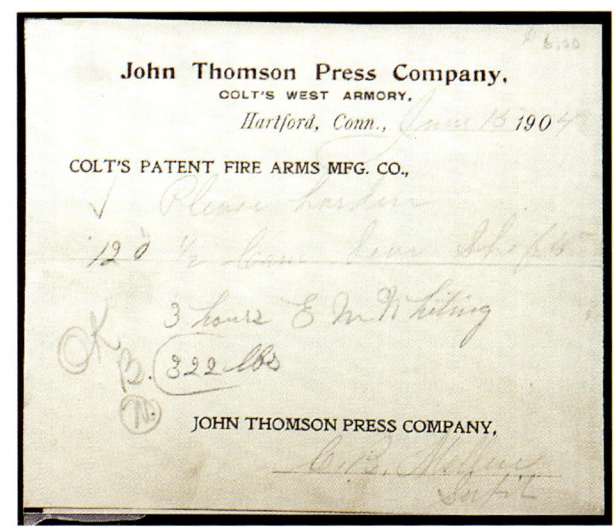

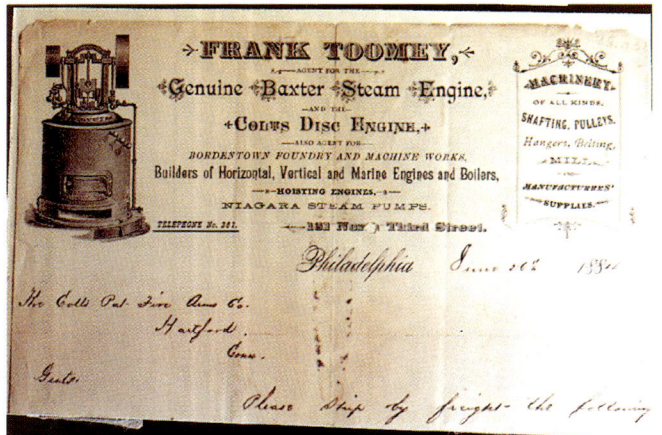

Price: $100-200

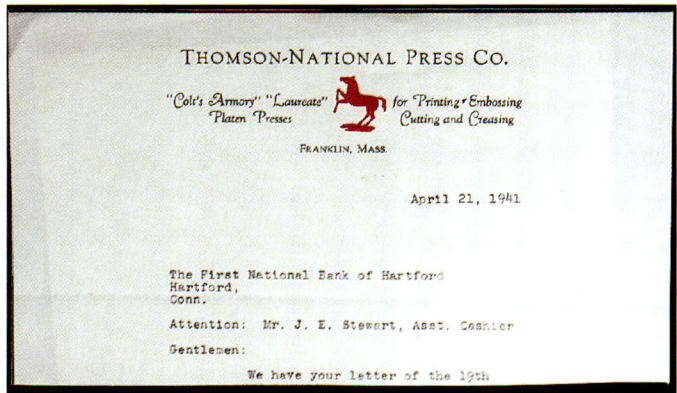

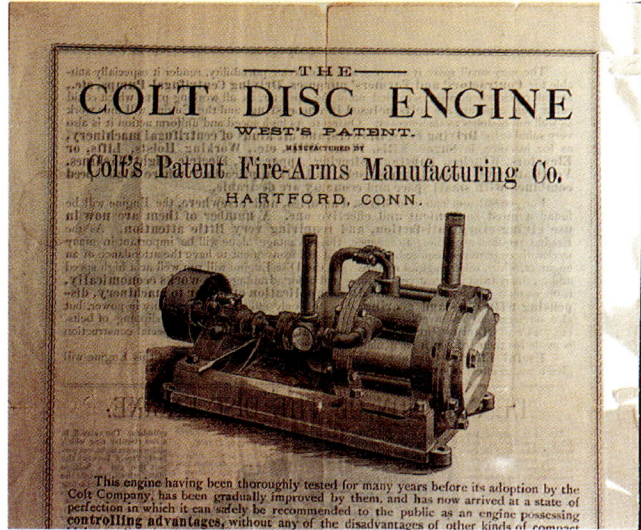

 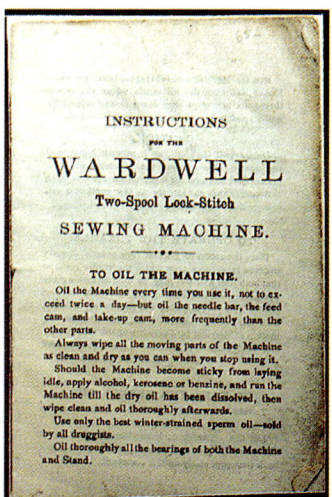

Prices for the five items above: $50-100

Price: $100-200

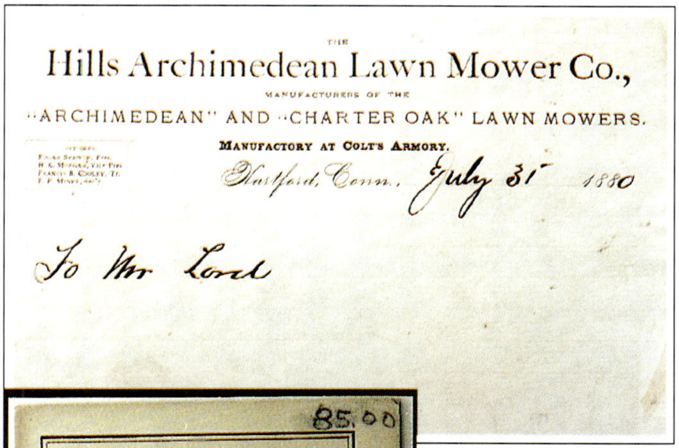

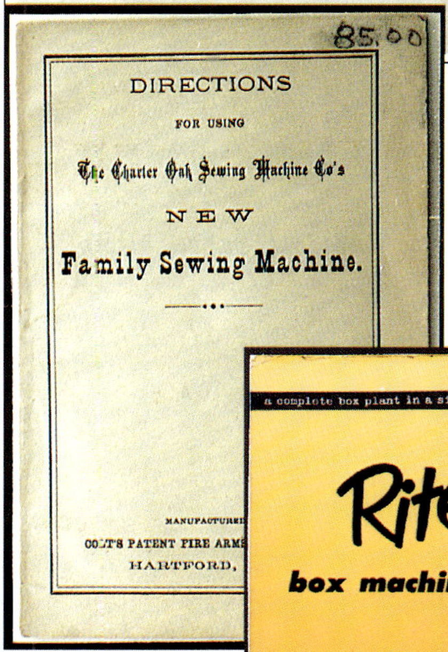

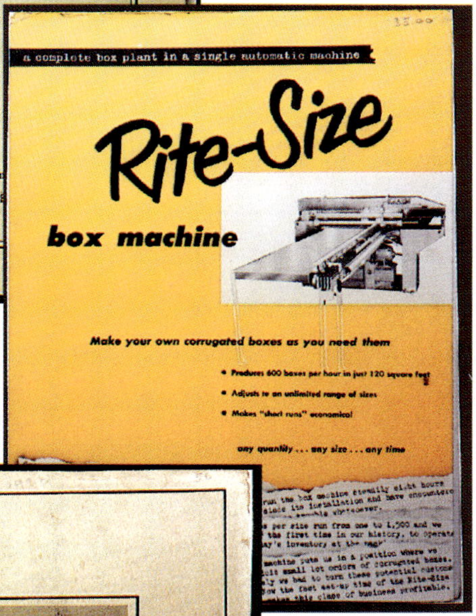

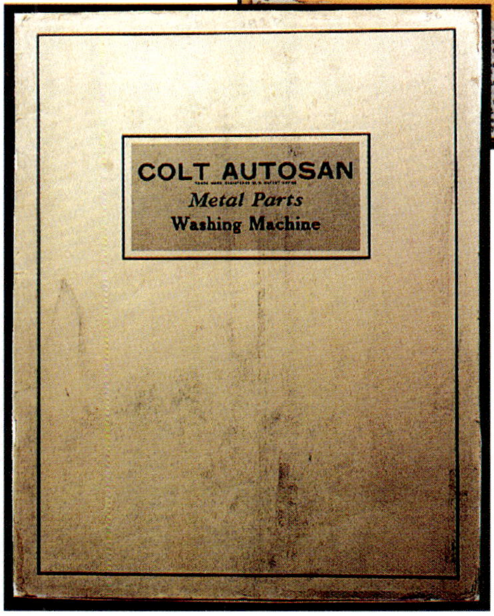

Price: $75-150

The Colt factory provided equipment and a trained work force that other companies used to manufacture their products at the turn of the century. Letterheads and manuals indicate that steam engines, lawn mowers, printing presses and sewing machines were manufactured by the Colt Manufacturing Company. In the 1920s, Colt diversified by buying companies making dishwashers, electrical products and plastics. The collection of letterheads and manuals pictured on these two pages are courtesy of the Tom Saady collection.

Prices for the four pictures above: $100-250

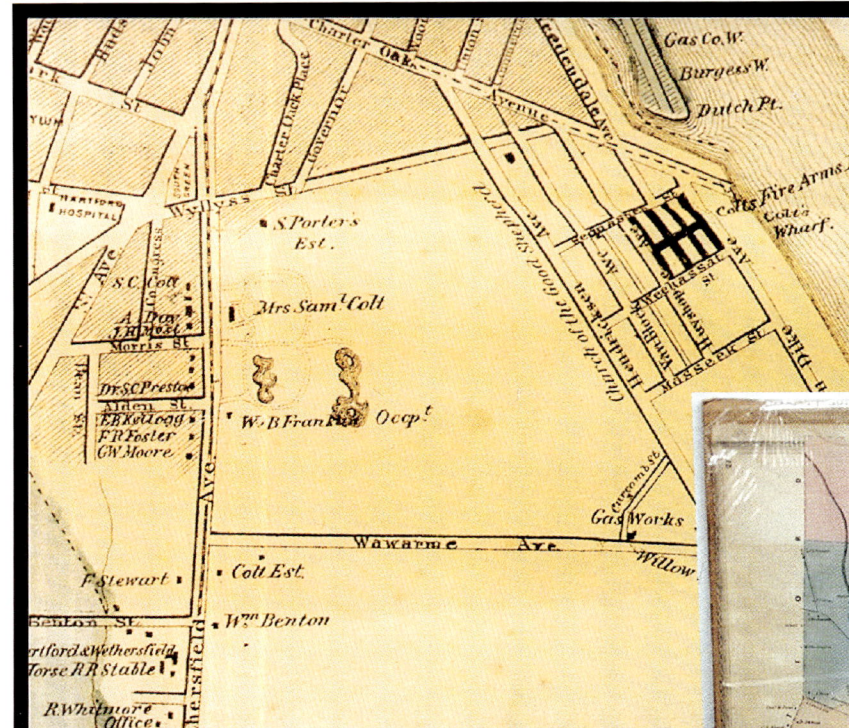

Few collectibles from the Colt Wicker Ware Manufacturing Company exist, so even a map labeling the company is prized. The company was established by Sam Colt in 1860 to utilize the willow cuttings from trees planted to protect the dike. **Price: $100-350**

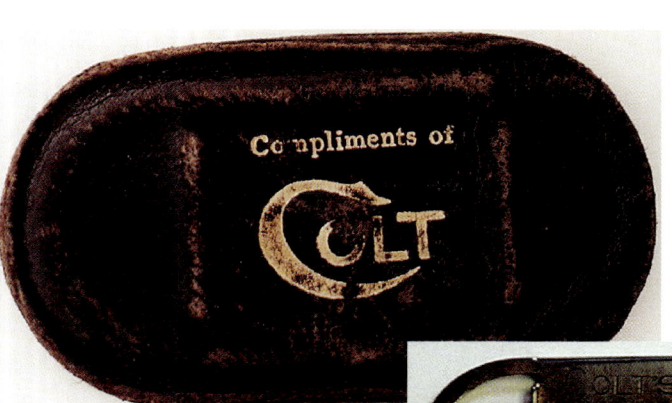

This cigar cutter is often incorrectly considered to be the first piece of memorabilia. The patent for the company making them is dated 1915, so this item would have to date from some time after that. Courtesy of the Mike Poulin collection.
Price: $150-250

Colt made adding machines for Federal from 1919 to 1922. Courtesy of the Norman Green collection. **Price: $2,500**

Calling card used by Sam Colt while he was at the New York University from 1841 to 1846. Courtesy of the Tom Saady collection. **Price: $800-2,000**

The standard style card used by Sam Colt throughout most of his gunmaking career. Courtesy of the Tom Saady collection. **Price: $1,000-1,500**

The logo on this wallet was used on literature given out to police officers from 1904 until the 1920's. The date of the wallet is unknown. **Price: $350-800**

COLLECTOR'S NOTE: Sam Colt freely gave his calling card to anyone he thought would be of help to his business. Although considered a paper collectible, they would be the first publicly distributed memorabilia. There are three known variations.

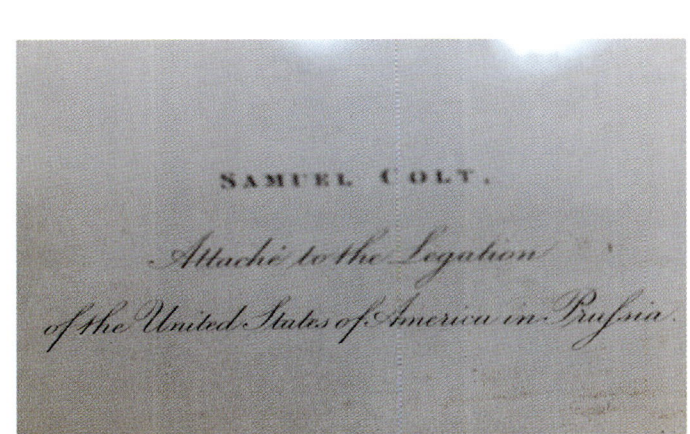

Sam Colt used this card when he attended the coronation of Czar Alexander II as an attaché to the U.S. delegation in 1856. Courtesy of the Tom Saady collection. **Price: $1,500-2,500**

This is a cover for the Colt's Armory Sewing Machine. The company organized May 15, 1872, and reorganized June 26, 1873, as the Charter Oak Sewing Machine Company. This decorative cover is thought to have been included in the Colt company exhibit at the 1873 Vienna International Exhibition. Courtesy of the Tom Saady collection and photo, information from the Butterfield and Butterfield auction catalog sale number 64-88, A-56 page 80. **Price: $6,500-10,000**

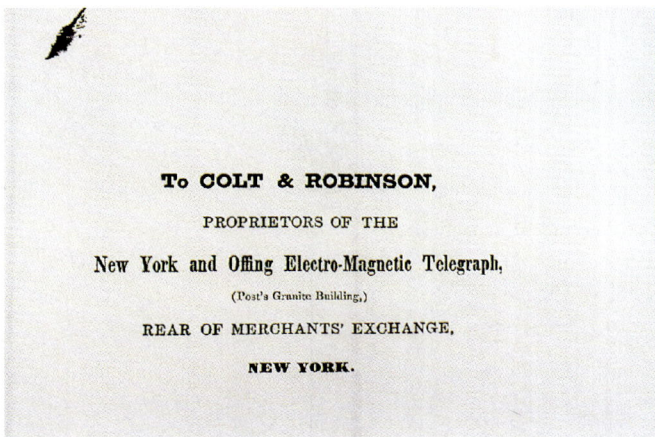

Sam Colt met Samuel Morse at the New York University and secured a franchise for Morse's telegraph. With William Robinson as a partner, Sam Colt incorporated the New York and Offing Magnetic Telegraph Association in 1846 and began selling shares and subscriptions. Few collectibles from this company of Sam Colt are known. Courtesy of the Tom Saady collection. **Price: $300-900**

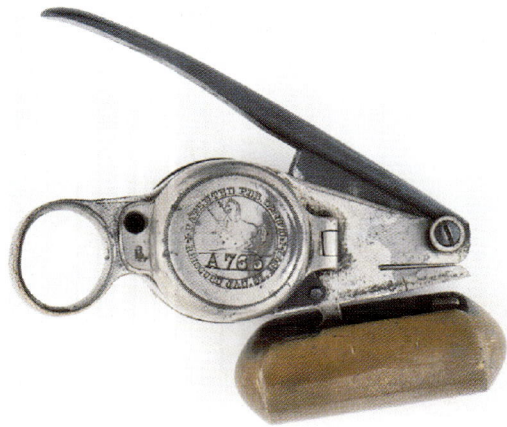

A railroad ticket punch known as a Railway Alarm Registry Punch was manufactured at the Colt factory for the A.W. Richmond Company during the 1870's. From the Wallace Beinfeld collection. **Price: $NEP**

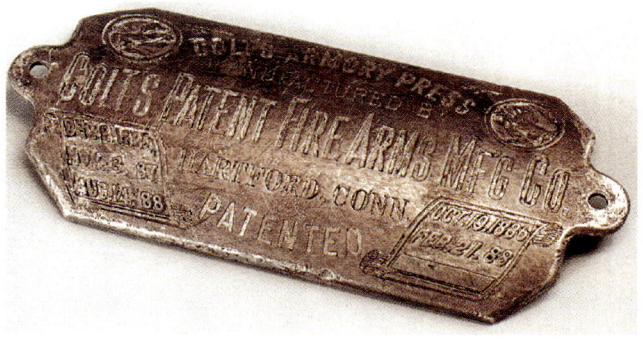

A plate from a printing press made by Colt. Courtesy of the Ron Lough collection. **Price: $150-250**

A keychain made for one of Colt's major distributors based on a design patented in 1875. Courtesy of the Ron Lough collection. **Price: $150-250**

A triple ribbon commemorating the unveiling of the Buckingham statue at Hartford on June 18, 1884. The connection of the Horse Guards and Colt for the event is unclear. Courtesy of the Tom Saady collection. **Price: $1,000-2,000**

A metal valve cover from the original Colt factory reportedly dating from prior to the fire of 1864. Courtesy of the Tom Saady collection.
Price: $1,000-1,500

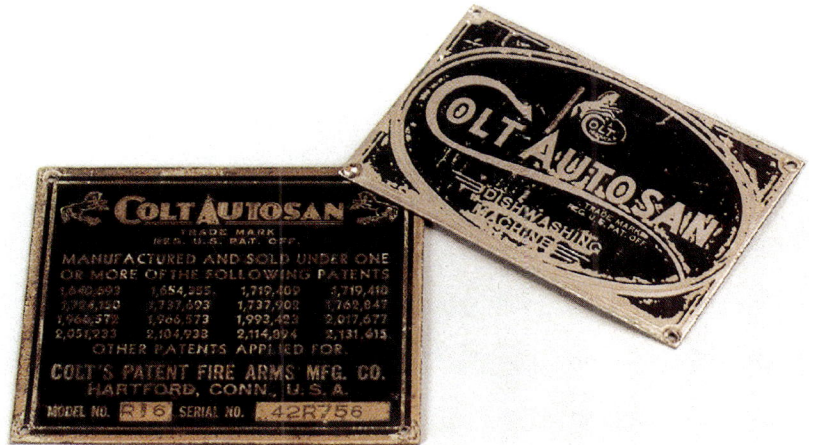

Colt manufactured the Autosan brand of commercial dishwashers into the 1950's. Courtesy of the Ron Lough collection. **Price: $100-150**

Chapter 3

PLASTICS

Colt went into the plastics business in 1920, with the acquisition of Conner and Lattin of Newark. Benjamin F. Conner would continue at Colt, eventually serving as president, from 1949 until 1955. The plastics products produced under the Colt logo are some of the most coveted Colt memorabilia today. The two basic types of products of the plastics division were ColtRock and Plastics. Early plastics were produced from a "phenol formaldehyde compound." The Colt president of the day, Samuel M. Stone, decided to call this material "ColtRock." The material also known as Bakelite, reportedly contained a percentage of asbestos and was used to manufacture heat resistent items such as smoking and electrical accessories.

Colt ceased production of ColtRock in 1935. A "synthetic resin composition" which replaced ColtRock was produced until the division was sold in 1955. This material which consisted of urea formaldehyde was called "Urea" by Colt. Today's collectors know it simply as plastic. The most common items made of Colt plastic and marked with the Colt logo are eyewash cups and a line of cosmetic containers. The Colt Plastics Company survives today as a major supplier of containers and closures (lids) for the pharmaceutical and cosmetics industry.

Two ten thousand gallon tanks located on the first floor of the Hartford factory contained formaldehyde and phenol. These chemicals were pumped to the fifth floor where they were boiled with wood flour, a dye color was added and then autoclaved to produce a colored plastic pellet. The dye was pressed into a thin sheet and ground into either a fine powder or coarse pieces before being added to the plastic pellets. The colored pellets were moved to the fourth and sixth floors. The sixth floor was the experimental model room. Production took place on the fourth floor. The pellets were pressed by hand into a heated steel mold, which was then subjected to 300° F steam and over a ton of pressure.

Use of pellets containing finely ground dye resulted in solid colors, whereas the use of a mixture of pellets containing coarsely ground dye would result in the variously colored onyx products. The excess plastic squeezed out of the mold is known as flash. Colt patented (2,353,995) a use for this flash by breaking it into small pieces and adding it to a plastic methyl methacrylate having a lower plasticizing temperature to make a decorative product such as ladies' compacts and artificial gemstones.

COLLECTOR'S NOTE: The most common ColtRock items are the Foursome electrical outlets. They were produced in 6 basic colors: red, walnut, black, green, onyx and mahogany.

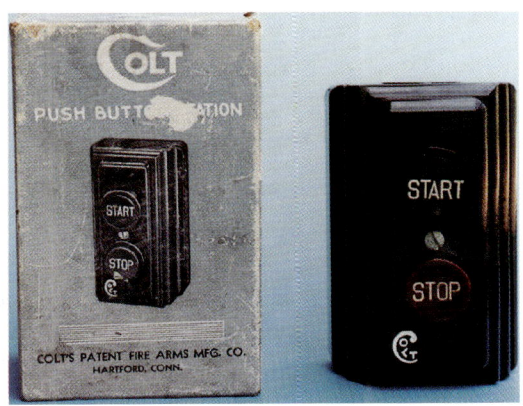

An electrical switch made of ColtRock with a unique Colt logo. Courtesy of the Dan Chesiak collection. **Price: $250**

The Colt Foursome label. **Price: $50-125**

Known only from a company advertising photo, the Foursomes were available in a master counter carton. Courtesy of the Colt Plastics Company files. **Price: $NEP**

The plug, also made of ColtRock, was made in two styles. Courtesy of the Dan Chesiak collection.
Price: $50-125

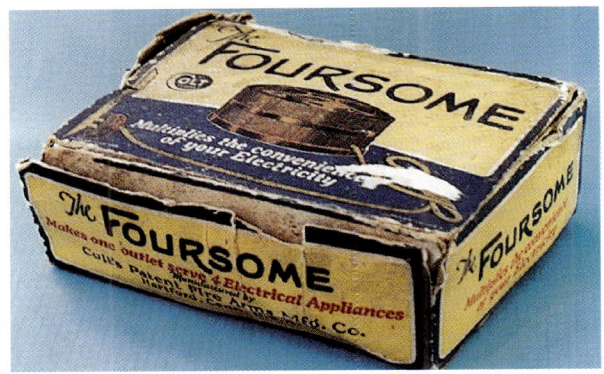

The plug is also marked with a Colt logo.
Price: $25-50

Boxes were colored to match the Foursome color. Courtesy of the Tom Saady collection. **Price: $150-300**

Also considered rare are the catalogs for ColtRock products. Two variations of catalogs are known with perhaps as few as 6 total examples existing. Courtesy of the Dan Chesiak collection. **Price: $500-1,000**

Mahogany Foursome. Dan Chesiak collection. **Price: $100-150**

Walnut Foursome. Dan Chesiak collection. **Price: $100-150**

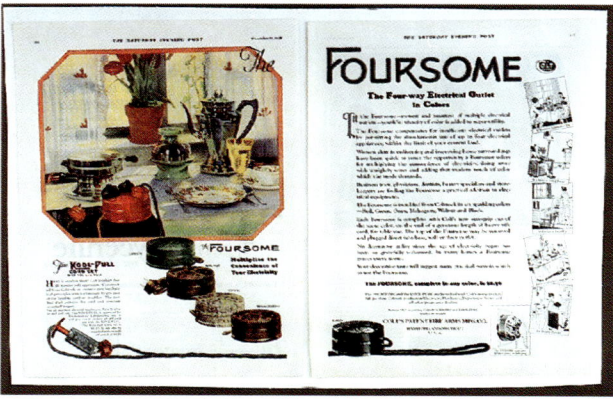

There may be as few as three published advertisements for Colt plastics products. *The Saturday Evening Post* (Nov. 17, 1928), *Modern Priscilla* (Nov. 1928) and an ad from *Vogue* and *Harpers Bazaar* (Nov. 1928) all presented the Foursome. Courtesy of the Colt Plastics Company files. **Price: $5-50**

The ColtRock catalogs also list the Kool-Pull electric cord set. Three examples are known. Courtesy of the Dan Chesiak collection. **Price: $500-1,000**

It is not known if two additional color ads were ever published. Courtesy of the Colt Plastics Company files.
Price: $NEP

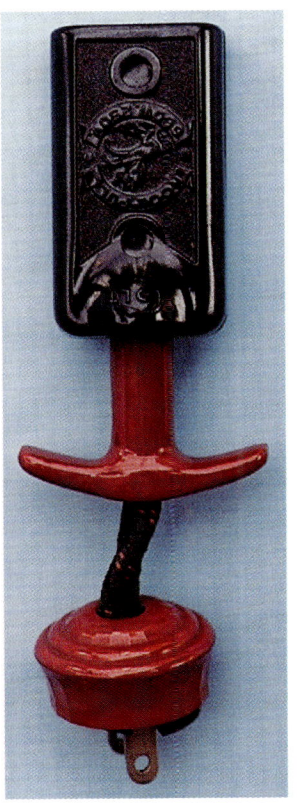

This may be a salesman's sample due to the short cord. Courtesy of the Dan Chesiak collection. **Price: $500-2,000**

This promotional photograph highlights the Kool-Pull. Courtesy of the Colt Plastics Company files. **Price: $NEP**

COLLECTOR'S NOTE: ColtRock tobacco accessories consist of the Tobac-A-Dor, Pipe-A-Dor, Jar, Jarette, Jarette Jr., Cigarette Book and the Smoke-Sette.

It is not known if these two color advertisements were ever published. Courtesy of the Colt Plastics Company files.
Price: $NEP

The ColtRock catalog lists some of the other major items produced such as the Tobac-A-Dor, Pipe-A-Dor and the Colt Jar. Even though the catalog promises these items in a variety of colors and pictures the Pipe-A-Dor in green, these three items are known only in walnut. Courtesy of the Dan Chesiak collection.
Price: $600-1,200

The Tobac-A-Dor was produced with a sponge in the lid to maintain humidity for the tobacco. Courtesy of the Dan Chesiak collection. **Price: $350-700**

The ColtRock Jar was patented in 1929. Courtesy of the Dan Chesiak collection. **Price: $350-600**

The ColtRock Pipe-A-Dor was patented in 1929. Courtesy of the Dan Chesiak collection. **Price: $350-800**

The ColtRock Tobac-A-Dor was patented in 1927. Courtesy of the Dan Chesiak collection. **Price: $350-700**

An additional ColtRock item was the Jarette. The Jarette was made in two sizes known to collectors as the Jarette (4-1/2 inches in height) and the Jarette Jr. (3 inches in height). Thought to have been produced in the basic 6 colors, a number of variations are known to exist which could be loosely considered to be onyx. One cobalt blue example is known. Two additional colors listed in company promotional photographs were SunBurst and BlueBlaze. Courtesy of the Colt Plastics Company. **Price: $250-1,000**

The Jarette logo. Photo courtesy of the Tom Saady collection. **Price: $1,000-2,500**

Red and black onyx Jarette. Courtesy of the Tom Saady collection. **Price: $250-1,000**

Walnut Jarette. Courtesy of the Tom Saady collection. **Price: $300-600**

Mahogany Jarette. Courtesy of the Dan Chesiak collection. **Price: $250-350**

Red Jarette Jr. Courtesy of the Dan Chesiak collection. **Price: $500-1,200**

Blue and white onyx Jarette. Courtesy of the Dan Chesiak collection. **Price: $250-1,000**

Red and black onyx Jarette Jr. Courtesy of the Dan Chesiak collection. **Price: $250-1,000**

Mixed red Jarette Jr. with black pull. Photo courtesy of the Tom Saady collection. **Price: $600-1,200**

This translucent Jarette Jr. is the only one known. Photo courtesy of the Tom Saady collection. **Price: $1,000-2,500**

A turquoise Jarette Jr. modified with a Smoke-Sette ring and black pull. Courtesy of the Tom Saady collection. **Price: $400-700**

A Jarette with the word "second" burned into the bottom. It is not known if indeed this indicated an imperfect product intended for a secondary market. Photo courtesy of the Tom Saady collection. **Price: $350-500**

COLLECTOR'S NOTE: The cigarette book, one of the most popular ColtRock items is best known from the cover title "The Courtship of Lady Nicotine." Three variations of cover designs are known, and in addition to the six basic colors, it was also produced in white. With three cover designs and seven colors, a total of 21 variations are possible. However, onyx, blue and green colors are unknown at this time.

A cigarette book. Courtesy of the Tom Saady collection. **Price: $1,500-2,500**

This photograph, labeled as blue, is the only evidence that the cigarette book was ever made in that color as no examples are known. Courtesy of the Colt Plastics Company files. **Price: $NEP**

COLLECTOR'S NOTE: The ColtRock Smoke-Sette is one item not found in the ColtRock catalog. The Smoke-Sette is a combination ashtray and cigarette holder.

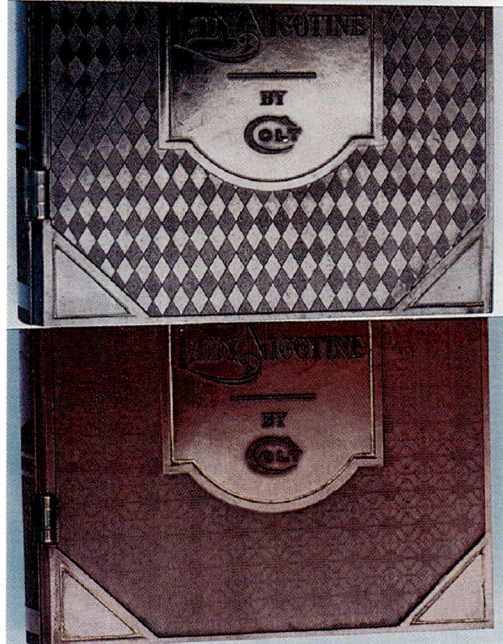

Three variations of cover design used on the cigarette book. Courtesy of the Dan Chesiak collection. **Price: $400-2,000**

Black, red and white cigarette books. Courtesy of the Dan Chesiak collection. **Price: $400-2,000**

Smoke-Sette logo. Courtesy of the Tom Saady collection. **Price: $350-600**

This promotional photograph shows the Smoke-Sette in the elusive SunBurst and BlueBlaze color in addition to conventional colors. Courtesy of the Colt Plastics Company files. **Price: $NEP**

A walnut Smoke-Sette. Courtesy of the Dan Chesiak collection. **Price: $350-950**

A red Smoke-Sette. Courtesy of the Tom Saady collection. **Price: $800-1,200**

A Jarette Jr. modified with a Smoke-Sette ashtray and a black Mr. Boston pull. Courtesy of the Dan Chesiak collection. **Price: $1,000**

A red and black onyx Smoke-Sette. Courtesy of the Dan Chesiak collection. **Price: $400-1,000**

COLLECTOR'S NOTE: The ball bearing assembly of the Tobac-A-Dor also served as the basis for another rare ColtRock item, a lazy susan known as the Serv-Round. They were made in two sizes 10" and 12" diameter, and until recently were thought to have been produced only in mahogany. Six examples are known, including a red one. Records ordering boxes indicate not only that they were intended to be packed in labeled boxes, but that Colt anticipated a yearly production of 1,200 10-inch and 400 12-inch Serv-Round.

The Serv-Round logo from the Dan Chesiak collection. **Price: $NEP**

A unique color pattern on the 12-inch Serv-Round. Photo courtesy of the Tom Saady collection. **Price: $2,200-3,000**

A 10-inch mahogany Serv-Round. Courtesy of the Dan Chesiak collection. **Price: $750-2,500**

An 10-inch Serv-Round in red. Courtesy of the Dan Chesiak collection. **Price: $2,200-3,000**

COLLECTOR'S NOTE: Additional items known to have been made of ColtRock are cigarette holders, whiskey shot glasses and a mechanical pencil.

A 12-inch mahogany Serv-Round. Courtesy of the Tom Saady collection and photo. **Price: $1,800-3,000**

Logo of the shot glass. It is not known why they were individually numbered. Courtesy of the Tom Saady collection. **Price: $80-125**

Five color variations are known. Courtesy of the Tom Saady collection.
Price: $80-125

Cigarette holder. Courtesy Dan Chesiak collection. **Price: $150-250**

Cigarette holder. Photo courtesy of the Tom Saady collection. **Price: $150-350**

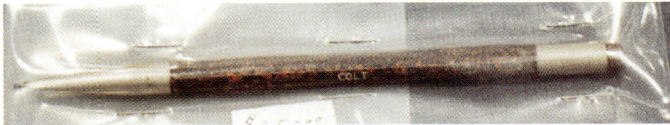

Mechanical pencil of ColtRock. Courtesy of the Dan Chesiak collection.
Price: $350-500

COLLECTOR'S NOTE: Colt ceased production of ColtRock in 1935 and switched all production to other plastics. The most common items made of Colt plastic and marked with the Colt logo are eyewash cups and a line of cosmetic containers. In 1955, the plastics division of Colt's Patent Firearms Manufacturing Company was sold to the Manufactured Products Corporation, which changed its name in 1956 to Colt's Plastics Company, Inc. The company continues to manufacture plastic containers and closures for leading pharmaceutical and cosmetic companies today. Close attention to the logos, however, should allow one to distinguish between Hartford production and post-Hartford production of plastic containers.

B.F. Conner was granted a patent for the eyecup in 1941. The eyecup was manufactured in three pieces from a synthetic resin composition. The base, cup and cover were made in a variety of colors so as to provide a number of combinations. The eyecup was intended for general usage and was not made exclusively for shooters. As the patent drawings illustrate, one variation was intended to serve as a cap for the bottle of eyewash. It is not known if that variation was ever made as no example is known to exist.

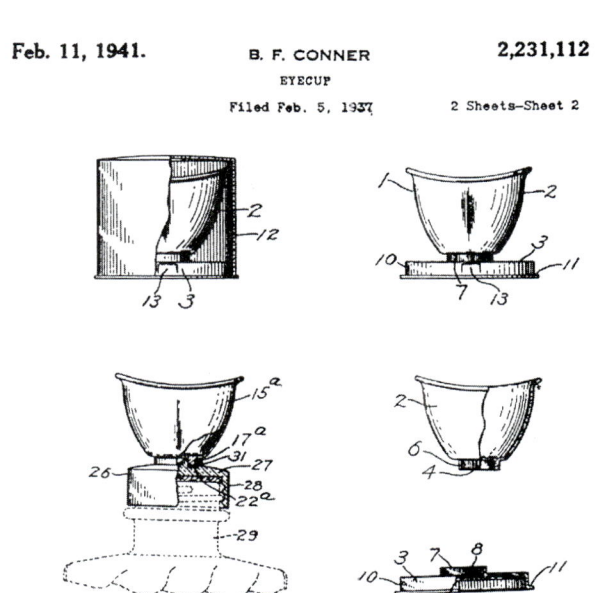

Eyecup patent drawings. **Price: $NEP**

Eyecup logo. Courtesy of the Ron Lough collection. **Price: $50-150**

Eyecup logo. Photo courtesy of the Tom Saady collection. **Price: $50-150**

Green, white and red eyecup covers. Courtesy of the Dan Chesiak collection. **Price: $100-250**

Black, purple and yellow eyecup covers. Courtesy of the Tom Saady collection. **Price: $40-80**

COLLECTOR'S NOTE: The purse make-up kit was patented in 1937 by B.F. Conner of Colt. All sections are interchangeable and any number of sections can be connected. Two designs of tops are known. Black, white, blue and red bottoms are known. Some kits are not marked with the Colt logo. White, red, dark blue, light blue, cream, brown and black and gold colors are known. Kits were provided with a spatula for application. Hartford production spatulas are known in two sizes and four colors. Post-Hartford spatulas are known in four shapes.

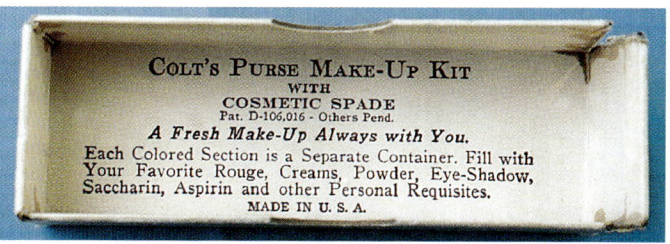

Original boxes are rare. Courtesy of the Tom Saady collection. **Price: $450-1,000**

Courtesy of the Ron Lough collection. **Price: $150-250**

Courtesy of the Tom Saady collection.
Price: $150-250

Courtesy of the Colt Plastics Company collection.
Price: $NEP

Courtesy of the Dan Chesiak collection.
Price: $150-250

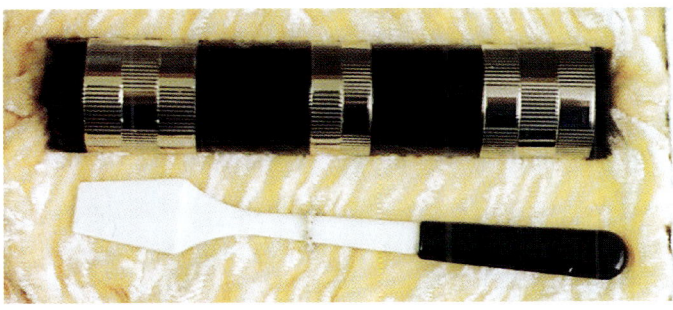

One of two presentation kits. Courtesy of the Colt Plastics Company collection.
Price: $NEP

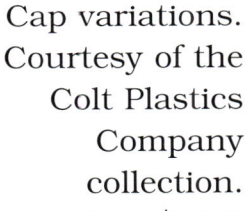

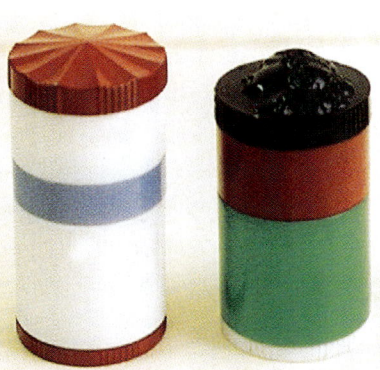

Cap variations. Courtesy of the Colt Plastics Company collection.
Price: $NEP

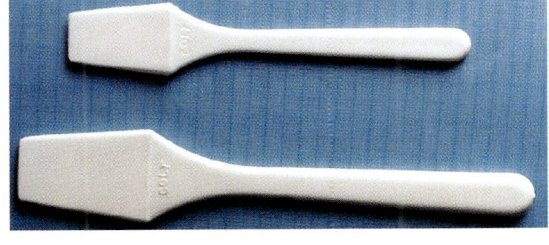

Courtesy of the Dan Chesiak collection.
Price: $10-25

Courtesy of the Colt Plastics Company collection.
Price: $NEP

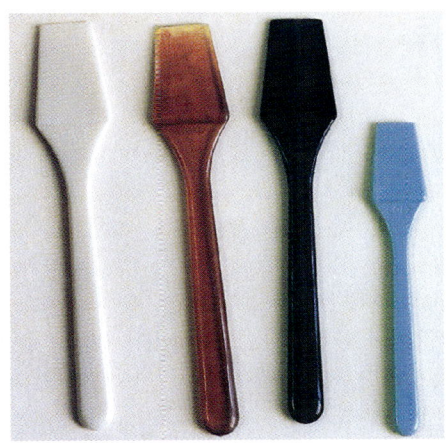

Courtesy of the Colt Plastics Company collection.
Price: $NEP

Courtesy of the Colt Plastics Company collection. **Price: $NEP**

COLLECTOR'S NOTE: Cosmetic containers were produced in two basic types—an air insulated double wall container and a plain single wall container. Colors that are known to exist include dark green, salmon, grey, pink, red, white and powder blue. Eight sizes of the insulated containers were offered in a 1955 price list. Other cosmetic containers appear to have been made for specialty purposes and include perforated lids, serrated lids and double lidded containers. It is not clear what a complete set of dressing table containers would consist of. A small plastic bracket to hold a number of small containers in a purse is known only from patent documents (2,217,644).

Courtesy of the Ron Lough collection. **Price: $250**

Courtesy of the Tom Saady collection. **Price: $150-250**

Purse Make-Up Kit without the Colt logo. **Price: $150-250**

1955 price list. Courtesy of the Dan Chesiak collection. **Price: $50-100**

Courtesy of the Tom Saady collection.
Price: $200-350

Courtesy of the Ron Lough collection.
Price: $75-200

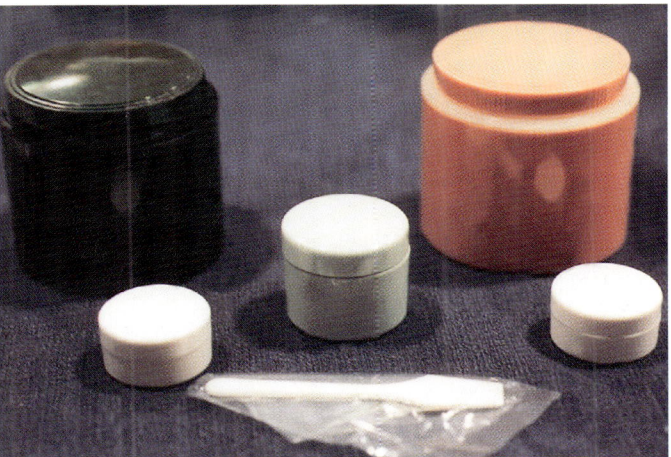

Courtesy of the Dan Chesiak collection.
Price: $75-350

Courtesy of the Tom Saady collection.
Price: $200-400

Courtesy of the Tom Saady collection. **Price: $200-350**

Courtesy of the Dan Chesiak collection.
Price: $75-200

Containers made for deMuir of Boston. Courtesy of the Tom Saady collection.
Price: $600-1,000

35

Powder container. Courtesy of the Tom Saady collection. **Price: $100-250**

Powder containers. Courtesy of the Colt Plastics Company collection. **Price: $100-250**

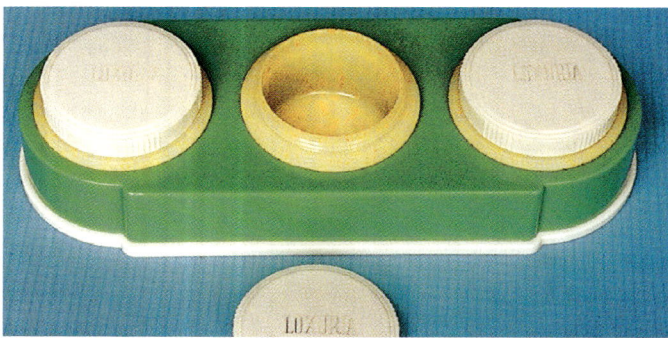

Marked "Luxuria". Courtesy of the Dan Chesiak collection. **Price: $250-400**

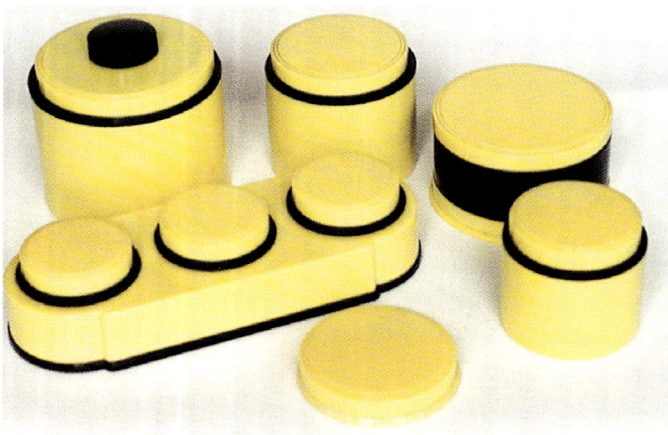

A vanity set. Courtesy of the Dan Chesiak collection. **Price: $1,500-2,500**

A vanity set consisting of a powder shaker and the following size jars: 8oz, 4 oz., 3 oz., 2 oz., 1/2 oz., 1/4 oz. and 1/8 oz. Photo courtesy of the Doc Palmer collection. **Price: $600-1,000**

Two-ounce sets. Courtesy of the Tom Saady collection. **Price: $250-750**

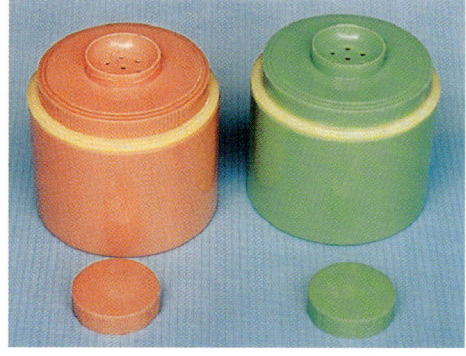

Powder containers. Courtesy of the Dan Chesiak collection. **Price: $250-350**

The purpose of the serrated lid on this container is unknown to the author. Courtesy of the Dan Chesiak collection. **Price: $250-350**

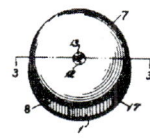  

1927 patent drawing. **Price: $NEP**

Courtesy of the Tom Saady collection.
Price: $250-350

Colt stack kit. Courtesy of the Dan Chesiak collection. **Price: $125-250**

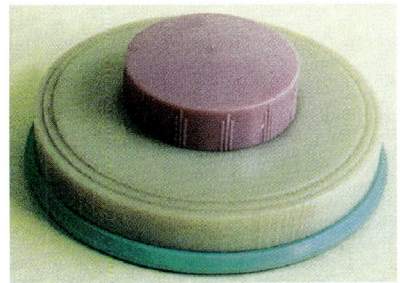

Colt stack kit. Courtesy of the Colt Plastic Company collection.
Price: $75-200

Pill container. Courtesy of the Tom Saady collection.
Price: $500-1,000

Logo of pill container. Courtesy of the Tom Saady collection.
Price: $500-1000

COLLECTOR'S NOTE: One of the first patents that B.J. Conner assigned to Colt's Patent Firearms Manufacturing company in 1928 was for a medical tablet container. Interestingly, this first item patented by the plastics division was to have been made of sheet metal. No metal examples of that pill container are known, but two plastic examples exist.

Pill container patented in 1938. Courtesy of the Colt Plastic Company collection.
Price: $NEP

COLLECTOR'S NOTE: A line of artificial gemstones manufactured from methacrylate were introduced in 1939, and marketed as ColtStones. Individual gemstones are unmarked so ColtStones are known from one example of stones mounted on a Colt marked display card, and one set of unmarked stones with a documented history. Another factory card is labeled for buttons, buckles and novelties. Several examples are known containing buttons and one buckle card is known. Nothing is known about what a Colt novelty would look like as no examples are known. As the individual buttons, buckles and ColtStones are not labeled they can only be authenticated when found mounted on salesmen's sample cards or if their history is documented.

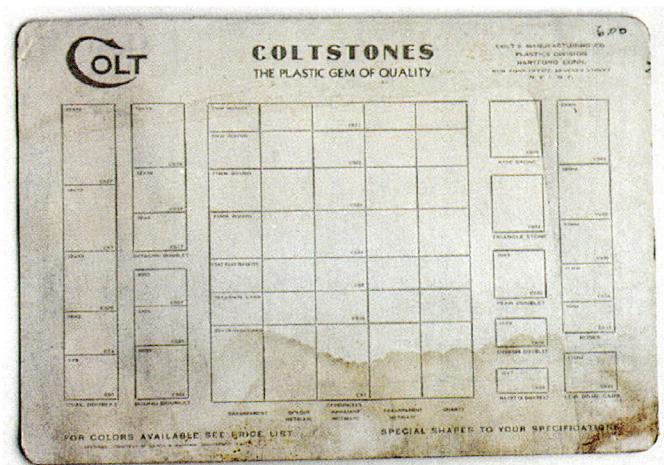

A blank salesmen's card. Courtesy of the Ron Lough collection. **Price: $50-150**

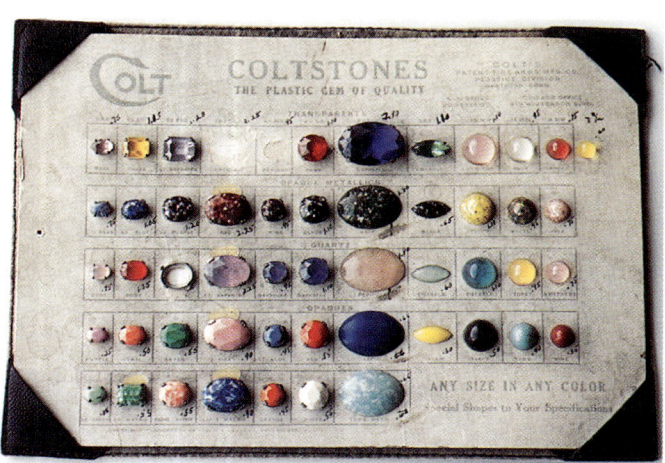

The only known card of ColtStones. Courtesy of the Ron Lough collection. **Price: $1,500**

The only known card of Colt buckles. Courtesy of the Ron Lough collection. **Price: $800-1,200**

Unmounted ColtStones. **Price: $NEP**

Shank buttons. Courtesy of the Dan Chesiak collection. **Price: $750-1,500**

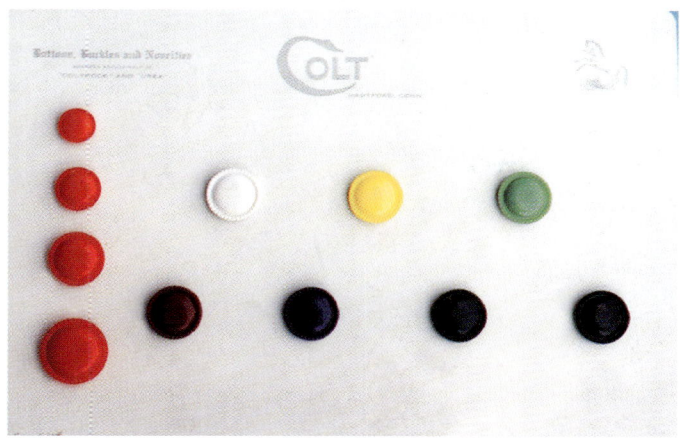

Shank buttons. Courtesy of the Dan Chesiak collection. **Price: $750-1,500**

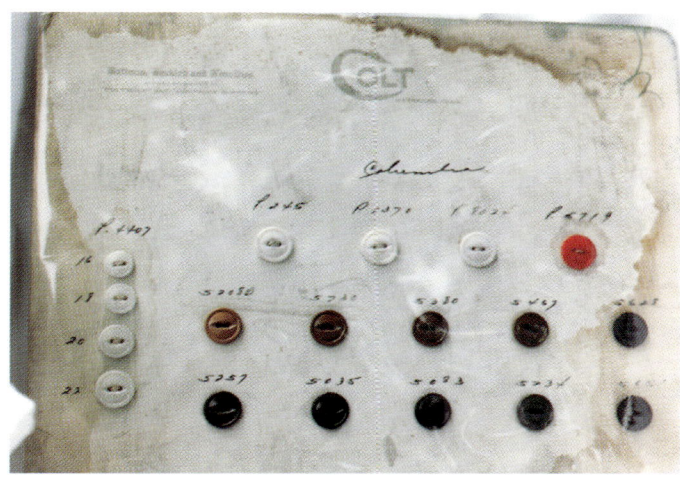

Photo courtesy of the Tom Saady collection. **Price: $900-1,300**

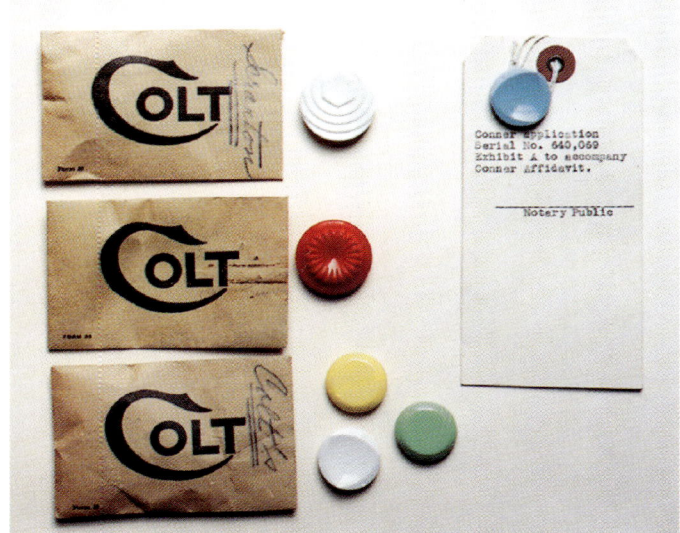

Samples of shank buttons submitted with the original patent application. Courtesy of the Tom Saady collection.
Price: $2,000

Courtesy of the Tom Saady collection.
Price: $1,000-1,500

COLLECTOR'S NOTE: The standard buttons appear to have been named for East Coast Universities. One card is labeled "baseball". It is speculated that the buttons were intended for nurses uniforms at university hospitals and for baseball uniforms.

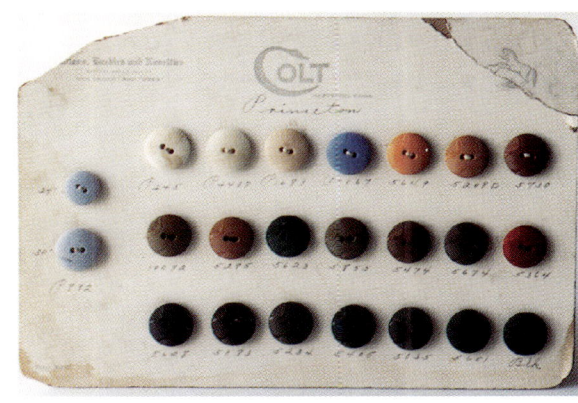

Courtesy of the Ron Lough collection.
Price: $1,200

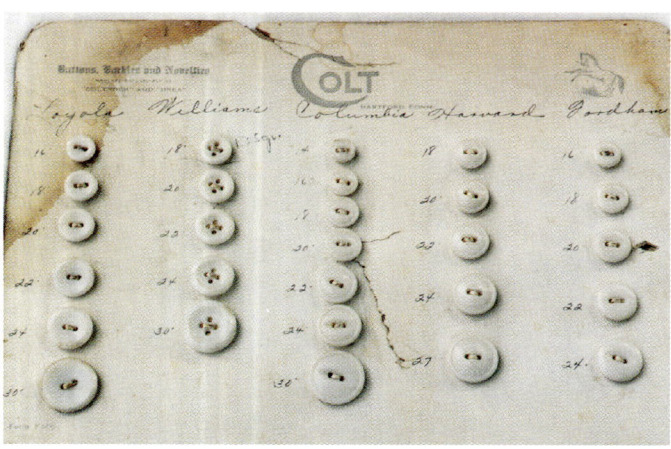

Courtesy of the Tom Saady collection.
Price: $800-1,300

Photo courtesy of the Tom Saady collection.
Price: $50-150

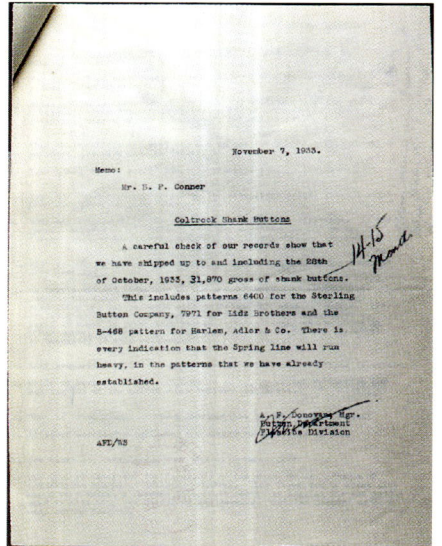

This memo indicates that Colt sold over 4.5 million buttons during a 14 month period in 1933. Courtesy of the Tom Saady collection. **Price: $50-250**

Courtesy of the Dan Chesiak collection.
Price: $75-200

COLLECTOR'S NOTE: The perfume button is an interesting combination of the base of a shank button and the top of the purse make-up kit. It was intended to be sewn to a cuff of a blouse or jacket to insure the wearer would not be without a supply of perfume.

Courtesy of the Wayne Becicka collection.
Price: $50-150

Courtesy of the Tom Saady collection.
Price: $50-150

COLLECTOR'S NOTE: Colt patented not only the ladies' compact but also the process for producing the glittered deco finish.

Courtesy of the Tom Saady collection. **Price: $600-1,200**

Courtesy of the Ron Lough collection. **Price: $1,000**

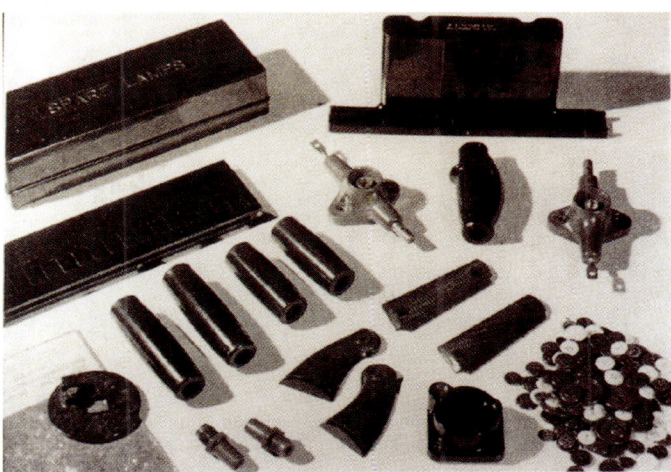

Courtesy of The Coltsman. **Price: $NEP**

Photo courtesy of the Tom Saady collection. **Price: $600-1,200**

Courtesy of the Colt Plastics Company. **Price: $NEP**

COLLECTOR'S NOTE: A number of additional items made by the plastic division of Colt during WWII were grips for the 45 Auto, the Commando and the .30 caliber and .50 caliber Browning machine guns, buttons for uniforms, magneto parts, molded cases for spare lamps for bombers, radio knobs, electrical grommets, and jar lids. Documents indicate that slide rules, dominos, checkers, watch crystals and Christmas tree bulb receptacles were also made by Colt. It is not thought that any of these items were marked. Patents issued to B.F. Conner and assigned to Colt illustrate bracelets and a jewelry box. It is not known if they were ever made or if they would have been marked.

Colt displayed its products at the Eastern States Exposition during 1949. Courtesy of *The Coltsman*. **Price: $10-25**

COLLECTOR'S NOTE: According to a Colt price list, bottle caps were produced in six styles in combinations of 10 sizes, jar caps in 19 sizes and tube caps in 5 styles and 4 sizes. Known only from patent documents is a container closure with applicator rod. It is not known if any of these plastic bottle caps were marked with the Colt logo. Bottle caps made for Mr. Boston and Rock and Rye are known to sport the Colt name.

Rock and Rye bottle and cap. Courtesy of the Dan Chesiak collection. **Prices: Item at left-$75-150; right- $300-500**

Courtesy of the Dan Chesiak collection. **Price: $50-75**

Photo courtesy of the Tom Saady collection. **Price: $25-50**

Mr. Boston cap. Courtesy of the Dan Chesiak collection. **Price: $20-50**

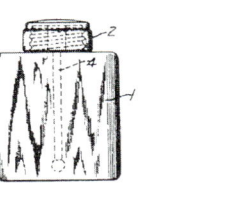 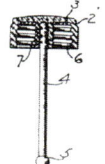 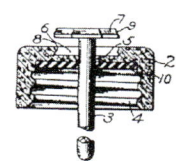

Patent drawing. **Price: $NEP**

COLLECTOR'S NOTE: Vigilant Colt collectors continue to discover the Colt logo, as used on the Carter Cube-Well. The Colt plastics division undoubtedly made these Cube Wells for Carter.

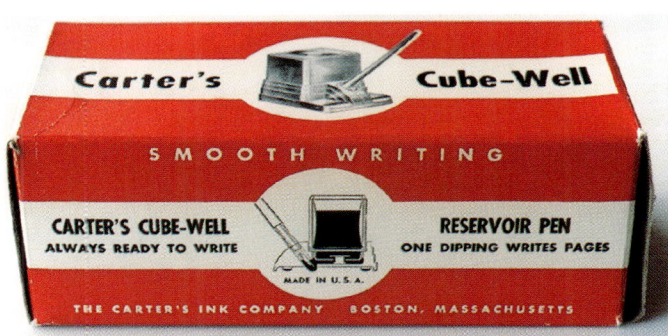

Mint boxes are rare. Courtesy of the Ron Lough collection. **Price: $350-500**

Colt logo. Courtesy of the Dan Chesiak collection. **Price: $250-500**

Authentic sets include a labeled pen. Courtesy of the Ron Lough collection. **Price: $75-250**

Components. Courtesy of the Dan Chesiak collection. **Price: $250-500**

Assembled. Courtesy of the Dan Chesiak collection. **Price: $250-500**

COLLECTOR'S NOTE: Post-Hartford production plastics can be distinguished by a close examination of the logos and method of fabrication.

Hartford produced plastics were made using a compression mold. **Price: $NEP**

Plastics made in a compression mold will have sharp edges and features.
Price: $75-200

Post-Hartford produced plastics use a flat-tailed version of the serpentine Colt. Photo courtesy of the Tom Saady collection. **Price: $20-50**

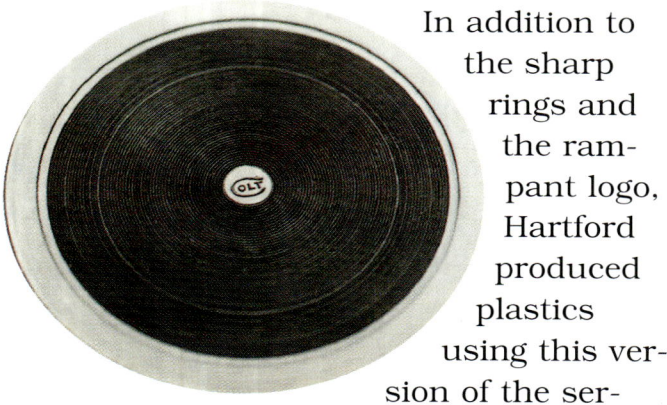

In addition to the sharp rings and the rampant logo, Hartford produced plastics using this version of the serpentine logo. Courtesy of the Tom Saady collection. **Price: $50-150**

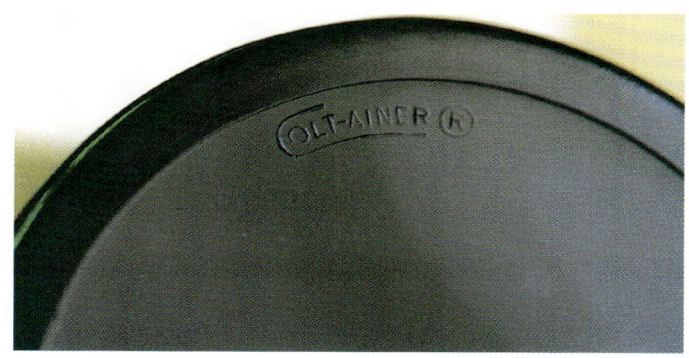

Trademarks of Colt-ainer (1967) and Colt-ier (1974) immediately identify contemporary plastic products. Also, the modern use of injection molding requires a smoother finish with fewer sharp edges.
Price: $20-50

Some Hartford-produced plastics used a plain version of the trademark. Photo courtesy of the Tom Saady collection.
Price: $50-150

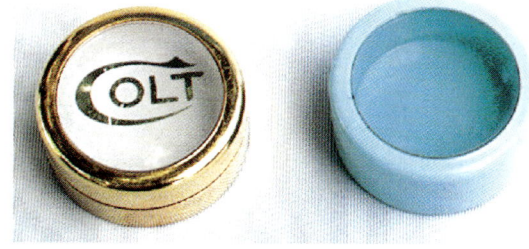

Post-Hartford containers made in 1970. Courtesy of the Tom Saady collection.
Price: $50-150

Post-Hartford Colt-ier container.
Price: $NEP

An assortment of sizes and colors of modern post-Hartford production lids.
Price: $NEP

The plastics division in 1947. Courtesy of the Tom Saady collection. **Price: $25-50**

Chapter 4
PATCHES

Emblem patches can trace their development back to the heraldic devices used on the shields and armor of European knights. The surcoat, or cloth worn over the knight's armor, became known as the coat of arms. It was decorated to allow the individual to be recognized on the battlefield. The design usually traced the family history of the individual it adorned. The design followed strict guidelines which were based upon the various pieces of the warrior's armor.

The emblem patch is best known for its use on the shoulder of uniforms as a decorative insignia. During WWI, the first such unofficial use occurred. Throughout WWII, emblem shoulder patches were required. Oil companies began using patches in the late 1920s and early 1930s for advertising promotions. In the late 1930s, the first Colt patch was issued as an advertising promotion.

Emblem patches may be printed, silk-screened or embroidered on cloth or felt. No silk-screened Colt emblem patches are believed to exist, and only one felt-printed emblem patch endures today. The majority of all Colt emblem patches are embroidered on cotton Dacron twill. A few Colt patches were embroidered on felt. Emblem patches may be manufactured either by hand or machine. The bullion blazer crest worn by Colt executives are all handmade. The remainder of all Colt patches are machine made.

The present day patchmaking involves several steps. A drawing of the patch is enlarged into a pattern which is used to program a computer. A computer program or tape controls a loom for stitching. The patch is then sized, cut, overlocked and tailed. There are two general types of machines, called looms, used for the embroidery stitching of patches. These machines are designed to provide laces for women's fashions, referred to as long goods. Some of the first machines that were modified to make patches were the Swiss-built Schflii looms. Accordingly, some patches are referred to as either Swiss or Schflii embroidered. The Schflii looms operate by moving a vertical wall of cloth around in front of an array of 340 stitching needles to create a design.

As the loom weaves, one color thread is sewn into as many as 340 patches simultaneously. The thread must be changed before stitching an additional color. Only one color cloth may be used. Different colored backgrounds are achieved by step stitching an additional thread color. Looms hold 10 or 15 yards of cloth either 48 or 60 inches wide. The size and shape of the patch, along with the amount of wastage, determines the number of patches that can be produced concurrently. The German-built Zangs and Plaven looms operate similarly. The Japanese-built Tajima looms operate by moving a sewing head, containing up to seven needles, around a fixed horizontal cloth mat. Machines may have 12, 20 or 24 heads. A computer controls the machine's head movements.

After embroidering is complete, material sizing occurs. The term "sizing" does not refer to the dimension, but rather to the spraying of starch on the backing. This process makes the order cloth's back rigid. Today, patches may be backed with different types of cloth such as crinoline or pellon.

Even more commonly a plastic heat seal is used. The plastic, when heated, bonds the patch and cloth allowing the patch to be ironed on to a uniform. Some plastic backings are bonded by pressure. After sizing, the material is cut into individual patches by a metal die in the shape and size of the desired patch. This is done by hand, as the die must be centered over the embroidery. After cutting, the edges of the patch are sewn to prevent raveling. This process, called overlocking, is done by a marrow machine. The top, bottom and edge of the border are all sewn, which may require the use of five or six spools of thread. The trailer of thread left over, called the tail, is either pasted or taped to the back of the patch, pulled through the stitching, or left free.

A variety of Colt patches exist. Generally, the early Colt patches were not overlocked but the later patches are. The handmade bullion blazer crests are attached by tack and clasp or plastic pocket flap. Patches made before WWII were sewn with cotton thread, while modern patches are sewn with Dacron, rayon or nylon. Variations which exist in Colt patches may be due to the thread's thickness, known as yarn denier. The two most commonly used are thin (100/2) and thick (150/2). Variations may also occur due to stitch size, which is commonly 1/6, 1/10 or 1/30mm. The denier causes size differences in the patch's lettering.

The same patch design manufactured by two different companies also varies. There are approximately 10 large companies, and as many as 80 smaller companies in the USA making patches at any given time. Patches from the same company may vary due to differences in cloth and thread color, the use of a different loom, or even differences from the same loom. The needles of the Schflii looms must be hand aligned for each patch job, and over a long production runs must be realigned. This results in some variation in individual patches.

All this makes the collecting of Colt patches both interesting and challenging. Collectors are of two types, those who lump similar items together and those who split minor variations into separate categories. It will be up to the individual collector to decide if differences in patches warrant their classification as different or simply a variation of an existing design. The collector is urged to heed Colonel Colt's advice to beware of counterfeits and patent infringements. Patches considered rare or uncommon will be reproduced by unscrupulous people if they are valuable.

Unless the history of a particular patch is known, it is almost impossible to determine the age. In fact, for most of the patches listed here, it has been impossible to identify the original manufacturer. The various Colt companies have probably used a variety of manufacturers over the years, however, records have not been located to identify which patches were issued by Colt. Indeed, a number of patches are known to exist that were not issued by Colt. Additionally, Colt has had patches made for internal use which were never distributed publicly. A collector should, therefore, not pay more than a patch is worth to his/her collection.

COLLECTOR'S NOTE: One of the best documented of the Colt patches has neither the rampant nor the serpentine logo. This patch was designed by E.J. Miller of Colt's engineering department in 1942, for use by members of the Machine Gun School and Colt Guard. In order to protect the Colt factory from Nazi paratroopers during W.W.II, Colt employees organized into a State Guard Volunteer Reserve Corp consisting of three men's units and the Colt Cadettes unit for women. The Guard and Cadettes were trained in the use of machine guns by a school established by Colt. This emblem worn by members of the Guard, the Cadettes and the Machine Gun School was granted a patent on January 26, 1943.

This is considered by some to be the first patch Colt distributed. It is thought to date from 1935 or 1938. **Price: $100-150**

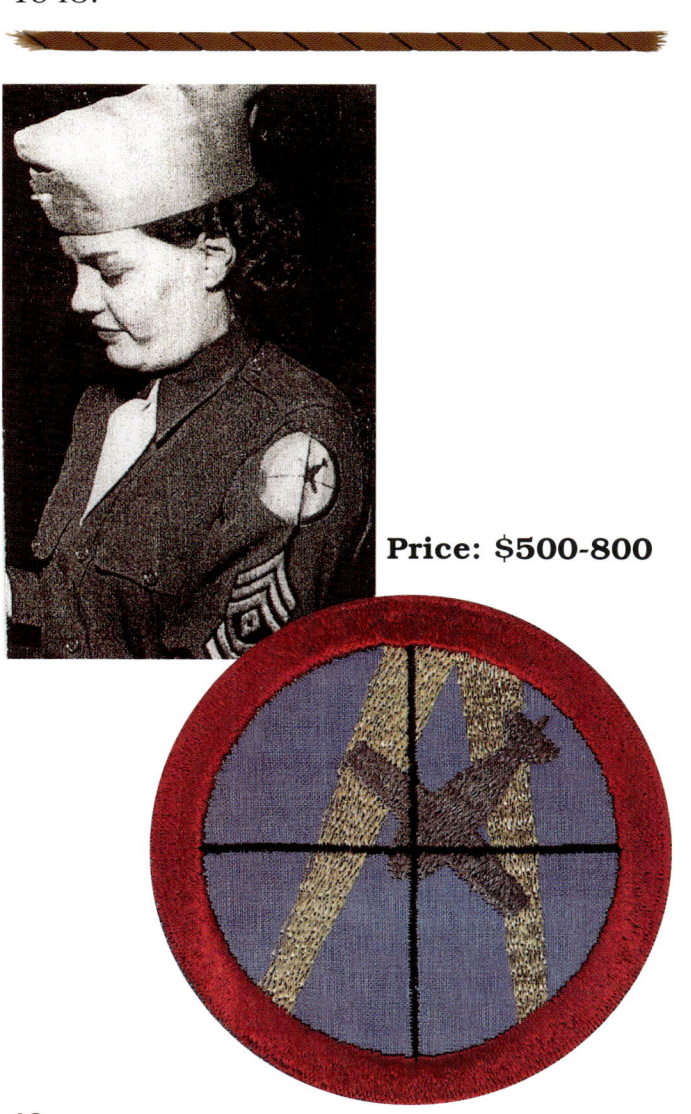

Price: $500-800

Variations are probably a result of the patch having been reissued by Colt over a period of time. The patches can best be distinguished by examining them from the back. **Price: (Top) $100-150, (Bottom) $50-100**

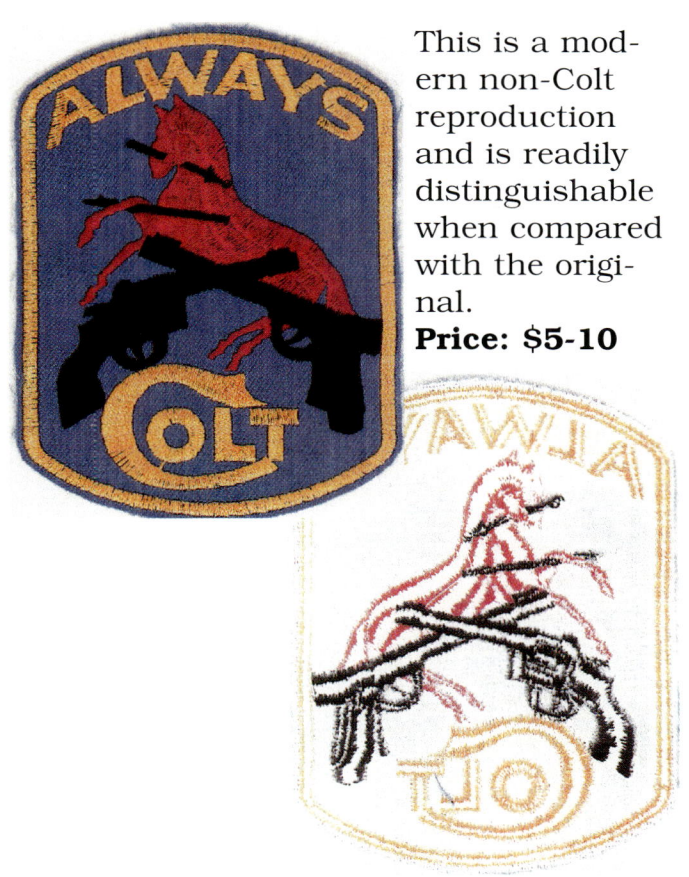

This is a modern non-Colt reproduction and is readily distinguishable when compared with the original. **Price: $5-10**

This patch represents a first series Match Target Woodsman with elephant ear grips. The gun was first manufactured in 1938. **Price: $75-150**

This patch represents a second series Match Target Woodsman having palm filler grips. The gun was manufactured from December 1947 until 1955.
Price: $75-150

This is a later reissue of the first series Match Target Woodsman patch. Courtesy of the Tom Saady collection.
Price: $25-75

A very good modern reproduction which can be distinguished from the back.
Price: $10

Several of these patches are known to exist and a best guess would date them from the 1940s. **Price: $100-150**

According to R.L. Wilson (The Rampant Colt, 1969, page 84, figure 124), this patch dates from approximately 1939.
Price: $75-150

This is the only printed Colt patch known. It is printed on felt. According to John Hintlian, it was one of the cheapest promotional items Colt ever issued and did not survive well. The patch represents a 3rd Series Match Target Woodsman which was introduced in 1955.
Price: $100-200

John Henry FitzGerald worked for Colt from 1918 until 1930. He was the expert in charge of the testing department of Colt's Patent Firearms Manufacturing Company. FitzGerald developed early ballistics procedures and developed standard training procedures for police departments around the country. He died in 1945. This patch honoring FitzGerald is thought to have been made about 1940 or 1944. The patch is pictured in R.L.
Price: $NEP

Wilson's book The Rampant Colt (page 85, figure 125) and in the Book of Colt Firearms by R.L. Wilson and D. Southerland (page 564, figure A). Mr. Wilson no longer has the patch and an original has not been located. The patch was reproduced in the mid-1960s and that reproduction is still being produced and sold today (1997).
Price: $2-5

Price: $30-50

This patch is listed in the book The Colt Armory by E.S. Grant (1982) as dating from the 1930s. Two variations in the large patch exist and minor variations exist in the stitching of four of the smaller patches. Colt reissued the patch in 1996 with the modern portrayal of the rampant Colt.
Price: $20-40

Price: $30-50

Price: $10-30

Price: $10-30

Price: $10-30

Price: $25

These patches are thought to have first been made in the mid-1950s. Variations are probably due to their having been reissued at later dates. The significance of the blue variation is unknown at this time. Courtesy of the Tom Saady collection.

Only 30 of these patches were made for the modern Colt pistol team. **Price: $250-350**

Price: $50-75

Colt sponsored police combat pistol matches which were held at Indiana University during the early 1960s. **Price: $30-50**

The Colt Pistol and Revolver Club was formally organized November 30, 1937. The club was open to all Colt employees and provided guns to those who needed them. In the fall of 1938, the Colt Club became a charter member of the Metropolitan Revolver League. The League brought together nearly all the pistol and revolver shooters in the Hartford area into one competitive group. Although a shortage of ammunition curtailed the League's activities during the war, the Colt Club survived until the 1980s.
Prices for above two patches: $250-500, $150-300

This patch commemorates the 125th anniversary of Colt.
Price: $100-150

Colt celebrated its 150th anniversary in 1986. This patch was distributed by the factory and never sold.
Price: $10-40

This patch was included in the "Colt Fast Draw Club" promotional kits and was also sold separately as item number 80 for 40 cents in 1962. Two sizes exist.
Price of each: $30-100

Colt operated an archery division from 1958 until 1967 and sponsored two tournaments.
**Prices from top to bottom:
$30-50; $15-30; $25-50**

54

These patches are thought to have been issued by the Colt factory. However, no records have been found to document their authenticity. They can be distinguished by closely examining the shape and thickness of the serpentine C.
Price of each patch: $5-15

55

Sold by Grand Prix Products Ltd., Stevens Point, WI in 1978. **Price: $15-40**

These oval patches are known to be non-factory releases.
Price: $3-7

Sold by Colt from 1983 until 1993.
Price: $15-40

Sold by Colt in 1993. **Price: $10-30**

This 3-3/4 inch diameter patch was offered in the 1968 accessory sales item (SPA-100) brochure as a brassard.
Price: $5-20

This 3-3/4 inch diameter patch was sold in a set of three patches from 1989 until 1992. **Price: $5-20**

Easily recognized by the silver border. **Price: $10-30**

Three and one-half inch diameter patch. **Price: $5-15**

Issued in 1991 for a short time. This patch has the name of the reorganized company, "Colt's Manufacturing Co." and the old style logo. **Price: $8-25**

Three and seven-eighths inch diameter patch. **Price: $5-20**

A non-factory reproduction that may date from 1968. **Price: $5-20**

This patch was issued in 1995 by the historical department of Colt. Proceeds from the sale of the 2,500 patches were donated to the Colt statue preservation fund. The rampant colt statue which sat atop the dome of the Colt Armory for 126 years was removed in 1990 and sold to an art dealer by the owners of the building. The Museum of Connecticut History at the Connecticut State Library purchased the statue through donations and museum funds. The patch was sold as Item B2906 in the Colt Wear Catalog. **Price: $5**

This four inch diameter non-factory patch is based upon the design of the 1968 Colt factory patch. It could be considered either a reproduction or a fantasy patch. Courtesy of the Vicki Otto collection. **Price: $5-10**

Colt re-emphasized its law enforcement products in 1995. This was partly due to legislation which restricted its sale of semi-automatic rifles to the public. This patch was given out at the 1995 Law Enforcement Trade Show and sold in the 1996 accessories catalog. **Price: $3**

This patch from 1995 is a reproduction. **Price: $10-15**

Manufactured in 1989. **Price: $5-20**

In 1995, Colt offered armorer training to police departments. These patches were made for the attendees of those two-day training sessions.
Price: $10-20

Given out from 1990 until 1993. **Price: $5-20**

Manufactured in 1993. **Price: $15-30**

This patch is thought to have been issued by the factory. **Price: $15-30**

Sold during 1995 and 1996. **Price: $3**

The advertising campaign "A Heritage of Colt Craftsmanship" was used during 1987 and 1988. This patch is surprisingly uncommon. **Price: $50-75**

Given out during 1990-1991. **Price: $30-50**

These four patches were sold during 1996. **Price: $3**

Colt reintroduced its black powder revolvers in 1974. The line was greatly expanded in 1979 with the Authentic Colt Black Powder Series. This patch dates from a promotional campaign in 1981. Two variations are known.
Price: $5-15

Mr. Bill Judd had this patch made to honor Bill Blankenship. Mr. Blankenship was a six-time national NRA pistol champion. He worked for Colt as a salesman and public relations person from 1971 until 1989, and is still active as a consultant today. Only 250 of these patches were made in 1974. This is only the second time that Colt has honored an individual by putting their name on a patch, John Henry FitzGerald being the first.
Price: $100-150

The yellow-jacketed variation was either a mistake or a prototype which makes it scarce. Courtesy of the Dan Chesiak collection.
Price: $30-50

These two patches vary slightly in the size of stitching and tailing, yet both patches were received from the factory on the same day. This patch was sold by Colt from 1989 to 1991.
Price: $5-10

This variation was apparently never publicly distributed and remains scarce.
Price: $50-100

Approximately 100 of these patches were made in 1966 for the jackets worn by employees on the test fire range at the West Hartford factory. **Price: $50-100**

This patch was distributed by the factory to celebrate the introduction of the Mark V line of pistols in 1982. **Price: $50-75**

This patch was sold in 1989 as a promotion for the Delta Elite pistol.
Price: $5-10

This patch, while offered for sale in the 1992 catalog, was never publicly distributed and is scarce.
Price: $75-125

COLLECTOR'S NOTE: The following ten photos illustrate that there are five basic types of bullion blazer crests that have been used by executives and the sales force at Colt. As these patches are handmade, patches will vary slightly. In addition, there are variations due to the manner in which the patches were attached to the blazer coats.

Mr. Don Mitchell had this blazer crest made in 1968. There were as many as 100 made. They exist with silver or gold lettering and are 3-1/2 inch in diameter.
Price: $250-600

Mr. George Wilson of the Metropolitan Police Department of Washington DC had this patch made for Mr. Bill Judd, who was the Colt salesman of that region at that time. The patch was made by the same company that made the patches for the FBI. **Price: $NEP**

This is considered to be one of the most desirable Colt patches. The sales force were given these patches late in the 1960s and instructed to sew them to a jacket. It is thought that as few as 30 may have been made. Two variations exist based on the backs.
Price: $100-150

Mr. Bill Judd had 12 additional patches made for his salesmen in 1978.
Price: $NEP

After receiving the blazer crest from Bill Judd, Mr. Bill Blankenship had 32 of these patches made to give to his salesmen and employees attending the industry shows. They were manufactured in 1985. These patches are a dark royal blue in color.
Price: $250-600

In the late 1980s, blazer crests were manufactured with a black background. They can be found both mounted to a black plastic pocket flap or unmounted.

The blazer crests used during the first part of the 1990s are light blue in color and can be found with clutch-type pin fasteners or plastic pocket flaps. Some that have been removed from the nameplate are unmounted. **Price: $250-300**

Price: $150-300

Price: $250-300

This blazer crest was made from a 1981 patch. The date was removed and the patch stitched to a leather back with tack pin fasteners. The patch is known to have belonged to Mr. Walt Gleason, who was a custom shop supervisor.
Price: $100-250

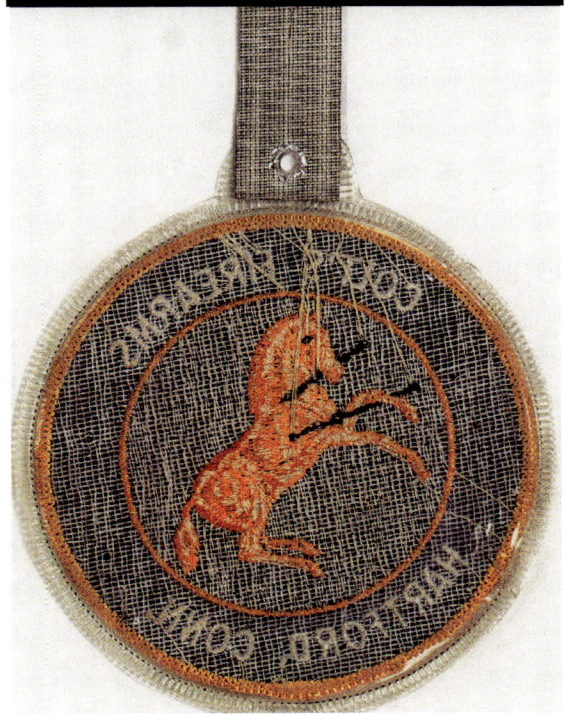

This version of a blazer crest was made by encasing a 1968 promotional patch in plastic and adding the leather strap so the patch could be worn with a company jacket. Since the original owner is not known, it can not be said with certainty that this is a "factory" patch. Courtesy of the Bob Kaminiski collection.
Price: $NEP

Two variations and sizes of a 1980 patch.
Price: $5-15

1981 patch. **Price: $5-15**

65

1982 patch. **Price: $5-15**

1969 California Regional Matches patch. **Price: $10-30**

1966 Combat Pistol Match patch. **Price: $10-30**

In 1996, Colt sponsored several rodeos and a rodeo team. **Price: $5-15**

1966 Pistol Champion-ship patch. **Price: $10-30**

The Colt's Commemorative Gun Collectors Association of America was founded in 1967. Mr. Wallace Beinfield designed this patch which was manufactured in 1968. The patch was reissued in 1975. The Association disbanded in 1979 with a membership of over 2,000. This patch is surprisingly uncommon as 5,000 were manufactured. **Price: $30-50**

Mr. Ken Condry patterned the Colt Collectors Association patch after the logo used for the club's pin. Approximately 500 of the original patches were made. In order to make the patch more closely resemble the association pin, 500 additional patches with the gold border were made in 1990. **Prices from top to bottom: $10-35; $5-25**

These patches were designed in 1988 by Mr. R. Sweeney. There were less than 20 of each design manufactured.
Prices from left to right: $15-50; $20-50

These two patches above were made for Pacific International Mercantile Corporation. Pacific International operated as a Colt distributor in California from 1972 until 1991. As a major distributor Colt allowed them to use the Colt logo. Approximately 250 of each design were made in 1974.
Price: $10-30

These two patches are known to have come from a desk at the Colt factory. They may be the factory originals upon which the reproductions are based, or they may be fantasy patches that were at the factory.
Prices from top to bottom: $50; $30

It is not known if these patches were ever released by the factory or if they are fantasy items. Two photos on top are courtesy of the Tom Saady collection.
**Prices from top to bottom are:
$100-150; $100-150; $10-30**

This fantasy patch was made in 1993.
Price: $5-7

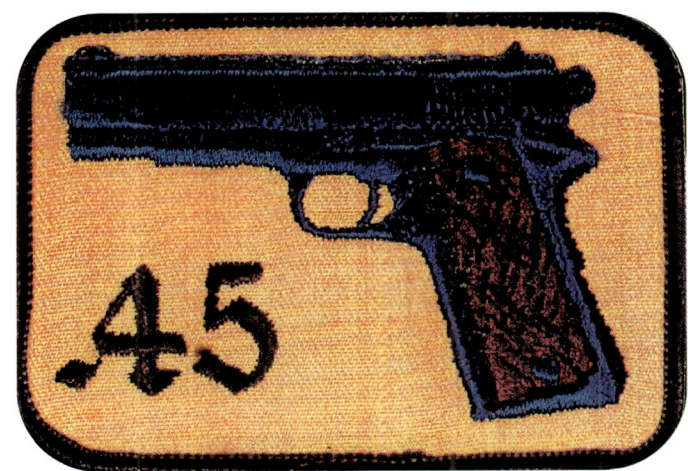

These are fantasy patches that were first made in 1978. They have been reproduced by a number of companies since that time, resulting in slight variations. They are still being produced today.
Price: $3-5, with the exception of the patch directly above, which is valued at $7-10

A 1996 fantasy patch.
Price: $5-7

These four patches above are all fantasy items, as Colt has never used blue as a color for the rampant Colt spears. **Price: $3-6**

Chapter 5
DECALS

Decals were first released by the Colt Firearms factory in the 1950s and were intended to be used for store front advertising. In the 1960s and 1970s a series of decals, also intended for store front advertising, were printed in four languages for Colt's European distributors. Colt has not released a store front decal since that time. In the 1980s and 1990s, decals and stickers have been made for internal use and are also available to the public through the Wares program.

This is the earliest known Colt decal. It was produced in October 1949, for the Autosan commercial dishwashing division of Colt. Courtesy of the Tom Saady collection. **Price: $50-100**

Decals issued for the firearms division are known to have been released in 1952. No examples were available for illustration. This is the original artwork upon which those decals were based. Courtesy of the Tom Saady collection. **Price: $120-150**

Made by the F.M. Decal Company of Hartford in 1957. **Price: $20-50**

COLLECTOR'S NOTE: The next nine decals are 5-1/2 inches in diameter, and were printed by the Palm Brothers Company of New York in 1964 and 1972.

French 1964. **Price: $15**

German 1964. **Price: $15**

French 1972. **Price: $15**

German 1972. **Price: $15**

Italian 1964. **Price: $15**

Spanish 1964. **Price: $15**

Italian 1972. **Price: $15**

Spanish 1972. **Price: $15**

English 1964. **Price: $15**

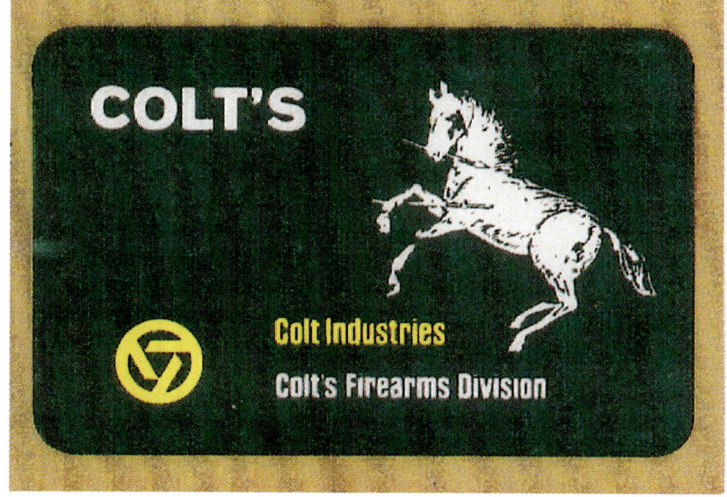

Decal, 3x2 inches printed by the Palm Brothers Company in 1968. **Price: $2-5**

Decal, 8x6 inches printed by the Palm Brothers Company in 1968. **Price: $15-30**

These decals from 1970 measure 6x9 inches.
Value of each item: $5-15

This decal was printed in 1965, 1969 and 1974.
Price: $5-10

77

This decal was printed in 1970 and again in 1974. **Price: $5-10**

This decal was released as part of a promotional campaign in 1981. **Price: $5-15**

These decals are actually parking stickers. Colt Industries used the gear logo from 1963 until 1990. Colt Manufacturing Company took over in 1990 and uses the CMC stickers even today (1996).

Price: $5-15

Price: $5-15

Price: $5-15

Price: $10-25

This is actually a temporary tattoo which is why the image is reversed. **Price: $ .10-1**

The Bravo-Zulu sticker was used by the president of Colt, Mr. Ron Whitiker from 1992 until 1995 to acknowledge exceptional employee performance.
Price: $20-50

Sold through the wares department from 1989 to 1991. **Price: $5-10**

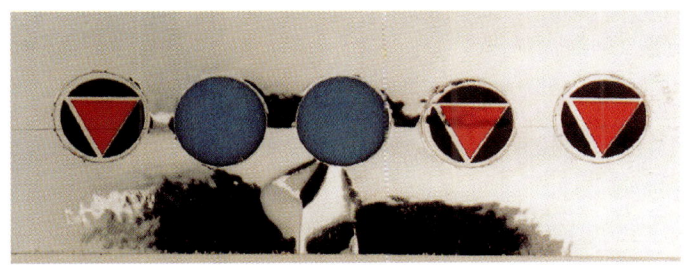

A sticker for the Delta Elite pistol grips issued in 1989. **Price: $5-15**

Sold from 1989 until 1991, this decal measures 3-1/2 inches on a side, and has a silver border that was impossible to photograph. **Price: $5-10**

A sticker given out in 1990.
Price: $1-5

Distributed during 1986, and never publicly sold, this decal is 3 inches in diameter and also has a silver border.
Price: $8-15

Either a decal or packing label from Colt Industries. **Price: $5-10**

Given out in 1996. **Price: $1-5**

Decals, from unknown date.
Price: $5-10

These decals were intended for use with a Plexiglas case to display a line of knives or holsters Colt introduced in 1972.
Value of each item: $15-30

Sold through the wares program during 1989 and 1990. **Price: $10-20**

Given out at the NRA show in 1996. **Price: $5-10**

It is not known if these decals came from the factory or if they are fantasy items.

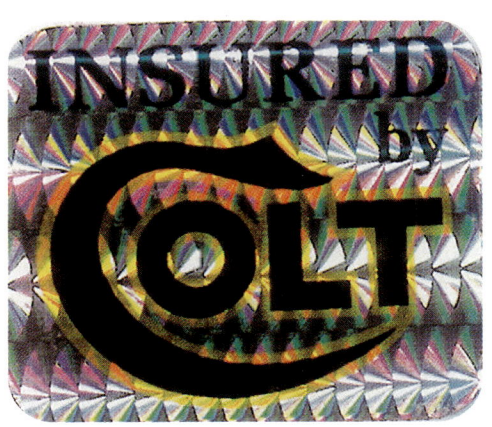

Price: $5-10

Price: $5-8 each

Fantasy bumper stickers and decals from 1993-1996.
Value of each item: $1-3

Chapter 6
BALL CAPS

Some of the Colt patches were offered attached to ball caps. Today Colt logos are being directly stitched onto the caps.

These ball caps were offered for sale through the Colt Wear Catalog in 1996.

Price: $17.00

Price: $16.00

Price: $18.00

Price: 12.00

Price: $17.00

Price: $9.00

Price: $18.00

Price: $17.00

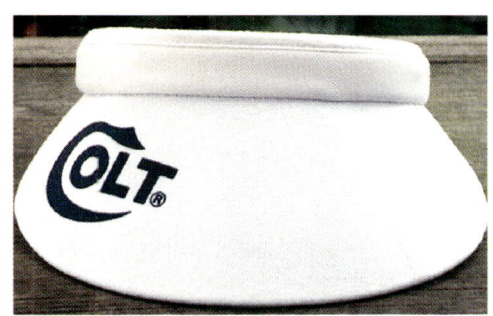

Price: $6.00

Price: $17.00

This cap, also offered for sale in the 1996 catalog, was available either sized or adjustable.

Price: $18.00

Price: $18.00

Price: $18.00

Three colors of hat bands were also available in the 1996 catalog. **Price: $3.00**

In 1996, Colt began sponsorship of a rodeo team.
Price: $15-30

Colt sponsored L.W. Miller in an ARCA Bondo/Mar-Hyde supercar series during 1995. These ball caps are one of the few collectibles from Colt's racing team. Photo at far left courtesy of the David Hoyte collection. **Prices from top to bottom: $50; $50; $75**

The advertising campaign, "Made Only in the USA," was in effect for only two years 1989 and 1990. This ball cap was available through the wares program for those years. Photo courtesy of the Stan Newman collection. **Price: $25-35**

These are prototype ball caps for the, "Made Only in the USA," advertising campaign that were not offered for sale. Photo courtesy of the Stan Newman collection. **Prices from top to bottom: $25-50; $25-50; $50-75**

Ball cap given to the sales force to wear.
Price: $25-50

The Colt M16 A2 was introduced in 1984.
Price: $25-50

Ball cap sold to law enforcement personnel in 1996. **Price: $9.95**

The Colt H Bar was introduced for civilian sale in 1986. Photo courtesy of the Stan Newman collection. **Price: $25-50**

This cap was given to those persons who completed a retail sales training program conducted around the country by the regional Colt sales managers and factory personnel during 1990 and 1991.
Price: $25-50

The Colt Delta Elite pistol was introduced in 1989.
Price: $25-50

A 1981 promotion for the Colt Black Powder revolver. Photo courtesy of the Stan Newman collection. **Price: $25-50**

Two variations of patches found on caps known to have been sold by the factory during 1991 and 1992. So many of these caps were made, they continued to be available into 1995.
Price: $25-50

A summer and winter cap having the same Colt patch. **Prices from top to bottom: $10-20; $25-50.** Photo at right courtesy of the Stan Newman collection.

Three additional variations thought to have been released by the factory. **Price: $25-50**

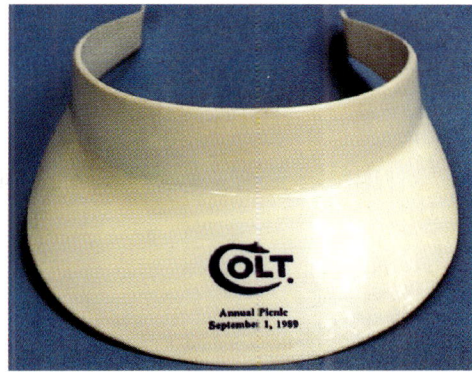

A visor given to employees at an annual picnic in 1989. **Price: $10**

Five prototype ski caps were ordered, only one is known to have been delivered, and they were never mass produced. Photo courtesy of the Stan Newman collection. **Price: $NEP**

Two stitched logo caps given out by the factory. **Price: $25-50**

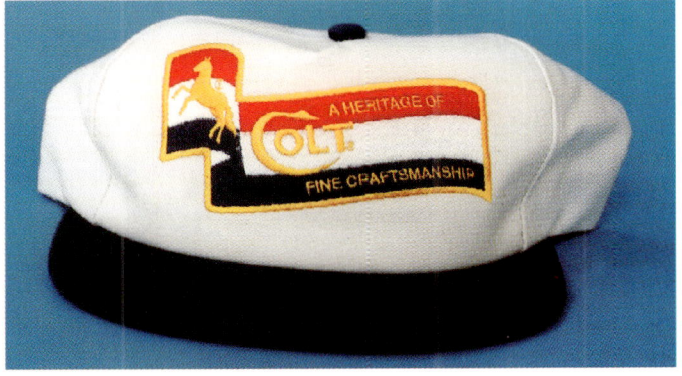

The advertising campaign "A Heritage of Fine Craftsmanship" was used during 1984 and 1985. **Price: $25-50**

These two pages are fantasy ball caps known to have not been released through the factory. **Price: $7-15**

COLLECTOR'S NOTE: Colt is the primary sponsor of the Colt Cup Rifle Matches that have been held every September since 1986. The matches are run by the Bell City Rifle Club of Southington Conn. and are held at the Blue Trail Range in Wallingford Conn. The event is limited to Colt or Colt authorized productions of the Colt Sporter and AR-15. In 1988, Colt gave out a standard ball cap. Since then, Colt has produced a limited number of caps for each year's event. The event was not held in 1992.

Caps. **Prices: directly above, $50; others shown $25-50**

This ball cap has a printed logo and is thought to have not been issued by the factory. **Price: $25-50**

Chapter 7
KNIVES

In 1971, Colt entered the knife business with the introduction of 13 different knives from the three manufacturers of Sheffield, Olson and Barry Wood. Each of the four Sheffield designs were available with either brown or black handles for a total of 8 variations. They were packed in a red flannel cutlery glove with a gold rampant Colt stamped on it. They included a Brown leather scabbard and were packed in individual boxes. There were 2,500 of each model made. They were sold as the Trailblazer, Mountaineer, Plainsman and Trapper under the Wilderness line of knives.

The line of all-purpose knives sold as the Sportsman line were made by Olson and came in three sizes. The original contract called for Olsen to supply 20,000 knives. However, at the start of production a fire destroyed part of the factory. A total of 1,000 Olsen knives of all three varieties are thought to have been accepted by Colt before the fire. They were also packed in the red flannel cutlery glove and included black leather sheaths.

The remainder of the contract was never filled. Some additional knives are known to exist which were rejected by Colt. These knives will have the Colt name partially buffed off. They were bought and resold by a major cutlery company in 1976 as irregulars. In addition, Olsen knife blanks stamped with the Colt trademark are known to exist. Some of these have recently been finished. Colt discontinued these knives in 1973.

BARRY WOOD

In late 1969, Barry Wood supplied a folding knife based upon his patent to Colt. Out of 35,000 MKI knives made by Wood 15,300 were supplied to Colt. The components were made by several contractors and assembled by Engineering Design and Services in Venice, California.

During the course of the four years he supplied knives to Colt, Mr. Wood continued to modify and improve his knives. He succeeded in creating a bewildering number of variations of what he considers to be just one knife, his MKI with a Colt logo. Most of the knives were produced with brown (natural canvas micarta) or burgundy (cordovan linen micarta) handles. There were 12 salesmen's samples made with black handles and one or possibly two with a stag handle. Collectors divide the knives into either three, four or five variations. Three major variations are presented here. All Barry Wood MKI Colt knives have the clearly visible Rampant logo present on the hinge pin, even when the knife is closed.

An assortment of Colt knives as offered in the 1972 catalog.
Prices: Sheffield $250-400, Wood $300-1000, Olsen $600-800

THE WILDERNESS LINE MANUFACTURED IN SHEFFIELD ENGLAND

1	U1010 Trailblazer, 7"	brown handle
2	U1011 Trailblazer, 7"	black handle
3	U1020 Mountaineer, 6"	brown handle
4	U1021 Mountaineer, 6"	black handle
5	U1030 Plainsman, 5½"	brown handle
6	U1031 Plainsman, 5½"	black handle
7	U1040 Trapper, 3½"	brown handle
8	U1041 Trapper, 3½"	black handle

THE WILDERNESS LINE MANUFACTURED BY BARRY WOOD

| 9 | U1050 Hunter, 3½ " | brown handle |
| 10 | U1051 Hunter, 3½" | black handle |

THE SPORTSMAN LINE MANUFACTURED BY OLSEN

11	U1110 All Purpose, 5½"	rosewood handle
12	U1120 All Purpose, 4½"	rosewood handle
13	U1130 Trout & Bird, 4"	rosewood handle

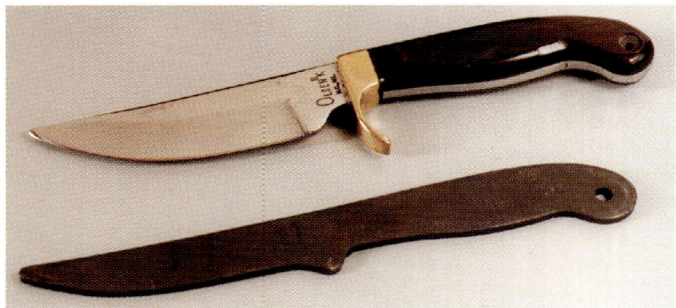

A non-Colt Olsen and a blank. Courtesy of the Ron Lough collection.
Price: $85-100

Logo stamp on the Colt Olsen blank. Courtesy of the Ron Lough collection.
Price: $125-150

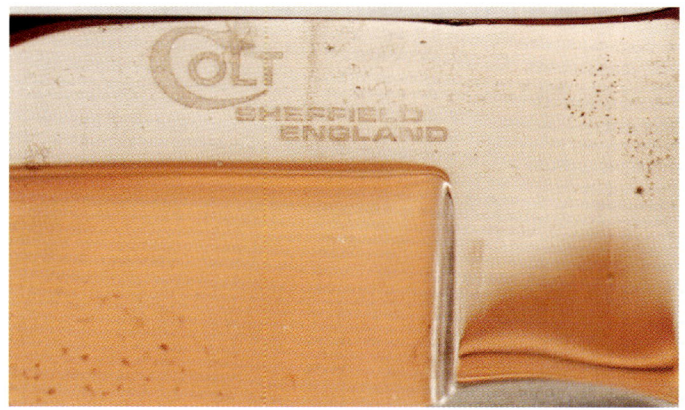

Logo stamp on the Sheffield knives. Courtesy of the Ron Lough collection.
Price: $350-375

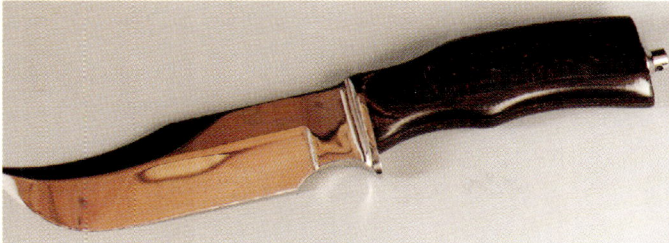

As few as 24 of these prototype Sheffield knives were made. They have a 6-1/2 inch blade and half were made with a black handle and the other half with a Brown Handle. Courtesy of the Ron Lough collection.
Price: $600-700

A dealer display case for Colt knives or holsters.
Price: $125-250

BARRY WOOD

The first 500s have the serpentine logo on the opposite side of the knife from the rampant logo. Photo courtesy of the Tom Saady collection.
Price: $1,000

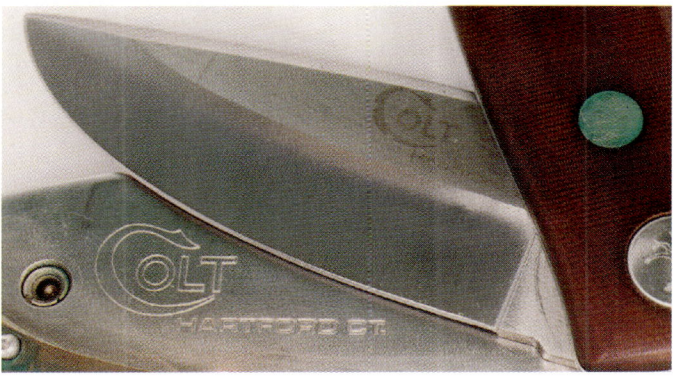

The next 2,000 not only have the rampant and serpentine blade logo on the same side of the knife, but have in addition, a large serpentine logo etched on the handle plate. All three logos are visible on the same side of the knife. Photo courtesy of the Tom Saady collection.
Price: $400-600

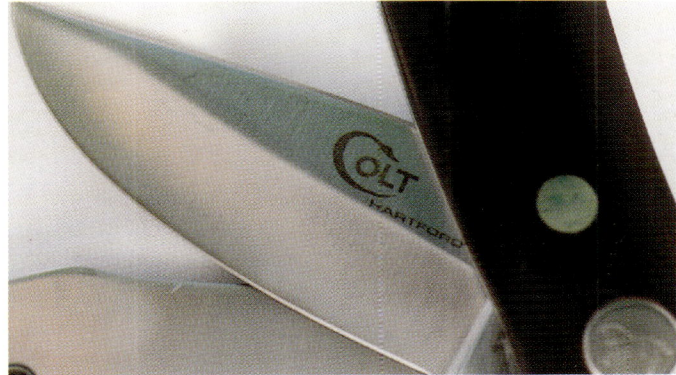

The large serpentine logo was left off the remaining knives, leaving the rampant logo on the hinge pin and the serpentine logo on the blade both visible at the same time. The handle was also changed from a rounded corner to a more angular edge which Mr. Wood called a "four-arc section". Some of these knives were made with the brown handles while most had the burgundy handles, some had handles that wrapped around the handle ends and some had handles with ends ground into a lightly flaring radius. Additionally some knives were made with a glossy finish to the handles. Other variations of this knife will have Stainless stamped at the base of the blade or U.S. Pat. stamped on the back of the blade. Photo courtesy of the Tom Saady collection.
Price: $350-450

The black salesmen's samples were packed in a tube. Courtesy of the Tom Saady collection. **Price: $1,000-2,000**

Tan and black sheaths were supplied, apparently at random, to those knives commercially sold. They were packed in Brown gun-style boxes. Photo courtesy of the Tom Saady collection.
Price: $350-500

An Italian replica of the Barry Wood reminds us to use caution and buy from reputable dealers. Courtesy of the Dan Chesiak collection. **Price: $200**

BOWIE

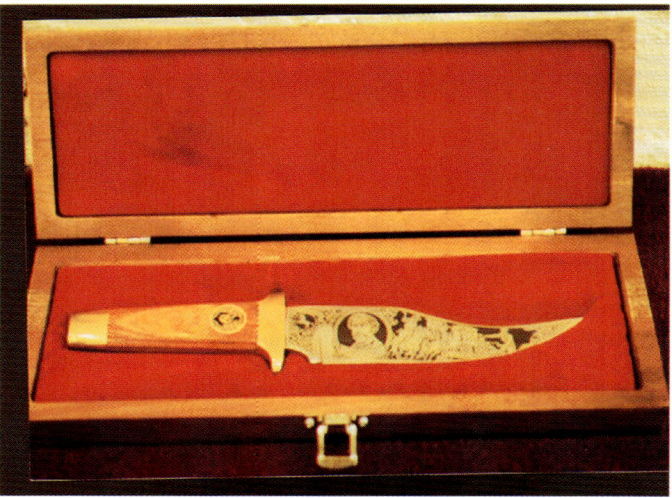

In 1977, Aurum Etching of Texas produced the Samuel Colt Collectors Bowie under license from Colt firearms. They were available serialized to the collectors, Colt or not, and some are reported without the medallion. **Price: $350**

This is thought to be a prototype from Aurum Etching. It depicts 17 of the presidents of Colt. Courtesy of the Ron Lough collection. **Price: $4,000**

BOKER

In 1978, Boker made 1,000 of these knives for Colt to be sold through Clearfield Hardware Co., Inc. of Pennsylvania. Courtesy of the Dan Chesiak collection. **Price: $250-300**

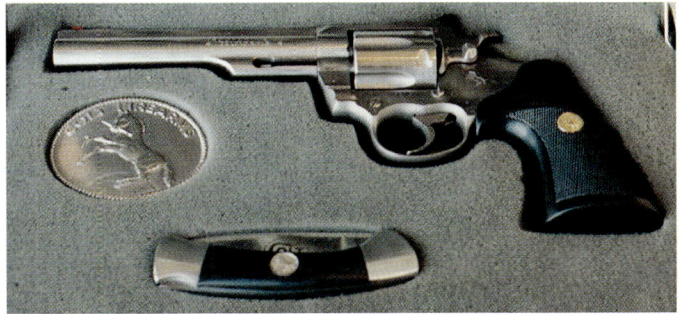

Three hundred of the Boker knives were cased with a Trooper MKIII and a buckle as the Clearfield Companion Set. The remaining knives were sold separately. **Price: $600-1,200**

BUCK

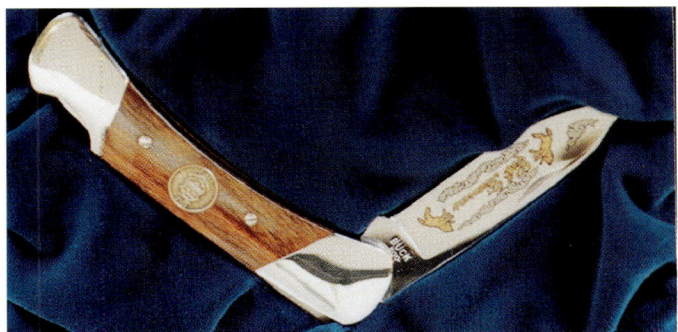

In 1983, Colt again offered a knife in their catalog. A serialized Buck with a custom shop medallion and etched blade was offered in a glass topped case until 1989. **Price: $250-350**

COLLECTOR'S NOTE: In 1986, Mr. Bill Judd, with Colt, commissioned two Buck knives to be engraved by Aurum Etching of Texas. They were to have been distributed through American Collectible Products.

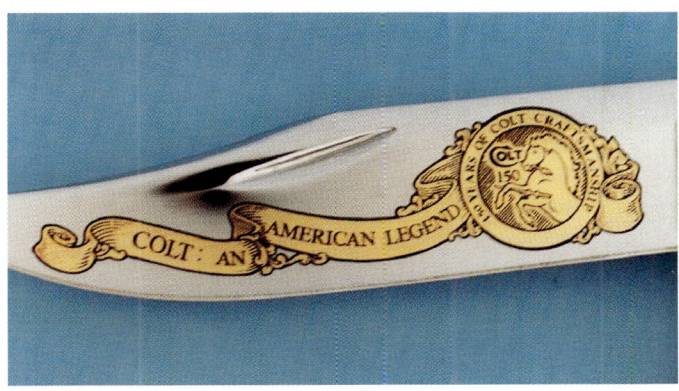

The Buck 110 folding knife was to have unlimited production throughout the year of 1986. It is thought that as few as 50 were actually made. Courtesy of the Dan Chesiak collection. **Price: $500**

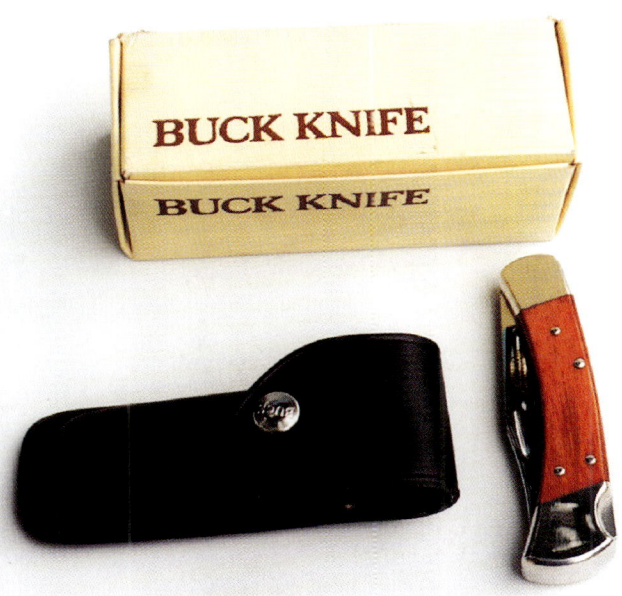

The Buck 110 came with a sheath and was packed in a Buck box. Courtesy of the Bill Judd collection. **Price: $500**

Some of the Buck 110's were custom cased. Courtesy of the Dan Chesiak collection. **Price: $500**

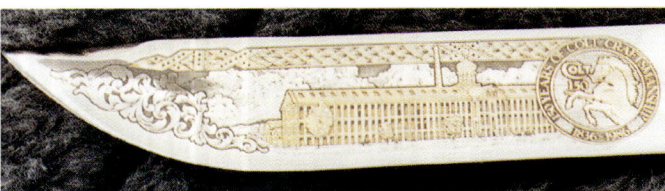

The Buck Custom 124 Frontiersman was serialized and was intended to be limited to 1,000. Serial number 15 is the highest number known and it is thought that as few as 20 were actually made. Reportedly the first knives produced were appropriated by executives at Colt, so American Collectible Products ceased production. Only four are known to have been commercially sold. Courtesy of the Dan Chesiak collection.
Price: $1,500-2,000

One of the Buck Custom 124 Frontiersman was custom cased and hung on an executive's wall at Colt. Courtesy of the Ron Lough collection.
Price: $2,500-3,000

COLLECTOR'S NOTE: Colt sold two Buck 525 pocket knives at the Colt Collectors Association meeting in Atlanta during 1996.

Only 75 of this design were made for the 1996 Atlanta show.
Price: $85

175 of this design were made for the 1996 Atlanta show. **Price: $85**

SCHRADE

The Schrade DE 555 knife, with serpentine and rampant Colt logos, was sold through the Colt catalog during 1989 and 1991. **Price: $35-75**

Two variations are known with either standard or modified leather awl.
Price: $35-75

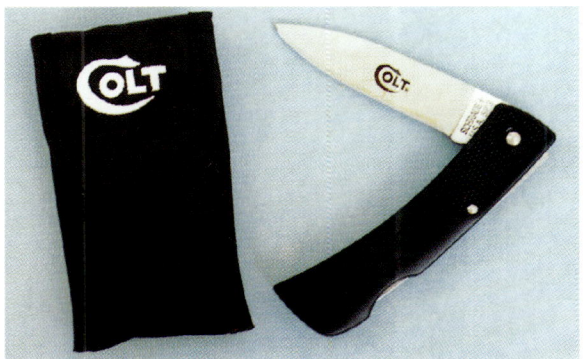

The base of the blade is marked Schrade.
Price: $50

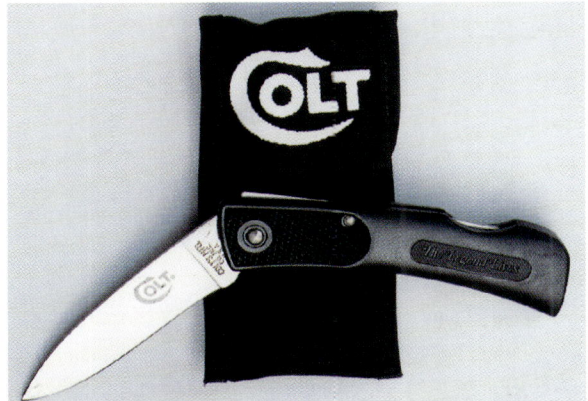

The base of the blade is marked "COLT'S MFG CO. INC." **Price: $32.50**

COLLECTOR'S NOTE: A Schrade with leather sheath offered during 1993 to present. Two variations are known.

A Schrade with a 150th anniversary medallion is known. It is not known how many were produced. Photo courtesy of the Stan Newman collection.
Price: $75-100

COLLECTOR'S NOTE: A Schrade knife marked "The Legend Lives" is still available today. Two variations are known.

No logo on blade. **Price: $52.50**

Serpentine logo on blade. **Price: $52.50**

CAMILLUS

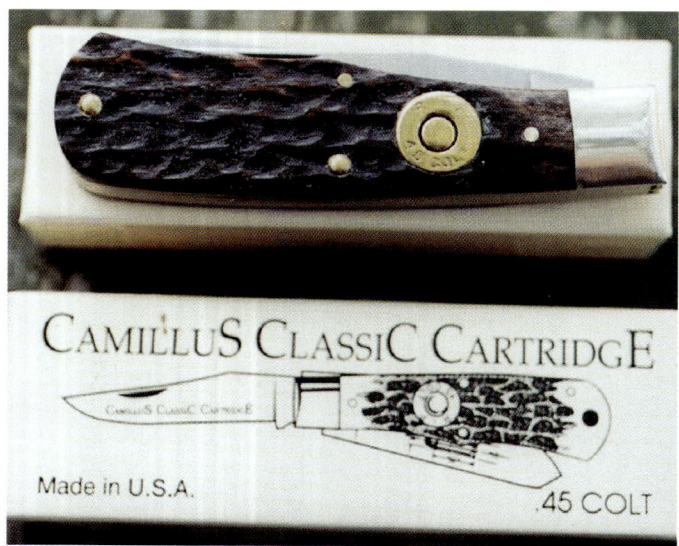

A Camillus with 150th anniversary medallion. Courtesy of the Jack Kelley collection. **Price: $75-100**

Colt by association is this 1996 Camillus cartridge knife celebrating the Colt 45 cartridge.
Price: $35

COLONIAL PROVINCE

A Colonial Province knife sold during 1992. **Price: $25-35**

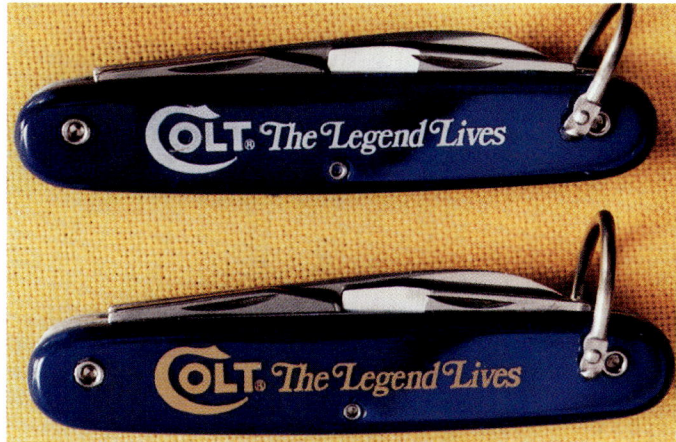

Another Colonial Province variation in two colors sold during 1992. Photo courtesy of the Stan Newman collection. **Price: $35-75**

WENGER

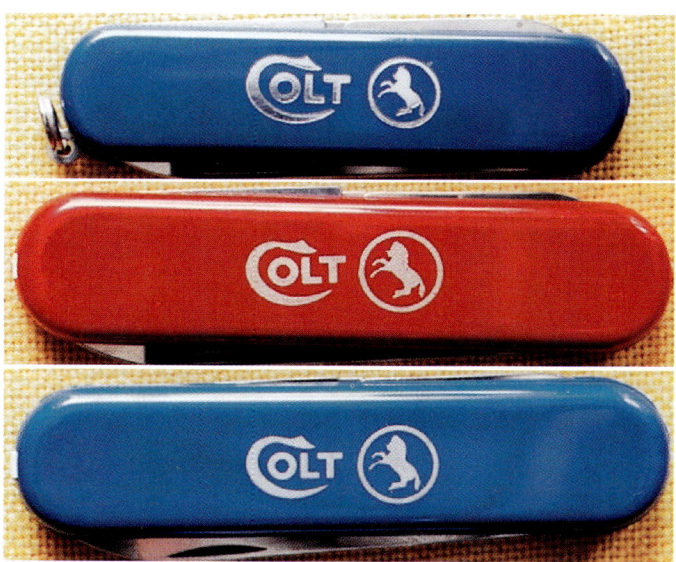

These knives made by Wenger were used internally as promotional and award items. Photo courtesy of the Stan Newman collection. **Price: $75-125**

CHINA

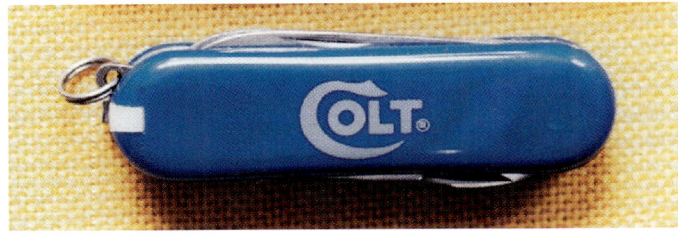

This knife, made in China, was given out at trade shows during 1991.
Price: $10-25

This knife, made in China, was given out at trade shows during 1996 and 1997. Only 500 were made.
Price: $10-25

ZIPPO

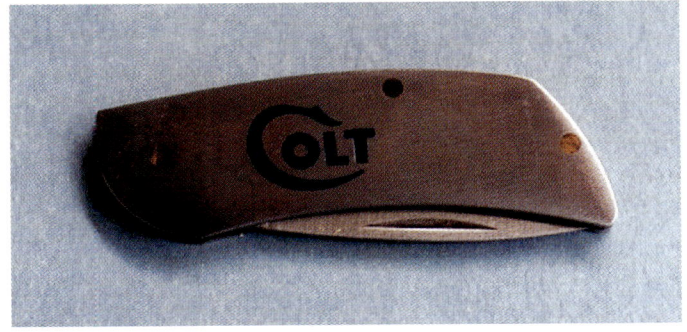

This knife, by Zippo, was distributed through the factory. **Price: $75-125**

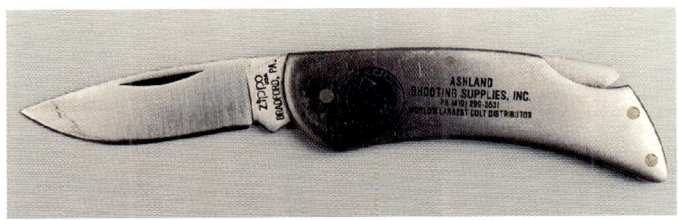

This Zippo was produced by Ashland Shooting Supplies as a gift for Colt executives and salesmen of the company. Ashland was a major Colt distributor. Photo courtesy of the Dan Chesiak collection. **Price: $125**

UNITED CUTLERY

In 1993, Colt licensed United to produce a line of knives.

The first United Colt knife was the CT1LTD, a limited edition Bowie serialized to 7,500. **Price: $NEP**

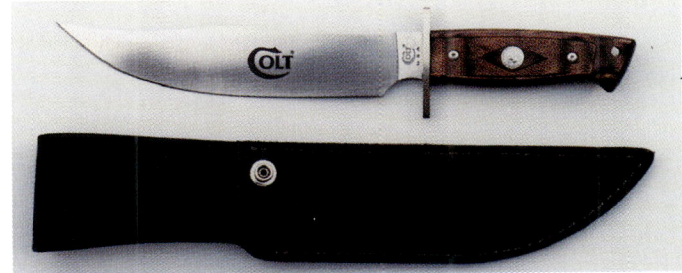

The regular Bowie CT1 was produced from 1993 until 1996.
Price: $59.99

A stand was available for dealer display of the CT1. **Price: $20-50**

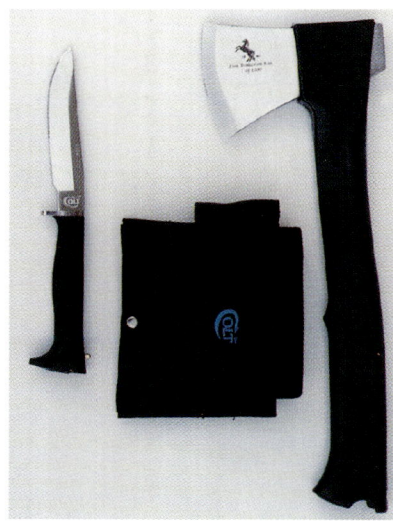

The CT2, an ax-knife combination, was not available until 1996. The first production run was serialized to 500. **Price: $50-93**

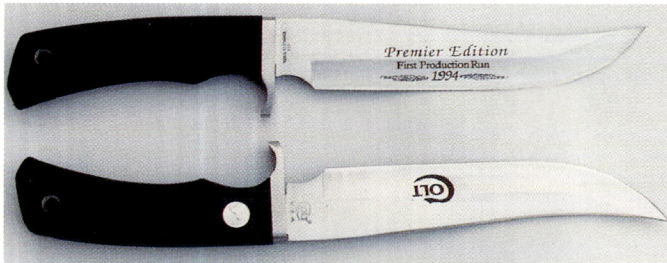

The CT3 Clip Point Hunter first production run was serialized to 500, and the remainder of the production was a standard non-serialized run.
Price: $50-80

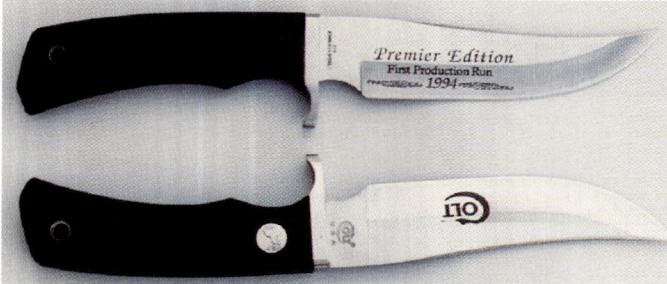

The CT4 Small Clip Point Hunter first production run was serialized to 500, and the remainder of the production was a standard non-serialized run. **Price: $39-74**

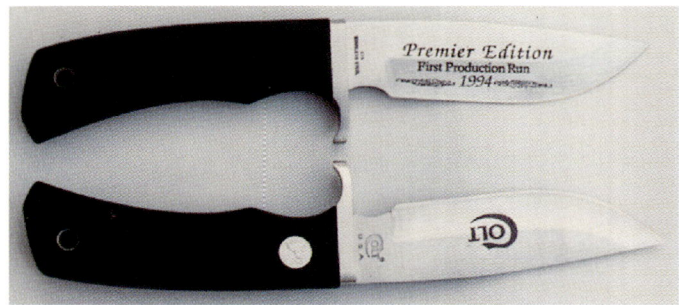

The CT5 Drop Point Hunter first production run was serialized to 500, and the remainder of the production was a standard non-serialized run. **Price: $39-74**

The CT5-L was released as a limited edition of 500 with a special belt buckle and plaque honoring Sam Colt as the first American tycoon. **Price: $79.99**

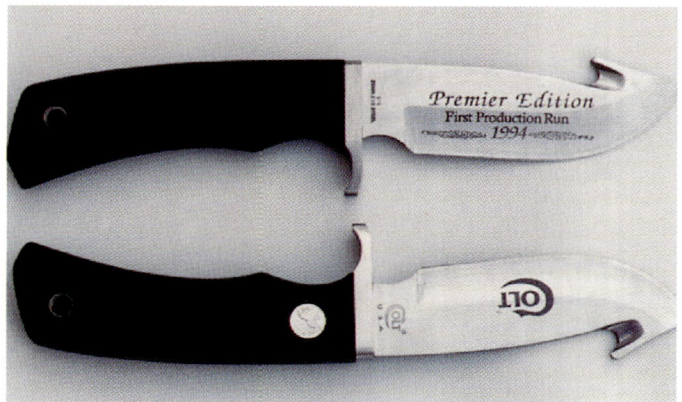

The CT6 Skinner first production run serialized to 500 and the standard production run. **Price: $42-80**

The CT-7 Serengeti Skinner standard production run and the CT7-B Serrated with black handle limited to 1250 knives. The CT-7 was also issued in a run of 500 first production knives. **Price: $55-112 ea.**

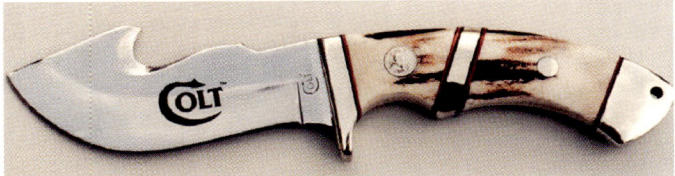

CT-7S Stag handle. **Price: $188**

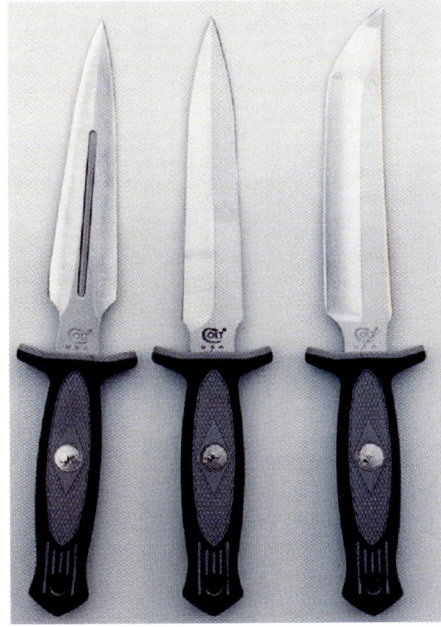

The CT8 Liberator dagger, CT9 Commander bayonet and CT10 Defender Tanto. These three knives were also available in a first production run serialized to 750.
Price: $42-82 ea.

The CT11 Sam Colt Signature Bowie issued in 1995 was limited to 1,000 knives. **Price: $260-538**

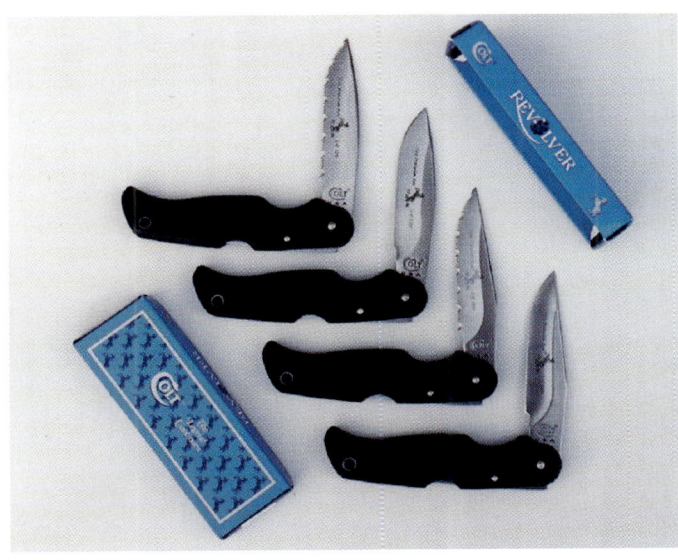

CT12 clip blade, CT13 serrated clip blade, CT14 drop-point blade and the CT15 serrated drop-point blade are all identified as Colt revolver lockbacks. The wheel used to roll the blade open is in the shape of a revolver cylinder. **Price: $60 ea.**

A dealer display case for the CT3, CT4, CT5, CT6, CT7-B and CT10. **Price: $125-250**

Shoulder holster for the CT8 or CT9.
Price: $20

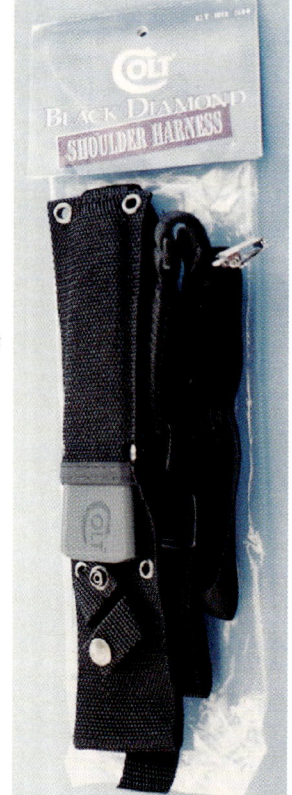

B.M.W. SOLINGEN

These knives made by B.M.W. Solingen are most likely fantasy knives. Courtesy of the Dan Chesiak collection.
Price: $350

It is not known if the 4 knives above were released through the factory or not. Courtesy of the Dan Chesiak collection.
Price: $50-100

TAYLOR

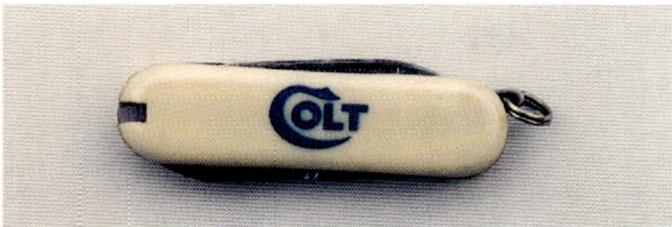

This knife made by Taylor is a fantasy. **Price: $5-15**

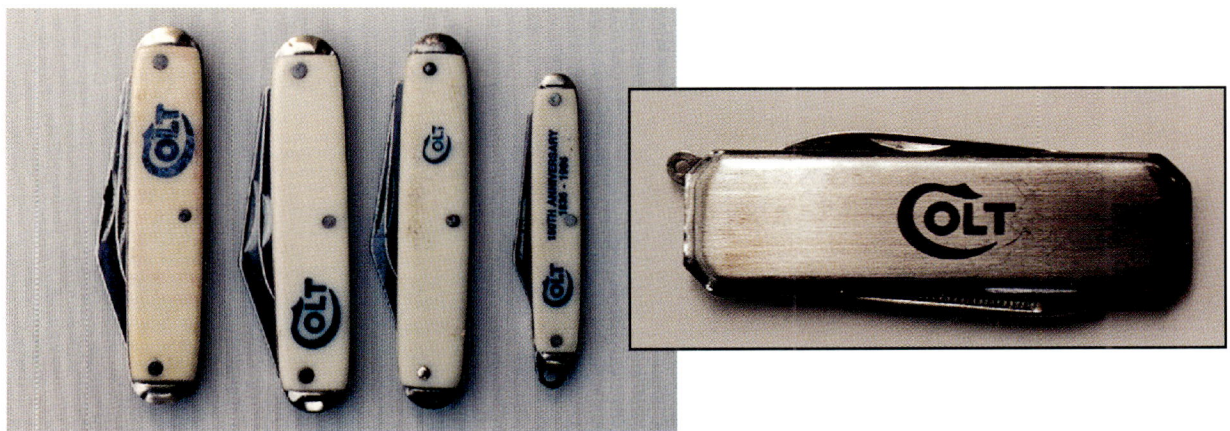

These knives made in China are fantasy knives. **Price: $5-15**

CASE

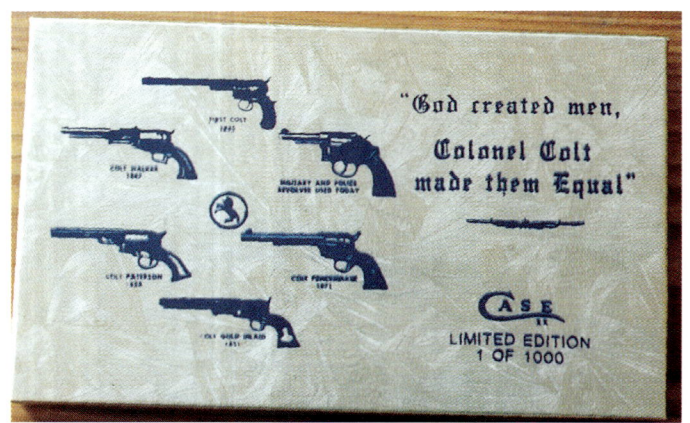

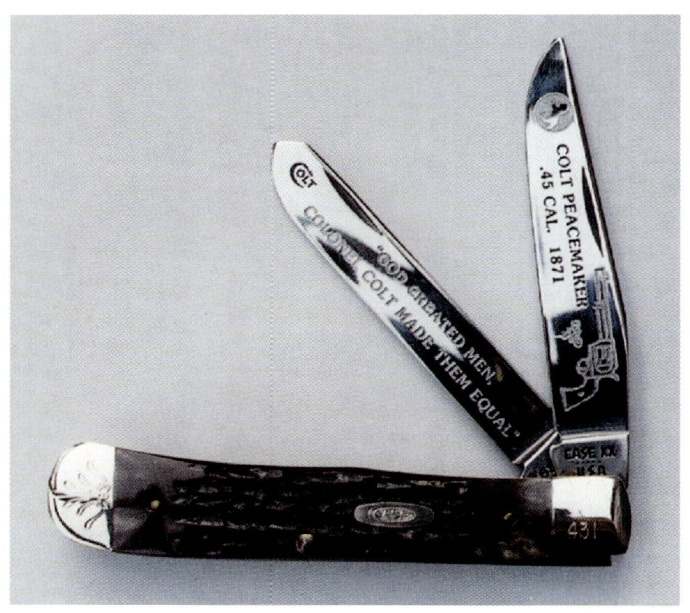

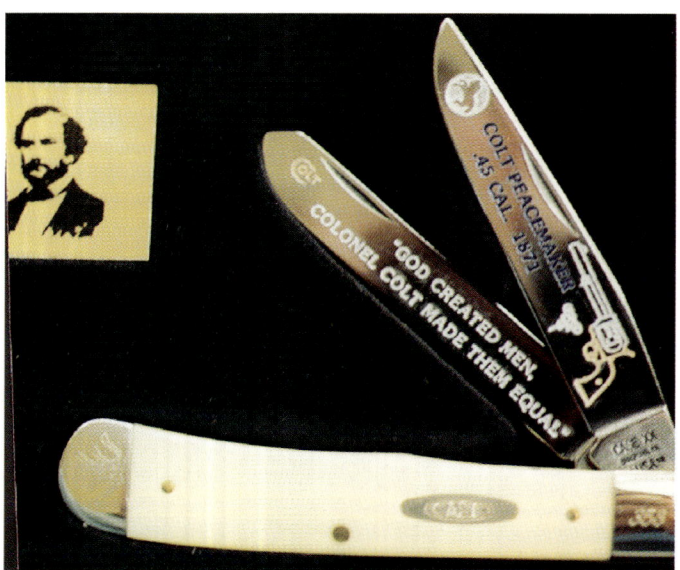

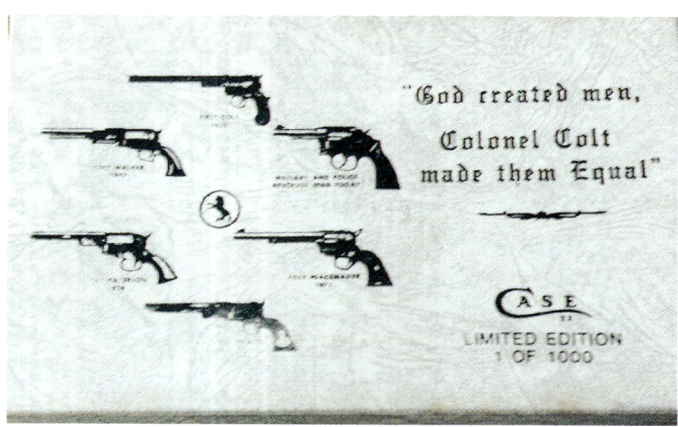

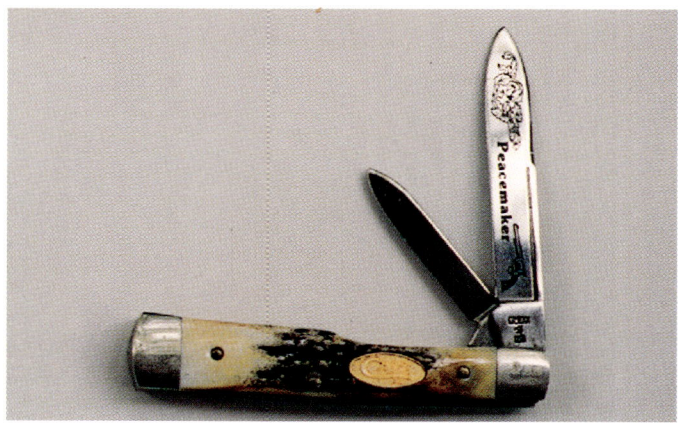

These three Case sets are also fantasy items that were never released through the factory.
Price: $50-100

Chapter 8
BUCKLES

Most buckles are made from brass which can be struck from a die. The die is made from a hob. The hob, made of steel, is engraved with the desired design and then hardened. Lead impressions are generally sent as proofs for approval so changes can be made before the hob is hardened. The die made from the hob will be a reverse image. When the die gets worn or breaks, a new die can be struck from the hob. There were several individuals at Colt who wanted a set of the lead proofs, so Colt required the manufacturer to supply several.

It is unclear when the first buckle was produced for distribution by the Colt factory. A buckle was offered in a 1962 sales promotion for the I.U. Combat Police Pistol Matches. It was available in either rhodium or gold plate and featured either the Single Action Army or the .45 automatic. No examples were available to photograph. The first mass-marketed buckles appeared in 1978. They were produced by Martek, for the Custom Shop, and came in ten different finishes. Brass, gold plate and rhodium were standard. Thirteen were made in solid gold and 250 were made in sterling silver.

An attempt was made to produce a color case-hardened blue. The dies could not stand up to the steel used for the buckles, so none were ever case-hardened. However, five steel variations of the buckle were produced. In 1979, a black variation was produced for inclusion with the blackpowder guns. A blue variation exists, and thirteen green buckles were produced for St. Patrick's Day.

Clearfield Hardware included a nickel-plated buckle with its Mark III companion set licensed through Colt. Martek would produce the 2nd edition buckle in 1979. It was produced in five finishes including a gold and rhodium. The sterling silver edition was limited to 500. Sports Style produced the third edition buckle in 1985. A sterling silver edition was limited to 1,000 and was encased in a walnut box having a pewter rampant horse. Standard editions were brass, rhodium, gold plate, nickel plate and rhodium and gold. A smaller version was produced both in silver & gold and silver & blue. Some variations are still available today.

There are probably more fantasy buckles bearing the name Colt than there are original buckles that were legitimately released through the factory. The most annoying of these are those marked "The World's Right Arm." The person responsible has not been found. Colt used the design and phrase "The World's Right Arm" in a 1909 advertisement. The first buckles seem to have been made in the 1950s. They were reproduced by almost every buckle company throughout the 1970s and early 1980s. Some are marked as having been made by Tiffany and Co., either in New York or London.

It is my opinion that neither Colt nor Tiffany ever had anything to do with the making or issuance of these buckles, because the buckles' logos and the logo of Tiffany and Co. are dissimilar. A couple of the companies may have actually licensed the buckles through Colt, but even this is unconfirmed. Another fantasy buckle is the Colt cameo. It was made by the same companies as "The World's Right Arm" and can also be found marked as from Tiffany. It was also produced by Adina, in silver, under license from Colt. A number of variations of buckles for the Army and the Navy are purported to have been made from shell casings either from the war or from Colt. No evidence has been found to support this claim.

Patterned after the 1962 I.U. combat buckle. Courtesy of the Marty Huber collection. **Price: $NEP**

Black variation from 1979. **Price: $50-100**

First edition brass buckle introduced in 1978. **Price: $30-50**

Also produced and sold through the custom shop in 1978 were these buckles available in black, turquoise and coral. **Price: $150-350**

250 were made in pure sterling silver and cased in a wooden box bearing a pewter Armsmear crest. Photo courtesy of the Tom Saady collection. **Price: $250-600**

A buckle presented to Bill Judd in 1978 as sales manager that was engraved by Howard Dove. Bill Judd collection. **Price: $NEP**

Concept artwork from Martek resulting in the second generation buckle in 1979. Courtesy of the Tom Saady collection. **Price: $150-200**

Second generation buckle from 1979 in brass. **Price: $20-35**

There were 500 made in pure sterling silver. **Price: $150-450**

Second edition buckle in rhodium. **Price: $25-40**

Second edition buckle in gold plate. **Price: $25-40**

Black Powder buckle from 1979. **Price: $100-250**

In 1981, this buckle appeared in an advertisement used by Colt. They were given to management and executives by Pacific International. **Price: $20-50**

COLLECTOR'S NOTE: These four third edition buckles were made by Sports Style in 1985.

Brass. **Price: $20-40**

Rhodium. **Price: $20-40**

Gold plate. **Price: $20-40**

Rhodium and gold. **Price: $20-40**

Nickel plated, small silver and gold and small silver and blue. **Price: $20-50**

This buckle was offered for sale to those persons purchasing a double diamond set of guns in 1986. The buckle is marked "150" to celebrate the 150th anniversary of Colt. **Price: $35-75**

Sold in 1986 to celebrate the 150 anniversary of Colt. This buckle is based on the medallion of the same design. **Price: $75-150**

Also sold in 1986 and marked with the 150th anniversary logo. **Price: $35-75**

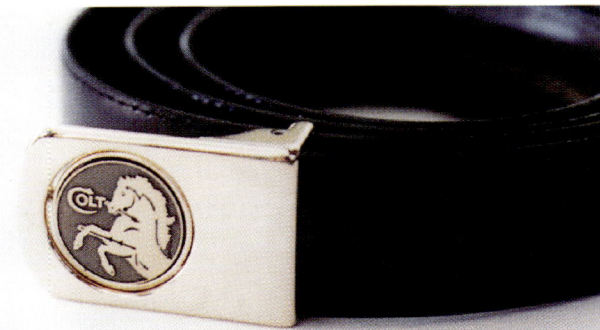

Similar to the 150 buckle, this belt and buckle were sold from 1989 until 1992. **Price: $35**

A ladies belt and buckle sold from 1989 to 1996. **Price: $35**

These buckles made by Aurum Etching in silver and gold were sold during 1988 through the Custom Shop. **Price: $30-50**

A similar buckle known only in gold is thought to date from the same time. **Price: $30-50**

COLLECTOR'S NOTE: The following three "The Legend Lives" buckles were available from 1992 until 1995.

Brass. **Price: $25-40**

111

Rhodium. **Price: $25-40**

Gold plate. **Price: $25-40**

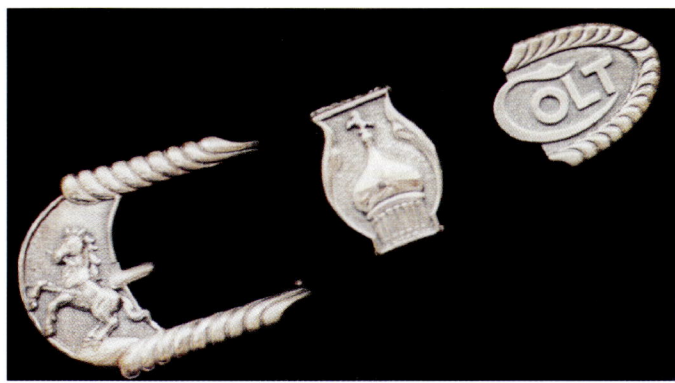

This buckle set is the creation of Francolini, a former custom shop engraver. **Price: $225**

These items are available through the Colt Wear catalog.

Price: $39.95

Price: $54.95

Price: $29.95

Licensed through the Colt Blackpowder Arms Company.
Price: $39.95

A Zippo buckle of uncertain date known to have been given out by the factory.
Price: $50-100

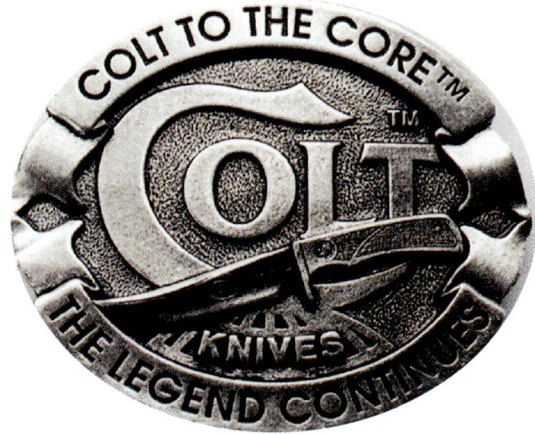
This buckle was available from January to June 1996, with the purchase of knives from United. United is licensed to use the Colt logo. **Price: $15-30**

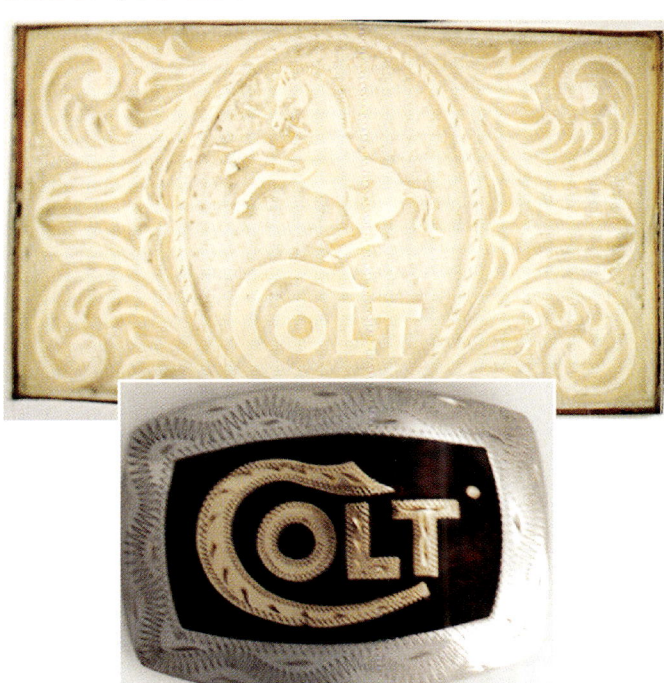

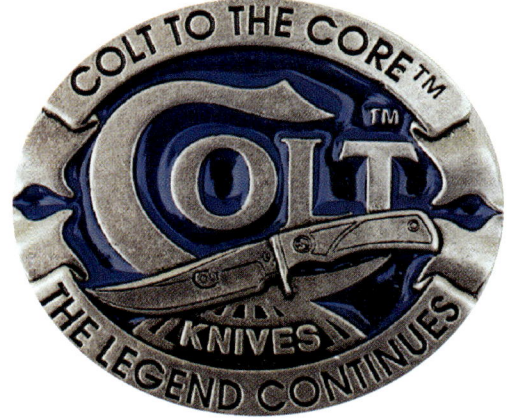
A blue variation was included with the CT5-L knife. **Price: $30-50**

These three buckles are also known to have been issued through the factory and were given to Colt employees. However nothing is known of their origin or date. Item at bottom from the Jack Kelley collection. Item at the top from the Jim Alaimo collection. **Prices from top to bottom: $NEP; $50-100; $300**

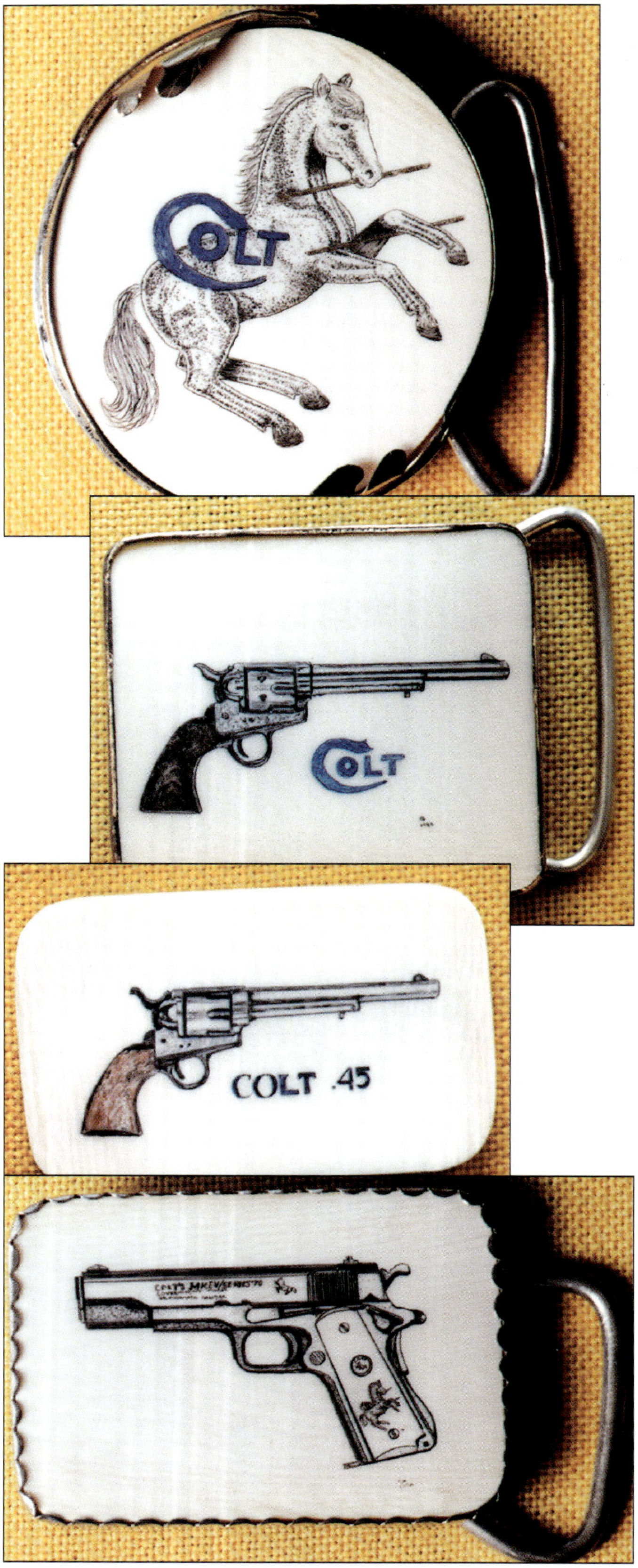

These are Colt prototype buckles that were never produced. Photo courtesy of Stan Newman collection. **Price: $NEP**

World's Right Arm. Fantasy Buckles.
Price: $3-7

Colt cameo. **Price: $5-15**

Colt cameo in a sterling silver limited edition by Adina. **Price: $50-100**

Marked Tiffany New York. **Price: $3-10**

Tiffany London mark. **Price: $3-10**

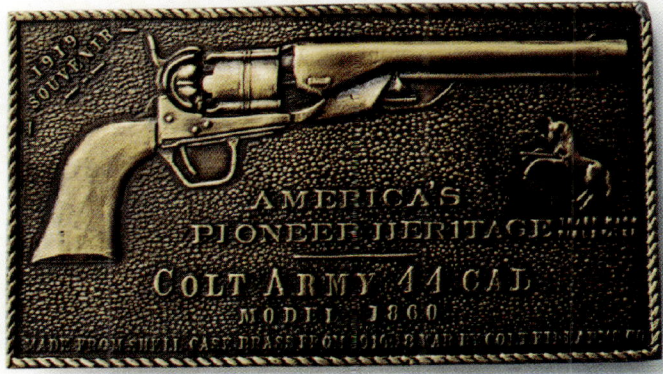
Colt Army. **Price: $3-10**

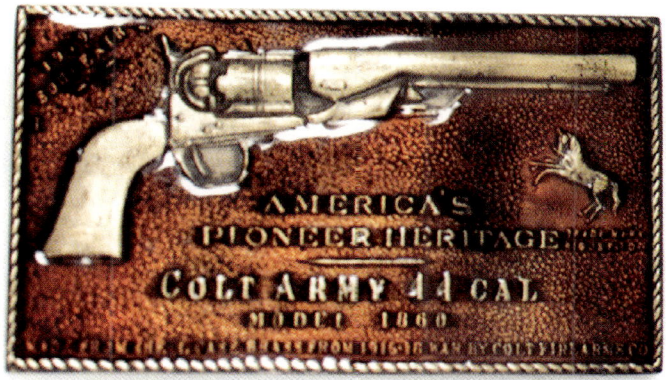
Colt Army variation. Courtesy of the Tom Saady collection. **Price: $3-10**

Colt Thompson. **Price: $3-10**

Colt shield. **Price: $3-25**

A fantasy buckle reproducing the logo of the Patterson capper made in 1996.
Price: $10-15

$10-25

$10-25

$16.95

$16.95

$5-15

$10-25

$10-25

$10-25

$10-25

$10-25

$10-25

$10-25

Some other fantasy buckles never released through the factory.

70-1 Walker Colt | 5670-2 .44 Dragoon Colt

70-5 1851 Navy Colt | 5670-6 .44 Rimfire Colt

70-9 Lightning Colt | 5670-10 Frontier Colt

670-13 1917 New Service Revolver Colt | 5670-14 .357 Magnum Python Colt

It is not clear if these buckles currently being sold are licensed. They are available in brass and gold and silver plate. **Prices: Above $25; Right $25 brass, $65 gold/silver plated**

5670-3 Texas Paterson Colt | 5670-4 1860 Army Colt

5670-7 Peacemaker Colt | 5670-8 Bisley Colt

5670-11 1895 DA Army Colt | 5670-12 1933 .38 Special Colt

5670-15 Army .45 Automatic Colt | 5706 M-16 Rifle

Chapter 9
JEWELRY

The idea of advertising using a lapel badge dates back at least to the 1840 presidential campaign. Paper illustrations protected with a piece of celluloid were used in the presidential campaign of 1888. The advertising buttons known today were patented by Whitehead and Hoag in 1896. Whitehead and Hoag, which incorporated in 1892, would become the largest manufacturer of advertising buttons. Companies making candy, chewing gum and tobacco had giveaway pins made. Whitehead and Hoag continued making pin-back buttons until the company was sold to Bastian Brothers in 1959 ("Price Guide to Collectible Pin-Back Buttons 1896-1986" by Ted Hake and Russ King 1991).

During their years of operation, they made pins for Colt including many of the identification badges. In 1938, the first pins and charms sold by Colt were made by the Robbins Company of Attleboro, Mass. The Robbins Company, established in 1892, is still in business today. They made pins for Colt until 1968. In 1968, Sports Style of New York made the most pins for Colt.

In 1984, Sports Style separated with Dick Miranda's company becoming ADStar in New York and Joe Miranda's company retaining the name Sports Style, but locating in Orlando. Sports Style made the 1971 pin sets and continues to make various items today. With the increase in internal and trade show giveaways from 1986 until today, a number of other vendors have supplied pins to Colt. Modern pins are usually either cloisonné or all metal. All metal pins are usually pewter, sterling or gold-plated brass. Pewter pins can be made using plaster or latex molds. Sterling and plated pins are usually cast.

The lost wax process is used to make individual waxes of the design. Each wax is attached to a wax tree and encased in plaster. The wax is burned out, leaving a cavity which can be filled with molted metal. After hand-finishing the piece is plated.

Cloisonné pins are made by applying different colors of powdered glass to a die-struck metal base. The metal base is made the same way as belt buckles. A design is transferred by pantagraph to a linoleum cut used to make a hardened hob. The hob is used to strike a reverse steel die which in turn strikes a copper base. The design must provide a border between colors which results in a metal dam to contain the powdered glass and separate the colors. The powdered glass color is positioned by hand with tweezers into the metal die-struck base. The piece is then fired at 1,500 degrees to produce the enamel colors. Each piece is then ground to expose the metal lines dividing the colors and hand polished. Due to the amount of hand labor, most cloisonné pins are made overseas. The type of back, known as a finding, which is put on the piece determines its use.

LAPEL PINS

This celluloid pin back may be the first mass produced publicly distributed piece of memorabilia from Colt. It is also prized by pin back collectors. Photo Courtesy of the Hake's Americana, York, PA. **Price: $800-1,200**

The pin was sold as a tie clip in 1941. No examples are known. Courtesy of the Tom Saady collection. **Price: $15-30**

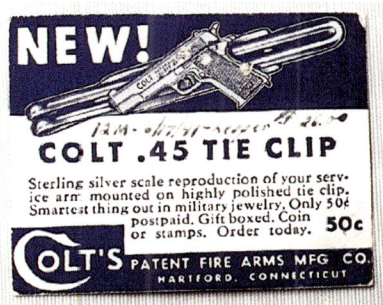

COLLECTOR'S NOTE: So many of these pins were sold that the shipping department was overrun with quarters. This pin is also stamped Robbins Co. and sterling.

Price: $75-150

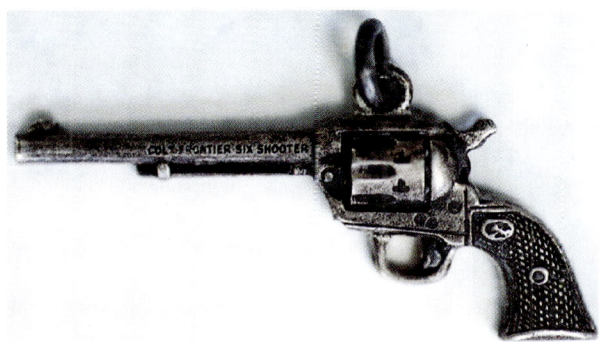

Price: $75-150

The first pin sold by Colt in 1938. It can be recognized by Robbins Co. mark and sterling stamped on the back. **Prices from top to bottom: $50-150; $5-15; $50-150; $5-15**

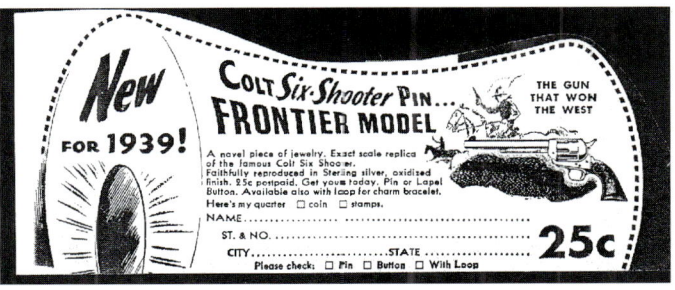

Price: $5-20

119

Price: $5-15

Price: $5-15

A union pin from 1941. Courtesy of the Mike Poulin collection.
Price: $250-500

Those employees contributing a suggestion to improve the efficiency or operation at Colt during WWII were given this pin. Courtesy of the Tom Saady collection.
Price: $125-250

Price: $10-25

An early style service pin from 1936. Over 250 service pins are known to have been given out yet this is the only known example. Courtesy of the Ron Lough collection.
Price: $1,000

This style service pin was introduced in 1945. The 25 year pins were silver, while all others were 10K gold. The 30 year pin was plain, the 35 year pin had a ruby stone, the 40 year pin had a sapphire, the 45 year pin had a emerald and the 50 year pin had a diamond. These are the only examples known.

Courtesy of the Tom Saady collection.
Price: $500-750

Price: $750-1,000

Price: $1,000-1,500

EIGHTY YEARS OF SERVICE IN THE EMPLOY OF COLTS IS RECOGNIZED by the Company as E. H. Kelly, superintendent of the Small Arms Division, 55 years with Colt's on March 1, pins a 25-year service pin on his son, E. R. Kelly, superintendent at Flower Street. President Samuel M. Stone, center, congratulates father and son.

The 25 and 50 year pins shown here are the very pins being awarded in this photo from "The Coltsman".
Price: $10-25

The Colt pistol and revolver club was organized in November 1937. The pin has the same logo as the patch and is 16mm in diameter. Courtesy of the Tom Saady collection. **Price: $75-300**

No examples of this pin have been found. The ad is from the company newsletter of WWII "The Coltsman".
Price: $NEP

COLLECTOR'S NOTE: These pins were offered for sale in 1968.

Price: $20-35

Price: $10-25

Price: $10-25

Price: $10-25

Price: $10-25

COLLECTOR'S NOTE: These pins were offered for sale in 1971. They were made as tie tack and cuff links in four finishes of three different gun replicas, Python, Automatic and Single Action Army. The four finishes were sterling silver, silver plate, 14kt gold filled and gold plate. Over 30,000 units or 1200 sets were manufactured by Sports Style of New York. Starter sets were sent to 100 dealers. Mr. Stan Newman relates one of his first jobs at Colt was to select 100 dealers having the name jewelry in their company name from Colt's list of dealers. The starter sets consisted of the 24 combinations of jewelry in their clam shell cases and a jewelry display rug. Slightly more than 100 of the rugs were made. Of the 100 starter sets sent out over 90 were returned to Colt by the dealers. The jewelry continued to occupy space at the Colt factory and provide controversy and is still common today. The display rugs were stored in a damp room and were mostly ruined and are rather scarce today.

Price: $15-25

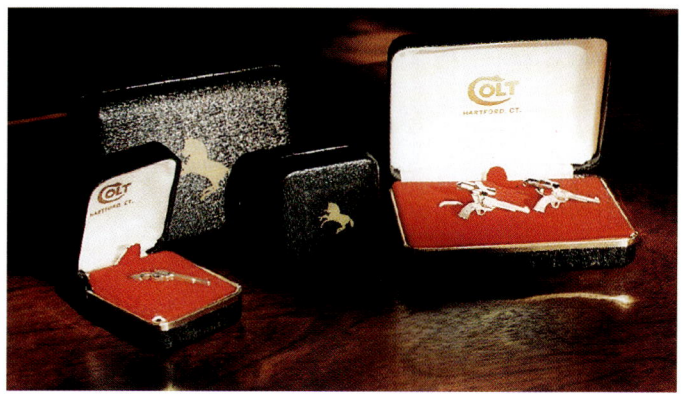

Price: $20-30

Price: $20-30

Price: $15-25

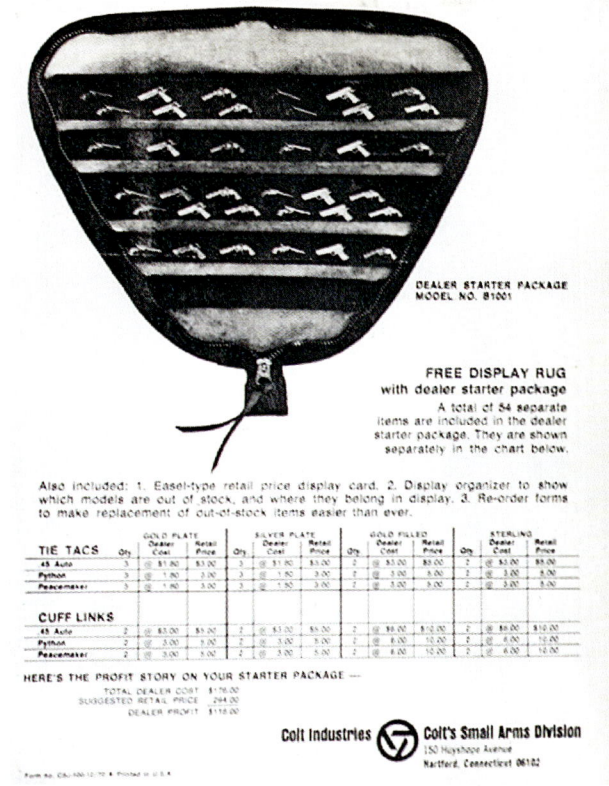

Prices: Ad $5-15; Item shown $100-125

In addition to the tie tac and cuff link sets made to sell, as few as 12 sets of gold rampant horse sets were made for the executives. Courtesy of the Ron Lough collection. **Price: $1,200**

1989 to present. **Price: $5**

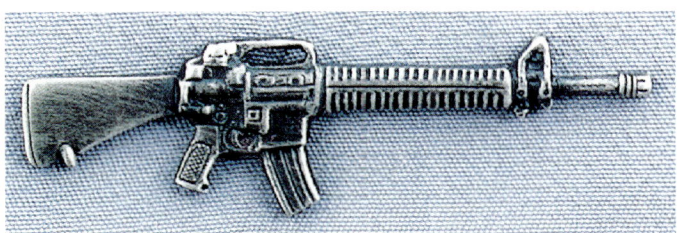

1989 to present. **Price: $5**

1987 to present. **Price: $5**

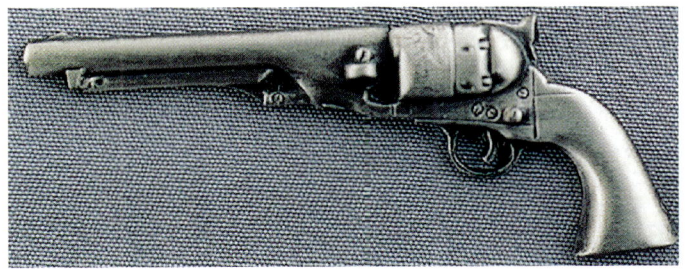

1989 to present. **Price: $5**

1987 to present. **Price: $5**

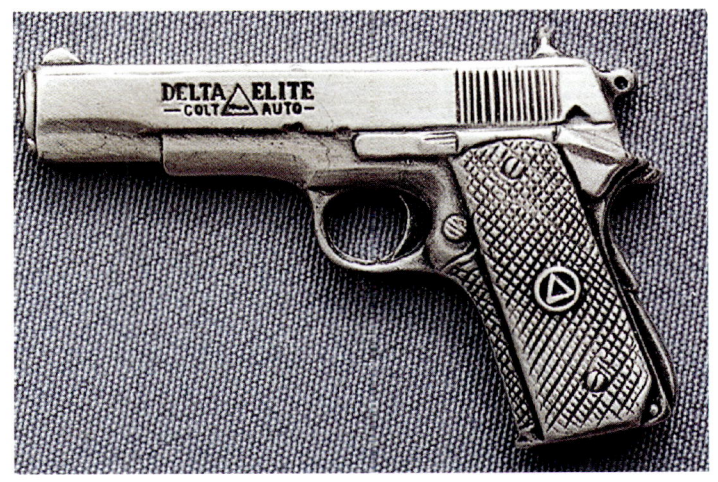

1989 to present. **Price: $5**

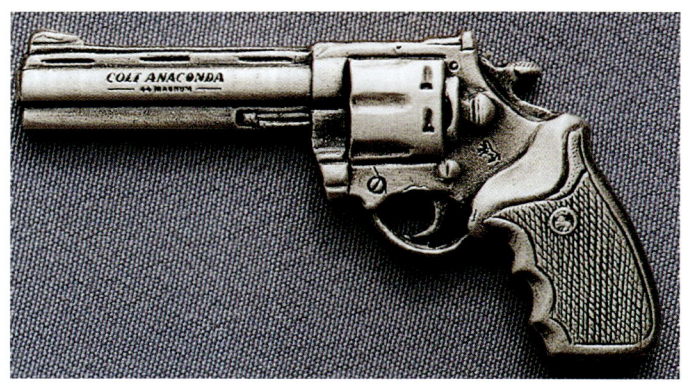
1992 to present. **Price: $5**

1992 to present. **Price: $5**

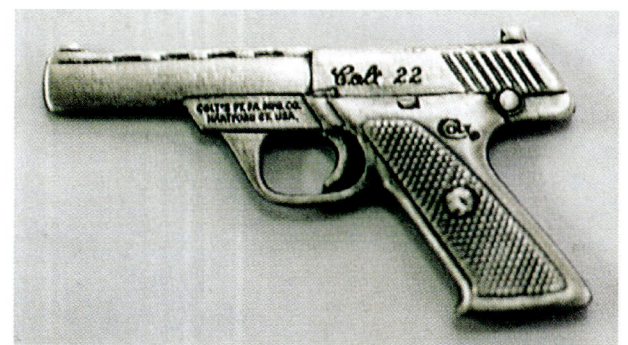
1995 to present. **Price: $5**

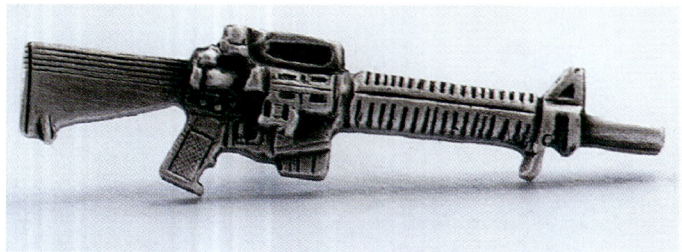
1996 to present. **Price: $5**

1979 to present. 17x20mm. **Price: $1-5**

1979 17x22 mm. **Price: $10-25**

1989 22mm. **Price: $10-20**

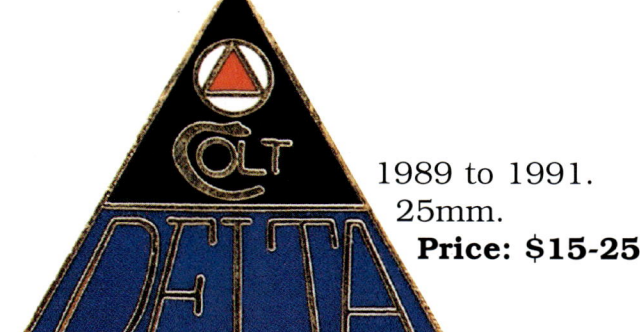
1989 to 1991. 25mm. **Price: $15-25**

1989 to 1992. 22x25mm. **Price: $10-25**

Given out at the 1993 CCA Show. 22.7mm. **Price: $5-15**

1989 to 1990. 20x24mm. **Price: $10-25**

Given out at the 1993 Shot Show. 16mm. **Price: $5-15**

1992 16mm. **Price: $5**

23mm given out at the 1995 Sahara Show. **Price: $10-20**

1993 to present. Sterling silver Francolini design. 23x18mm. **Price: $35**

The king Cobra was introduced in 1987. 16mm. **Price: $1-5**

1993 to present. Sterling silver Francolini design. 27x30mm. **Price: $35**

Sold from 1989 to 1992. 26mm. **Price: $15-35**

Plastic giveaway version. 25mm.
Price: $5-20

Although listed in the 1992 price list distribution was limited. 29x22mm.
Price: $10-25

Given out with ball caps in 1990 and 1991. 22x29mm.
Price: $20-40

Sold during 1992. 22x29mm.
Price: $10-25

Made from a grip medallion. 13mm.
Price: $10-25

Sold in 1986. 25mm.
Price: $25-50

Plastic giveaway version. 20x25mm.
Price: $5-20

Internally distributed in 1991. 25mm.
Price: $25-50

Plastic giveaway version. 20mm.
Price: $10-25

Sold during 1986. 13mm. **Price: $20-35**

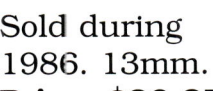

Sold during 1986. 13mm. **Price: $20-35**

Three sizes and variations. **Price: $5-25 ea.**

This pin represents the M231 port firing weapon made for the Bradly during 1979. **Price: $50**

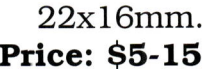

22x16mm. **Price: $5-15**

22x16mm. **Price: $5-15**

30x15 mm. **Price: $35-50**

COLLECTOR'S NOTE: The following three photos illustrate pins made for Colt sponsored Police Combat Pistol Matches during the early 1960's. Pins, medals, buckles, bolos and patches were given out.

1961 43x10mm. **Price: $35-50**

1963 Southern Regional Police Combat Pistol Matches. **Price: $35-50**

According to Jackie Frascarelli, these pins were actually made for Colt at one time. They are now widely reproduced. 22mm. **Price: $2-5**

Beginning in 1987, Colt awarded a safety pin for years of service. 25mm.
Each item is valued at: $25-50

Photo at right is courtesy of the Norman Green collection.

Representatives of the Safety committee were given an identification pin to wear. 77x36mm.
Price: $35-50

Starting in 1983, Colt began having pins made especially for a particular event or show and dating the pins. These pins were given away in addition to the ball caps at the annual Colt Cup rifle matches in Wallingford Ct. 25mm.
Price: $25-50 ea.

1996 Shot Show. 22 mm. 2,500 made.
Price: $10-20

1997 Shot Show. 24 x 21mm. 2,500 made.
Price: $5-10

1997 Shot Show. 22mm.
Price: $5-10

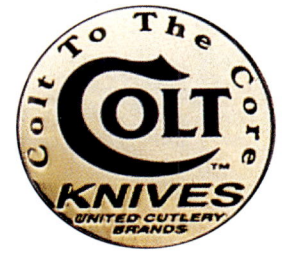

1994 Shot Show. 27mm. 5,000 made.
Price: $25-35

1995 NRA Meeting 12x22mm. 2,500 made.
Price: $15-25

1995 Shot Show. 28x28mm. 5,000 made.
Price: $15-25

1996 NRA Meeting 18x22mm. 2,500 made.
Price: $10-20

Only 250 were made for the 1996 CCA Meeting.
Price: $15-25

European Commonwealth. **Price: $10-25**

COLLECTOR'S NOTE: Colt flag pins are the product of the military sales division. The first pins were developed by Rob Roy and were made for Malaysia and Thailand. The pins were made to be worn and given out when potential customers from foreign countries visited the factory. Not available to illustrate are pins for Peru and Portugal.

Greece. **Price: $10-25**

Bahrain. **Price: $10-25**

Jordan. **Price: $10-25**

Egypt. **Price: $10-25**

Kuwait. **Price: $10-25**

Malaysia. **Price: $10-25**

United Arab Emirates. **Price: $10-25**

Saudi Arabia. **Price: $10-25**

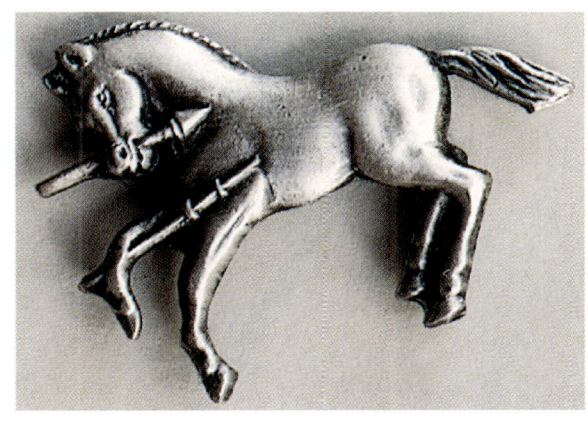
Sold from 1987 to present. **Price: $5**

Thailand. **Price: $10-25**

Sold from 1989 to present. **Price: $5**

Turkey. **Price: $10-25**

14K gold sold from 1993 to present. **Price: $20**

14K gold charm sold from 1990 to 1993.
Price: $20-40

Sterling silver pin made by John Guest. They were also available in gold.
Price: $100 silver, $250 gold

24K gold earrings sold from 1990 to 1992. **Price: $35-50**

Sterling silver pin made by Robert Phillips. **Price: $65**

Sid Bell sterling silver pin made in 1970. Over 200 were supplied to Colt, some are known to be numbered. These pins were offered in the 1992 collectible catalog but were never sold. **Price: $50-100**

Sterling silver rampant Colt pin from Earl Whitney. Mr. Whitney has been providing these pins since the early 1970's. He also has them in "3-D," as a bolo and in 14K gold. **Price: $21**

COLLECTOR'S NOTE: The Wadsworth Athenaeum in Hartford CT., exhibited "Sam and Elizabeth: Legend and Legacy of Colt's Empire" from September 8, 1996 to March 9, 1997. The next three items, were produced to be sold in the museum gift shop during that exhibition.

Pin. **Price: $24**

Rampant Colt earrings. **Price: $29**

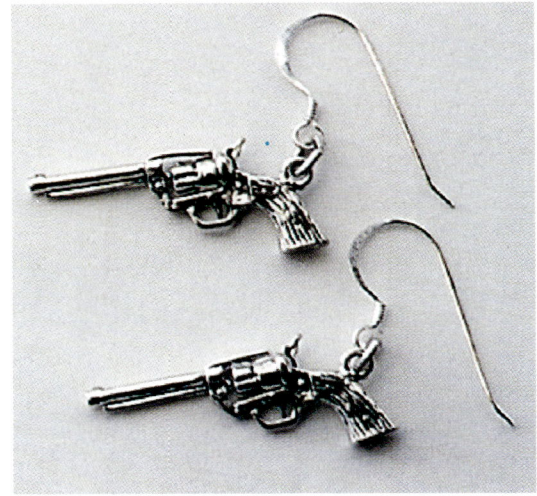

Revolver earrings. **Price: $18**

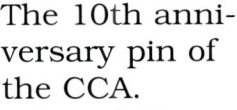

The Colt Collectors Association was founded in December 1980, with 42 members. The association logo was designed by Mr. Ben Lane and Mr. W.H. Fluitt machined a prototype from which the club pin was made. 45mm.
Price: $35

The 10th anniversary pin of the CCA.
Price: $35

A set of Colt firearm replica pins made by John Adams Sr.. Mr. Adams is an engraver who worked for Colt at one time.
Price: $10

It is not known if these pins were ever issued through the Colt factory, or if they are fantasy pins. The first six photos appear courtesy of the Norman Green collection.

19mm. **Price: $5-15**

26mm. **Price: $10-15**

Price: $5-15

Price: $5-15

Price: $5-15

Price: $5-15

Price: $5-15

Price: $5-15

Price: $5-10

Price: $5-10

Price: $5-10

Price: $5-10

Price: $5-10

COLLECTOR'S NOTE: These are fantasy pins never released through the Colt factory.

Price: $1.25

Price: $2-7

Price: $2-7

Price: $2-7

Price: $2-7

Price: $2-7

Price: $2-7

Price: $2-7

Price: $2-7

Price: $2-7

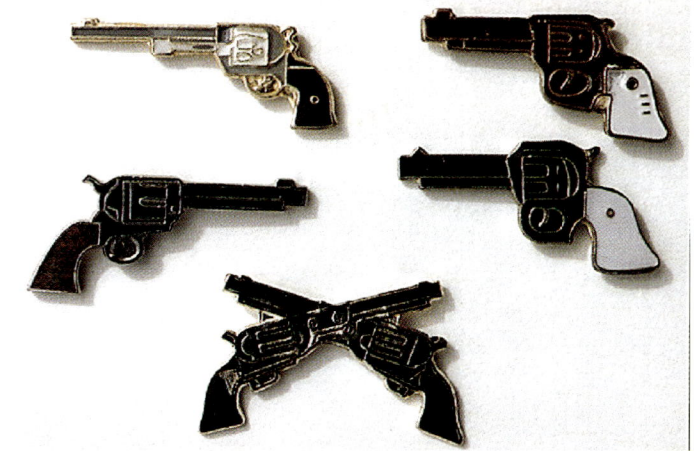

Price: $2-7

Price: $2-7

Price: $2-7

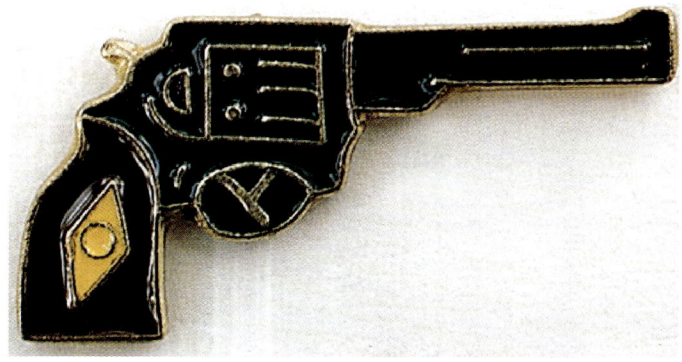

Price: $2-7

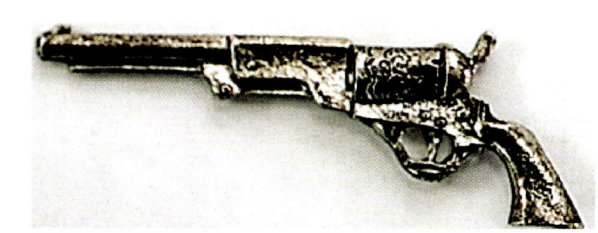

Price: $2-7

Price: $2-7

Price: $2-7

 Price: $2-7

 Price: $2-7

 Price: $2-7

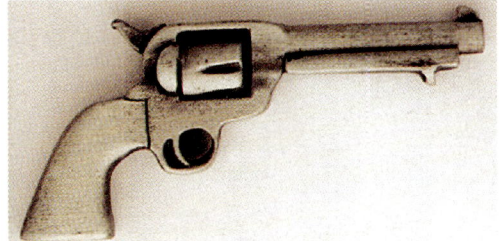 Price: $2-7

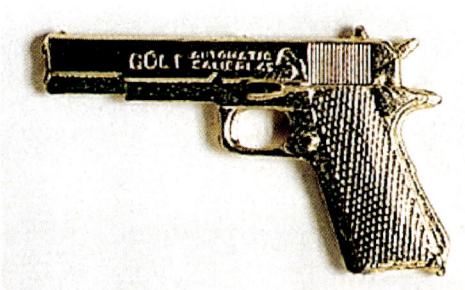 Price: $2-7

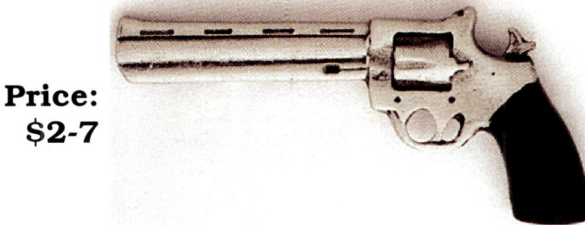 Price: $2-7

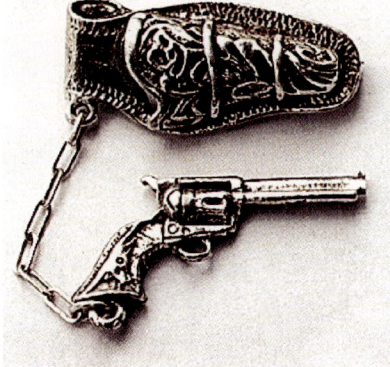 Price: $40

 Price: $2-7

 Price: $40

 Price: $2-7

 Price: $2-7

 Price: $2-7

Price: $2-7

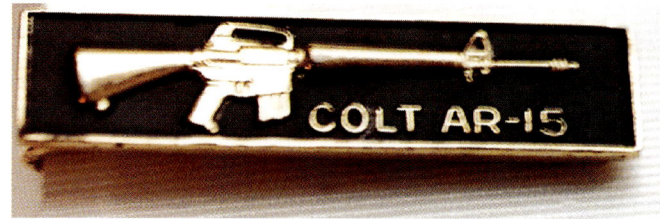

Price: $15-30

Price: $2-7

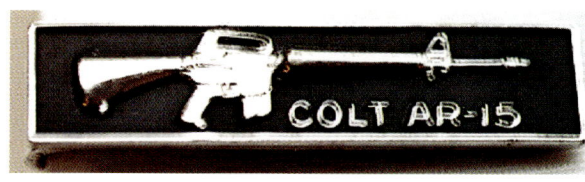

Price: $15-30

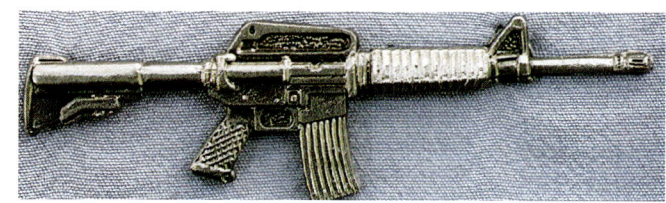

Price: $2-7

 Price: $2-7

 Price: $2-7

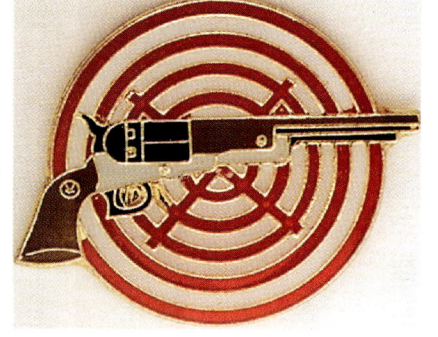 Price: $2-7

Price: $9-7

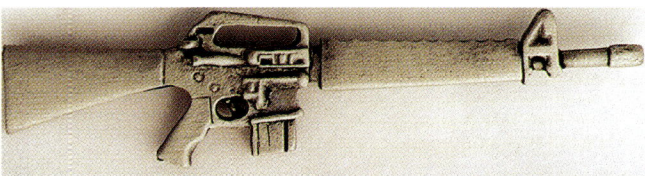
Price: $2-7

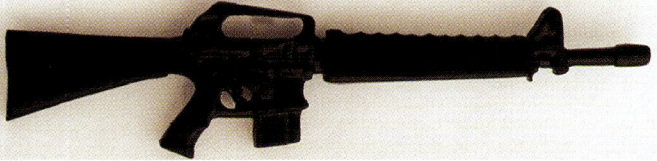
Price: $2-7

Salesman's pin. 37mm.
Price: $15-30

Customer pin. 55mm.
Price: $10-20

1970 promotion. 89mm.
Price: $10-20

Some fantasy non-factory bolo ties. These are available in gold or silver and with black or white cords.
Each item is valued at: $10

PIN BACKS

Colt gave away a hunting trip to Vermejo Park Ranch in New Mexico during 1984. The following two pin backs, were used to promote that contest.

The Colt union went on strike in 1986. **Each item is valued at: $15-30**

Salesman's pin back 1989 and 1990 56 mm. **Price: $5-20**

STICKPINS

COLLECTOR'S NOTE: Colt has advertised only one stickpin for sale, a sterling silver rampant horse that apparently was never produced. However, five stickpins are known to have been produced through the factory.

Price: $20   **Price: $20**   **Price: $35**

Price: $35   **Price: $50**

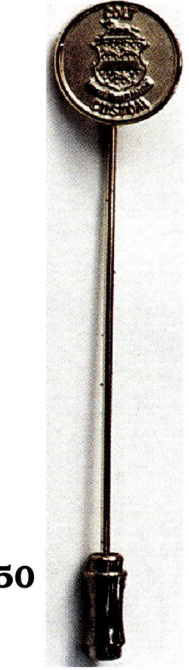

CUFF LINKS

An early two part cuff link made by Whitehead and Hoagg possibly in the 1930s.

Value of item: $50-100

COLLECTOR'S NOTE: Cuff Links were part of the 1971 sets of jewelry sold by Colt. Four finishes and three styles were available.

Price: $15-20

Price: $10-15

Price: $10-15

Sterling silver cuff links made by Francolini and sold by Colt from 1994 to present.
Price: $50

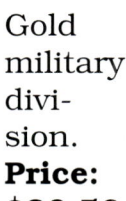
Silver military division.
Price: $30-50

Gold military division.
Price: $30-50

Internally distributed.
Price: $20-40

One of two known prototype samples.
Price: $50-100

COLT INDUSTRIES JEWELRY

Colt was owned by Colt Industries from 1963 until 1990. From 1963 to 1973, they used a gear logo instead of a rampant or serpentine logo. Jewelry having the gear logo of Colt Industries is of little interest to most collectors of Colt memorabilia.

Service pin. **Price: $100**

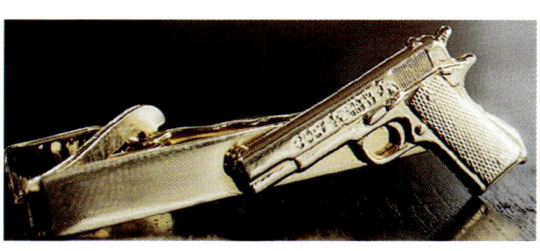
Sold in 1968. **Price: $20-40**

Plain tie bar. **Price: $20-40**

The Trouper MKIII was introduced in 1969. **Price: $15-30**

Sapphire tie bar. Courtesy of the Mike Poulin collection. **Price: $30-50**

Late 1960s. **Price: $15-30**

Plain tie tack. **Price: $20-40**

Sapphire tie tack. **Price: $30-50**

TIE BARS

Sold in 1968. **Price: $20-40**

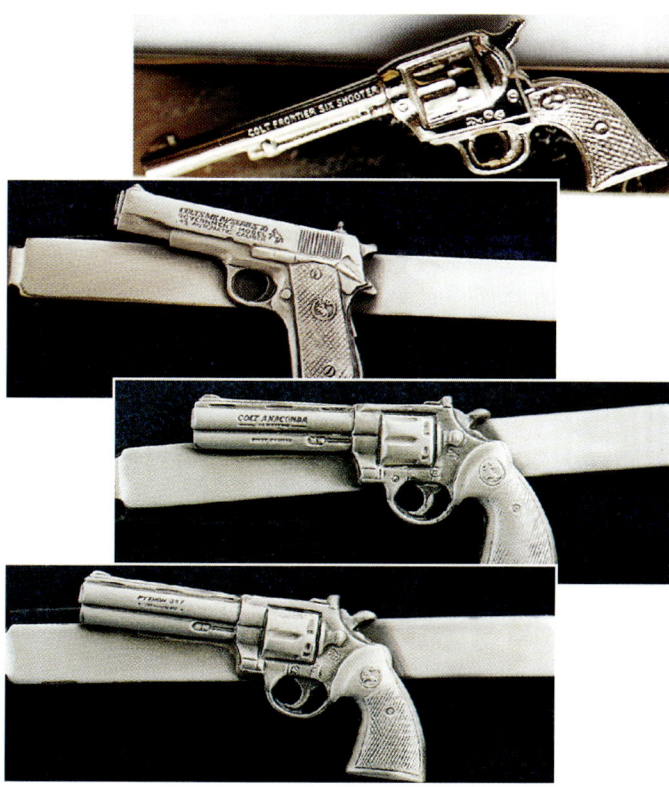
All of the 1992 lapel pins were supposed to be available as tie bars. These are the only ones known to have been issued. **Each item is valued at: $10-20**

Two other tie bars sold during 1992.
Each item is valued at: $10-20

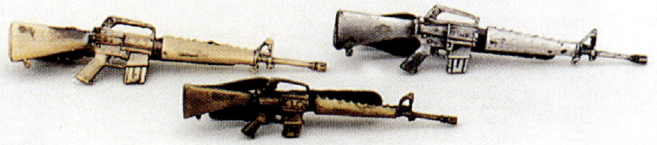

This pin representing the AR-15 was available in three variations.
Price: $10-20

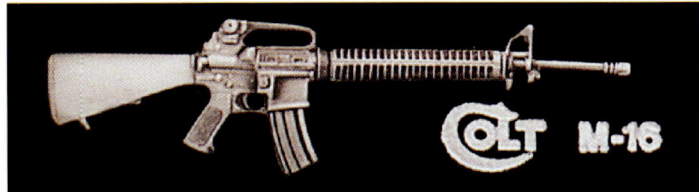

Pewter M16. **Price: $10-20**

Custom Shop prototype. One of two known. **Price: $50-100**

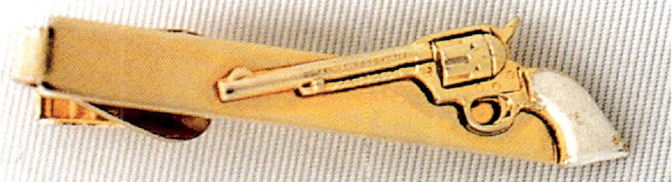

These are thought to have been made for or by Jay Scott. Colt owned the Jay Scott company which made pistol grips from 1974 until 1988.
Each item is valued at: $50-100

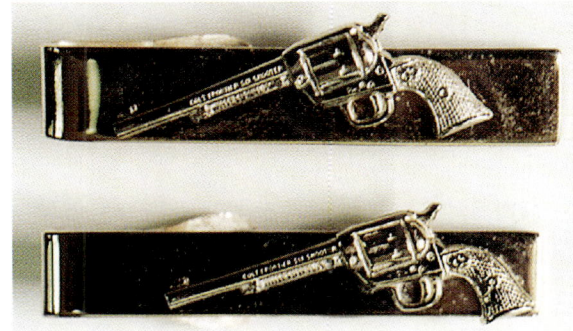

Two variations of a modern tie bar.
Price: $10-20

These are non-factory fantasy tie bars.

Price: $5-10

Price: $5-10

Price: $5-10

 Price: $15-30

Price: $40

BUTTONS

One of the earliest memorabilia items is this button thought to date from 1856. Colt also made and sold buttons out of plastic and Coltrock from the 1930s through the early 1950s.
Price: $1,000

Colt sold these button sets starting in 1992. **Each item is valued at: $25-50**

 Other Colt buttons can be found on the salesmen's jackets from the 1970s and 1980s. **Price: $10-20**

A Francolini button cover sold 1995. **Price: $35**

This is most likely a fantasy button done at the same time and by the same person responsible for all the non-factory buckles such as "The World's Right Arm." **Price: $5**

BOLO TIES

One of the earliest known bolo ties was offered in a 1962 sales promotion for the I.U. combat police pistol matches. It was available with either the single action army revolver or the .45 automatic. No examples are known to photograph, however a similar bolo slide is thought to date from the same time. Courtesy of the Marty Huber collection.
Price: $150-250

Available through the Custom shop in 1978. A red "coral" color was also available. **Each item is valued at: $150-200**

Another bolo thought to date from the 1960's. Courtesy of the Dan Chesiak collection.
Price: $50-100

A present from Colt to those people who attended the 1992 Colt Collectors Show in Hartford, CT.
Price: $35-50

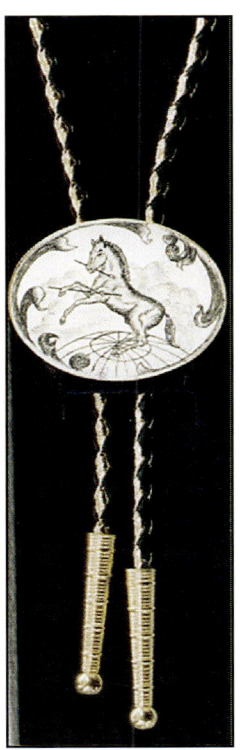

Sold in 1992:
Price: $25-35

Price: $25-35

Given out by Colt.
Price: $25-35

Given to his friends at Colt by Al DeJohn.
Price: $35-50

Price: $35-50

Non-factory bolo's made by John Guest.
Price: $125 silver, $275 gold

Chapter 10
TIES

Colt had a number of ties made to give away to their dealers and friends. Three different patterns were made, the Rampant Colt, the Factory Dome and the Armsmear Crest. Each of the three designs were made in three colors; red, blue and green. As fashions changed, Colt had two sizes made, one narrow made by Olynn and a wide tie made by W.M. Chelsea Ltd. There are thus 18 different variations of these ties. Twelve additional ties have since been made including three still available.

Narrow crest ties by Olynn. Courtesy of the Jim Alaimo collection.
Value of each item: $40-100

Narrow red dome tie by Olynn. Courtesy of the Jim Alaimo collection.
Price: $40-100

Wide green dome tie by Chelsea. Courtesy of the Norman Green collection.
Price: $40-100

Wide crest ties by Chelsea. Courtesy of the Jim Alaimo collection.
Value of each item: $40-100

Wide green rampant tie by Chelsea. Courtesy of the Jim Alaimo collection.
Price: $40-100

Wide red rampant tie by Chelsea. Courtesy of the Jim Alaimo collection. **Price: $40-100**

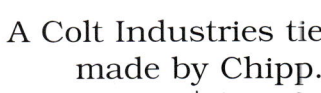

A Colt Industries tie made by Chipp. **Price: $50-150**

Salesmen were given this tie and handkerchief made by Stockpole to wear at trade shows during the 1970s. **Price: $50-150**

This tie was made to celebrate the 150th anniversary of Colt. **Price: $150-250**

An alternative salesmen's tie was this one by Macaseta Ltd. **Price: $50-150**

A Colt Industries tie made by J. Press. **Price: $50-150**

Sold during 1996. **Value of each item: $29.95**

A factory tie, maker unknown. Courtesy of the Dan Chesiak collection. **Price: $150-200**

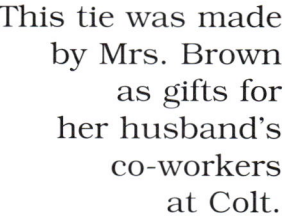

This tie was made by Mrs. Brown as gifts for her husband's co-workers at Colt. **Price: $100-150**

Made for Larry Wilson by J. Press. Larry Wilson collection. **Price: $300-500**

Made for the board of directors of the CCA in 1983. Courtesy of the Jim Alaimo collection. **Price: $50-180**

Sold during 1995. **Price: $30.00**

Chapter 11
KEY CHAINS

Key rings have been around for some time. They were first widely used for advertising at the 1892 Columbia Exposition. The development of a key chain had to await the existence of beaded chain, which was first used for lamp pulls in the 1920s. In the 1930s, the addition of electric starters to the automobile led to the widespread need for a chain to hold the keys. The 1940s evolution of plastics made key rings and key chains a popular and common advertising promotion.

This is perhaps the most abundant of all Colt memorabilia. First given out in the 1950s, it is still available. At one time, Colt was going to put one of these screwdriver key chains in the box with every gun sold. Several hundred thousand were made, enough to occupy several pallets at the factory. Some were nickel plated at the factory to make them special.
Price: $5-25

This medallion, key chain celebrated the 125th anniversary of Colt in 1961. These were given out with every gun sold during that year.
Price: $20-50

An early change purse, key chain. Photo courtesy of the Stan Newman collection.
Price: $50-100

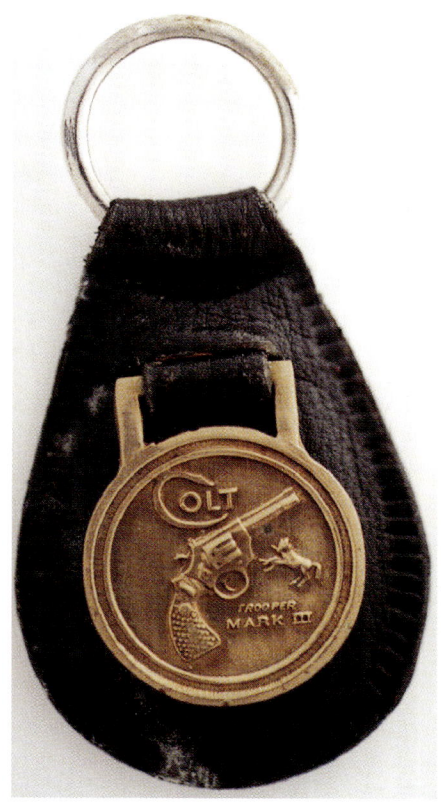

The Mark III was introduced in 1969.
Price: $50

These key chains are thought to date from the 1960s.

Price: $25-50

Price: $25-50

These key chains are thought to date from the 1970s.
Value of each item: $25-50

Price: $30-50

Price: $30-50

1981. Courtesy of the Stan Newman collection.
Price: $25-50

Price: $20-40

Sold during 1986.
Price: $25-50

Sold during 1987 and 1988. **Price: $25-50**

The 10mm Delta Elite was introduced in 1988. **Price: $20-25**

Sold during 1989 and 1990. **Price: $20-25**

Sold during 1992. **Price: $20-25**

Prototype samples considered during 1992. Five of each were made. Courtesy of the Stan Newman collection. **Value of each item: $35-75**

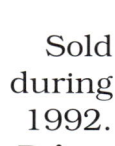

Sold during 1992. **Price: $20-25**

Given out at the annual NRA Show in 1992. **Price: $5-20**

Photo depicts example of the serpentine Colt logo which appears on the following three key chains.

Sold during 1996. **Price: $17.95**

Given out at the annual NRA Show in 1994.
Price: $10-25

Prototype key chains made for the Custom Shop.
Value of each item: $80

Given out at the 1994 Law Enforcement Show.
Price: $15-25

Other key chains known to have been given out through the factory.

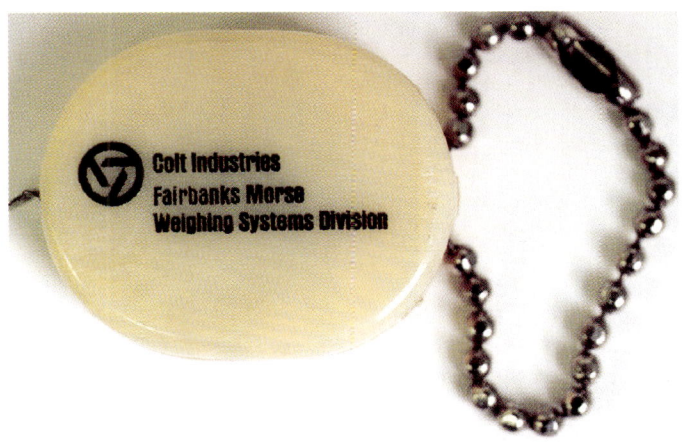

Given out at the 1995 military show.
Price: $20-35

Price: $35

155

 **Price: $10-25**

Price: $25-50

Colt Collectors Association key chain.
Price: $20-50

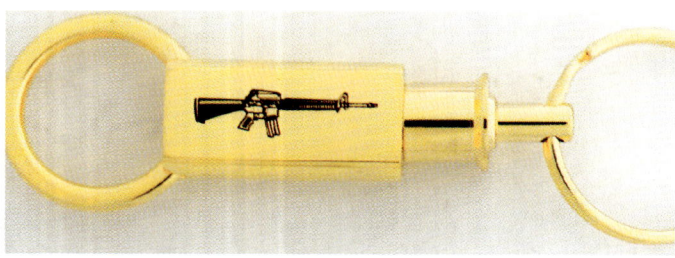
Price: $10-25

 Sold at the Wadsworth Athenaeum as part of an exhibition.
Price: $9.95

Price: $25-50

This Zippo key chain was released through the factory.
Price: $25-50

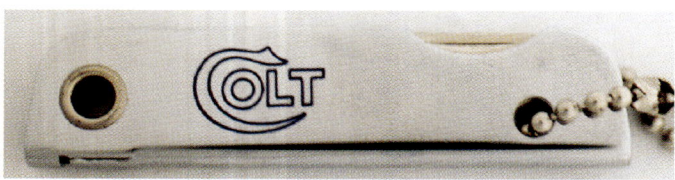
Price: $20-50

COLLECTOR'S NOTE: Fantasy key chains not issued through the factory. These can be easily distinguished by comparison with the authentic logo.

Price: $5-15

Price: $5-15

Price: $5-15

Price: $5-15

Korean-made cap pistol, key chains sold in 1995. **Value of each item: $6-10**

Price: $5-10

Price: $5-10

This non-factory key chain is available in gold and silver.
Price: $5-10

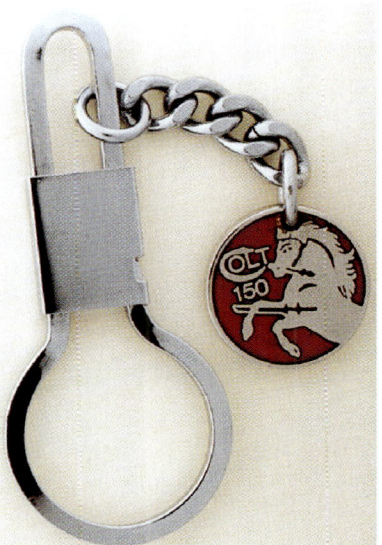

Most likely a fantasy non-factory item.
Price: $5-20

157

Chapter 12
BADGES

During WWI, concerns over espionage led to the use of the first identification badges at Colt. Prior to that time, Colt simply locked the factory doors during work hours. These early badges were all made by Whitehead and Hoagg. Most of these early badges were consigned to the metal drives of WWII, making them rare today. The first photo metal badges were used just prior to WWII. These badges were color coded to restrict unauthorized movement of employees in the factory. Plastic laminated photo ID badges have been used since the 1960s. Today, Colt zealously controls its badges to prevent unauthorized entry into its factory, making the modern badges highly collectible.

A pre-WWII badge. Courtesy of the Tom Saady collection. **Price: $300-500**

A pre-WWII badge. Courtesy of the Mike Poulin collection. **Price: $500-800**

Courtesy of the Steve Freeman collection. **Price: $150-250**

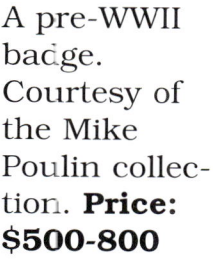
This badge is known to have been given out 8/20/1941, and thus it is felt that this style badge was used just prior to, and during, WWII. **Price: $150-250**

COLLECTOR'S NOTE: These badges were used by salaried employees during and after WWII. Colt operated three plants during the war and the color code of the badge identified which plant and which division the employee was working. White frames were used at VanDyke and the main office. Yellow frames were used at Flower Street.

Courtesy of the Dan Chesiak collection. **Price: $150-250**

Courtesy of the Mike Poulin collection. **Price: $75-150**

Courtesy of the Mike Poulin collection. **Price: $100-250**

Courtesy of the Steve Freeman collection. **Price: $50-150**

Courtesy of the Mike Poulin collection. **Price: $250-350**

Courtesy of the Dan Chesiak collection. **Price: $50-150**

Courtesy of the Dan Chesiak collection. **Price: $100-250**

The blue and yellow frame indicate access to both Park Street and Flower Street. Courtesy of the Tom Saady collection. **Price: $150-250**

Price: $75-150

COLLECTOR'S NOTE: The next three badges were used by hourly employees during WWII. The number corresponded to the employee's time card. These badges were also made in orange and white.

A vest badge from WWII. Courtesy of the Mike Poulin collection. **Price: $400-800**

Price: $75-100

Photo is courtesy of the Mike Poulin collection.

Price: $50-100

Price: $50-100

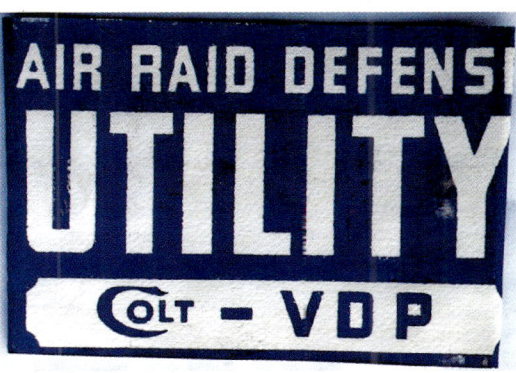

An arm badge for the factory guards during WWII. Courtesy of the Dan Chesiak collection. **Price: $200**

Guard badge. Courtesy of the Ron Lough collection. **Price: $250-350**

A hat badge for the Colt guards during WWII. Photo courtesy of the Tom Saady collection. **Price: $300-600**

Modern nickel hat badge. Courtesy of the Bill Judd collection. **Price: $250-350**

 Modern nickel vest badge. Courtesy of the Ron Lough collection. **Price: $250-350**

Visitor badge. Courtesy of the Ron Lough collection. **Price: $150-200**

Modern gold hat badge. Courtesy of the Norman Green collection. **Price: $250-350**

Modern factory badges are difficult to find. **Price: $50-75**

 Modern gold vest badge. Courtesy of the Norman Green collection. **Price: $250-350**

Also difficult to find is the Colt factory badge for the Colt Collectors Association. **Price: $50-100**

Colt Industries badges. **Price: $30-50**

 A CCA badge for the 1986 meeting in Hartford. **Price: $15-25**

Chapter 13
BAGS

Colt advertising bags may not be of interest to most collectors, but they do provide for an inexpensive collection. In addition, they should raise the question of what was intended to be placed in the bag. Cloth gym and range bags have been used since the 1970s as internal awards and for sale to the public.

1982 Family Day. **Price: $5-10**

1990 Family Day. **Price: $5-10**

1991 Advertising campaign. **Price: $10-20**

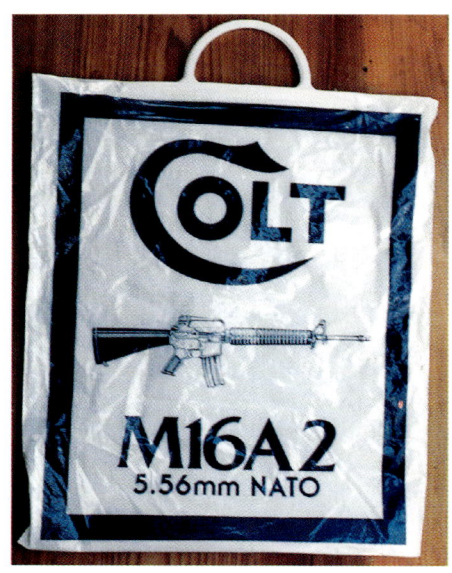
Dedication of the M16A2, April 12, 1984 at the Hartford Plant. **Price: $3-10**

1996 and 1997 Shot Show. **Price: $2-5**

1989 Advertising campaign. **Price: $5-10**

1993 Colt Collectors Show. **Price: $5-15**

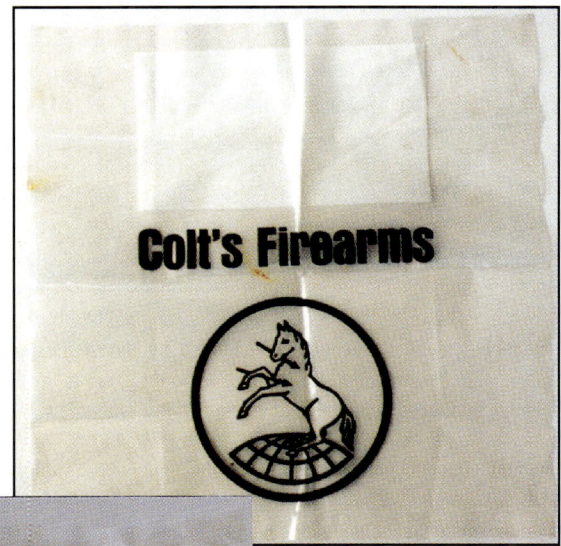

Early parts bags. **Value for each item: $2-5**

During the 1980s, Colt had luggage made by Emmebi of Italy. As many as four sets may have been made. As few as one of the briefcases may have been made.

Price: $175-250

Price: $175-250

Sheffield knife glove from 1971. **Price: $20-30**

Price: $300-500

1985 gun case. **Price: $5-15**

1986 buckle case. **Price: $3-5**

1987 employee safety award. **Price: $20-40**

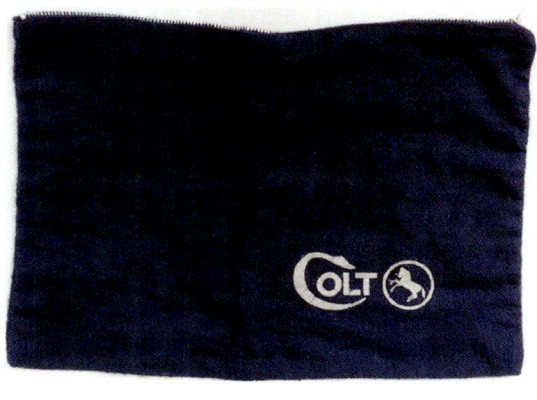

Zippered case possibly for money or papers. **Price: $5-15**

1987 employee safety award. **Price: $15-30**

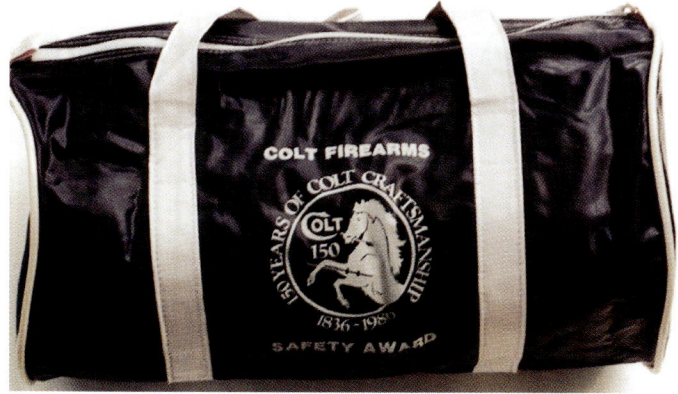

1986 employee safety award. **Price: $15-30**

Sold during 1989. **Price: $20-40**

1989 promotional bag. **Price: $25-30**

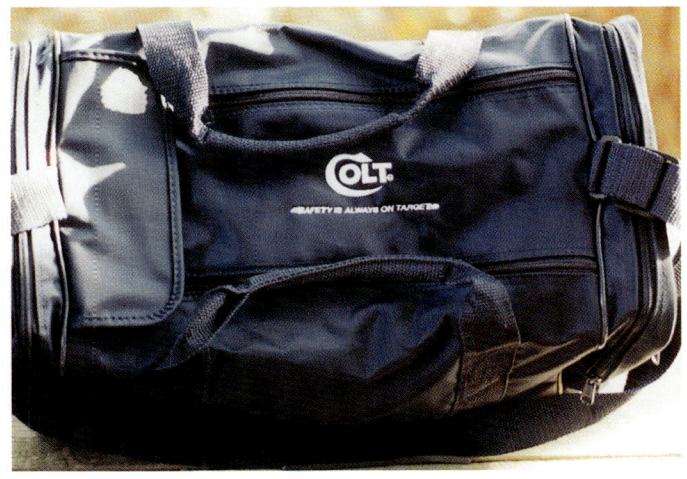

1990 employee safety award.
Price: $50-100

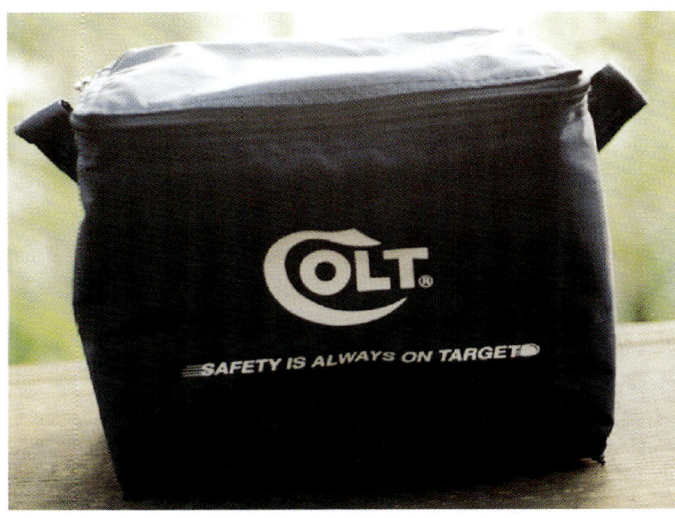

1993 employee safety award.
Price: $15-30

Sold during 1995. Also available in royal blue and black. **Price: $110**

The following three bags were sold during 1996:

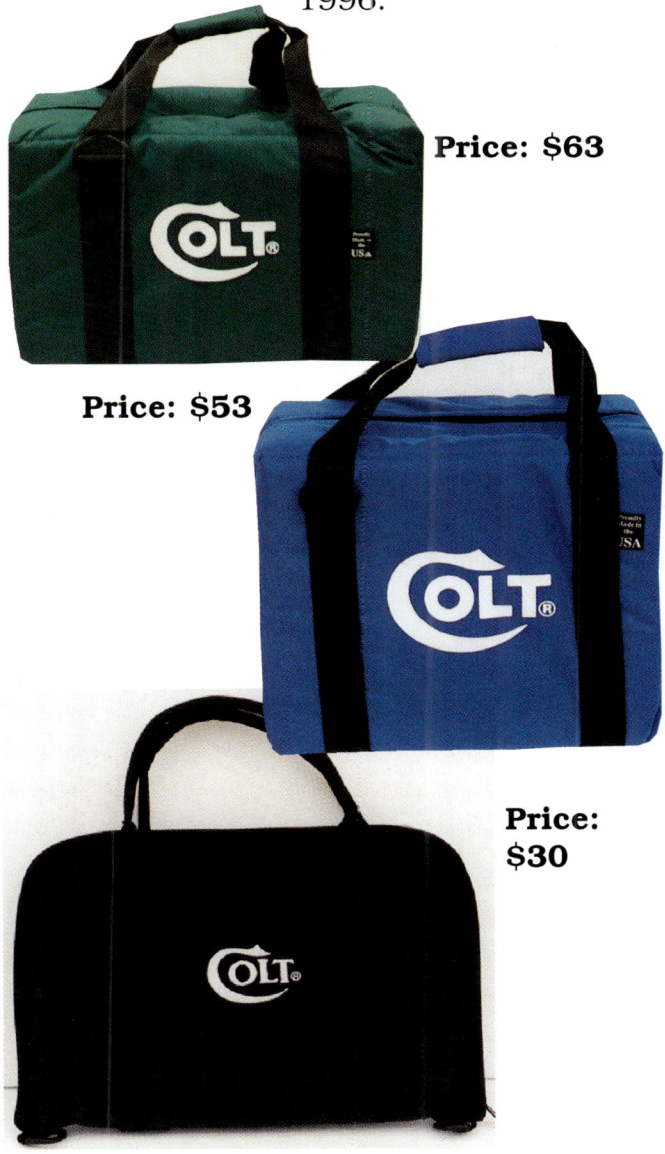

Price: $63

Price: $53

Price: $30

Chapter 14
SHOP SUPPLIES

Items that one could expect to find in a gun shop are brought together in this chapter. A bore gauge and a factory tool room tag may date from prior to World War II. Also included are items sent to dealers such as counter mats or counter displays and shooting accessories intended for sale to the public.

In the late 60s Colt developed several product lines directed toward personal security and law enforcement. The most common products offered to the public were the telshot items including an aerial flare kit, a tear gas kit and 12 gauge cartridges intended to scare birds. The telshot technology was developed by the Pyrodynamics Division of Colt. Telshot was named for the Telstar satellite which was the days big news. The basic principal of all the telshot devices was the use of a time delay fuse on a fired projectile. A cartridge could be fired to some distance before the time delay fuse would ignite a charge. That charge could be tear gas, a flash charge, a sonic charge or an explosive charge.

Products sold to law enforcement agencies include handcuffs, 12 gauge tear gas cartridges and a bomb disposal kit. Other security items produced and not available to picture here included a public address system, a facial identification kit and a shotgun having eight barrels.

Other experimental products being developed by the division, not included here, were plastic preloaded removable cylinders, plaster bullets, a retro rocket bullet, a caseless projectile, and several experimental cartridge rounds. An additional project resulted in an explosive cartridge that operated an electric switch or produced a rotational force to turn bolts or extend an actuator.

Tool room tag from the factory. To remove an item from the tool room the borrower would leave his tag in place of the tool. Photo courtesy of the Tom Saady collection. **Price: $150-300**

Reproduction from 1995, that is almost impossible to distinguish from the original.
Price: $5

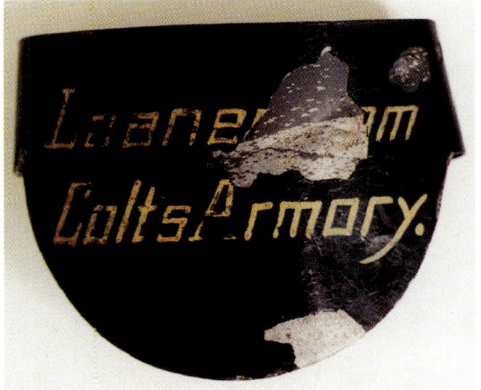

A band that was to be placed on items removed from the armory.
Price: $20-50

Counter mats:

Dates back to 1968. **Price: $50-150**

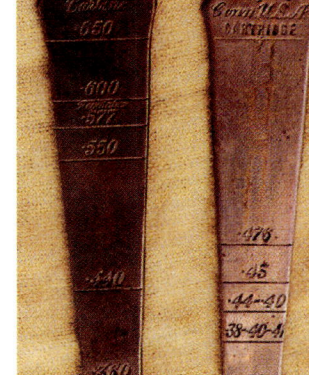

An early bore gauge.
Price: $50-100

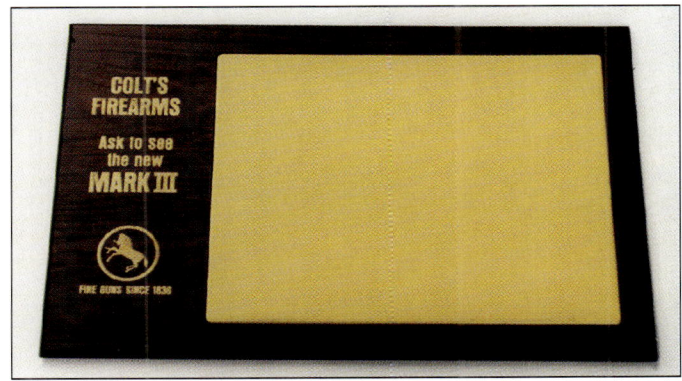

From 1969. **Price: $50-150**

Dates back to 1991. **Price: $20-35**

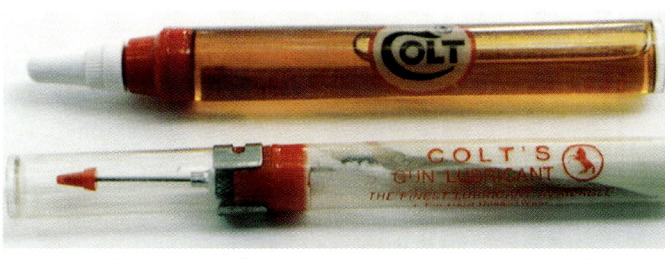

Gun lubricant from 1968 (top) and 1972 (bottom). **Price: $5-15**

Modern oiler bottle. **Price: $20-35**

This mat, given out in the 1970s, had become a valuable collectible until it was reissued and sold by Colt in 1996. **Prices: $14.95**

It is not clear what this item is, or whether it was made by the factory. It may be a prototype counter mat. Courtesy of the Tom Saady collection. **Price: $200-400**

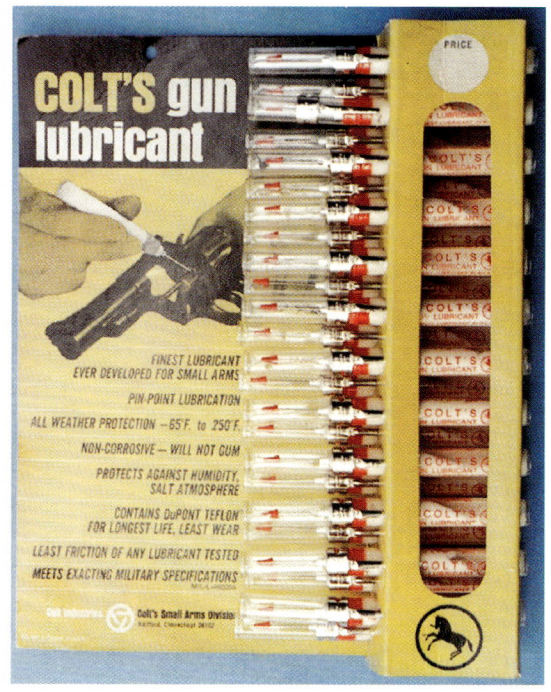

A dealer display of gun lubricants. **Price: $150-200**

A 1982 dealer display rack. Photo courtesy of the Norman Green collection.
Price: $50-75

Dealer display rack. Photo courtesy of the Norman Green collection.
Price: $120-150

One of five prototype cleaning kits.
Price: $50-100

An advertisement showing a stocked rack. **Price: $10-20**

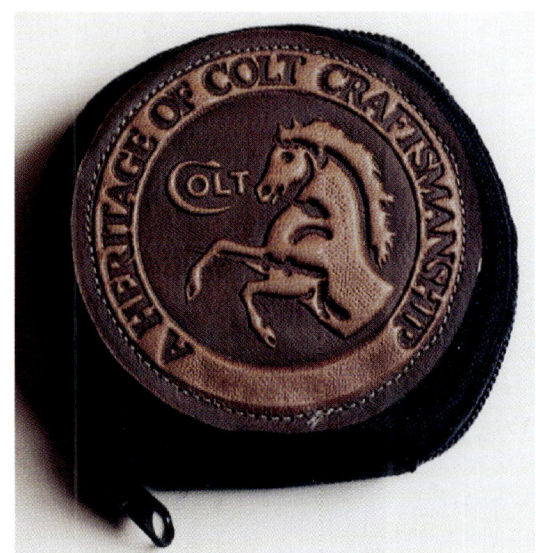

Cleaning kit from 1987. Courtesy of the Tom Saady collection.
Price: $15-30

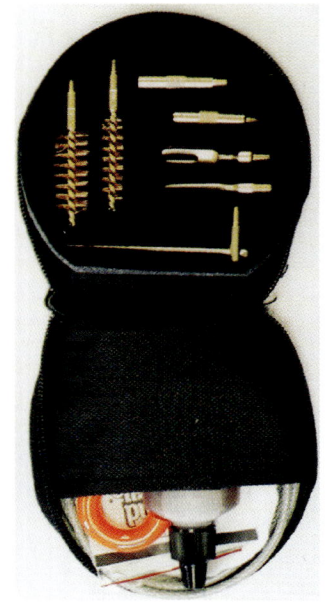

Sold in 1995 and 1996. **Price: $29.95**

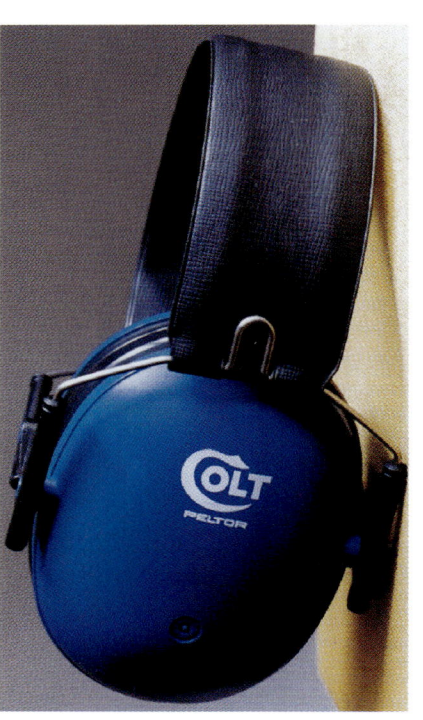

Gold and black variation.
Price: $30-50

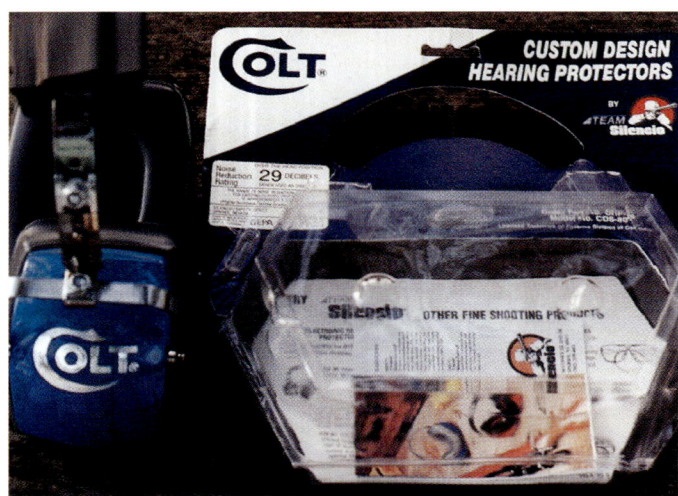

Hearing protectors sold by Silenco, from 1990 until 1995. **Price: $10-30**

White and blue variation.
Price: $30-50
Photo courtesy of the Stan Newman collection.

Hearing protectors by Peltor, sold by Colt starting in 1995. **Price: $29.95**

Safety glasses given to those CCA members who visited the factory in 1992.
Price: $15-30

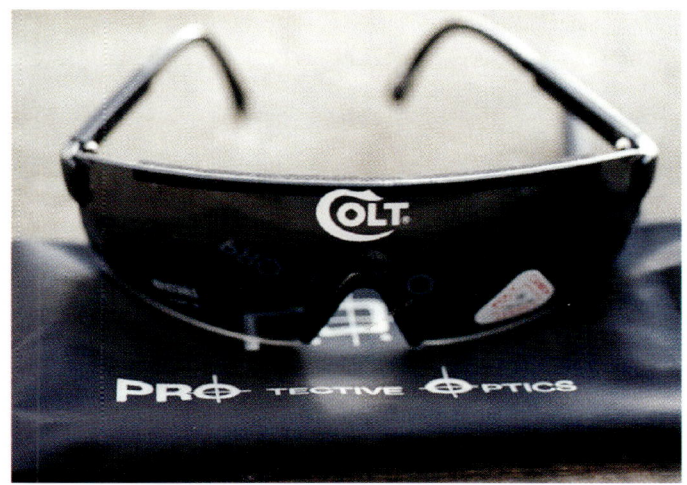

These shooter's glasses are available in 7 colors. A deluxe version of shooter's glasses is not marked Colt.
Price: $28.95

1987 gun cloth. **Price: $7**

Dates to 1990. **Price: $7**

From 1996. **Price: $2.95**

Prototype gun cloth. **Price: $20-50**

Prototype gun cloth **Price: $20-50**

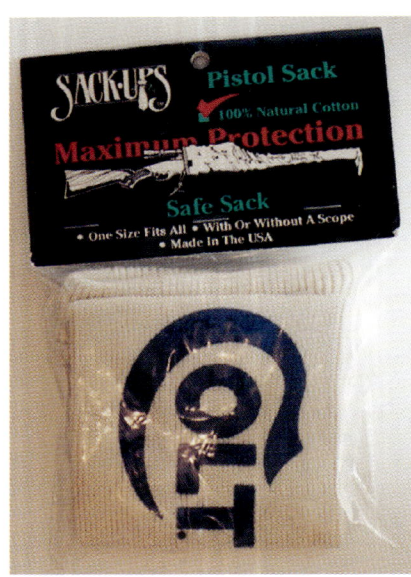

A pistol sock giveaway.
Price: $20

Automatic barrel bushing wrench.
Price: $10

A 1969 giveaway promoting the MKIII.
Price: $10-25

A towel for shooters sold in 1996.
Price: $7.95

Modern screwdrivers.
Value of each item: $5-25

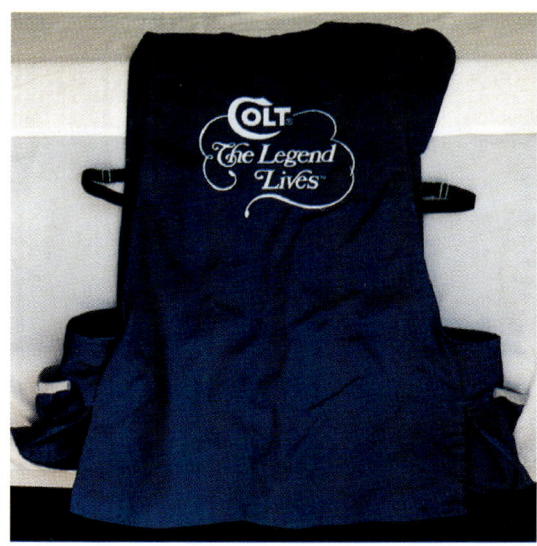

A shooting jacket from the Charleton Heston Celebrity Shoot in 1991.
Price: $250-500

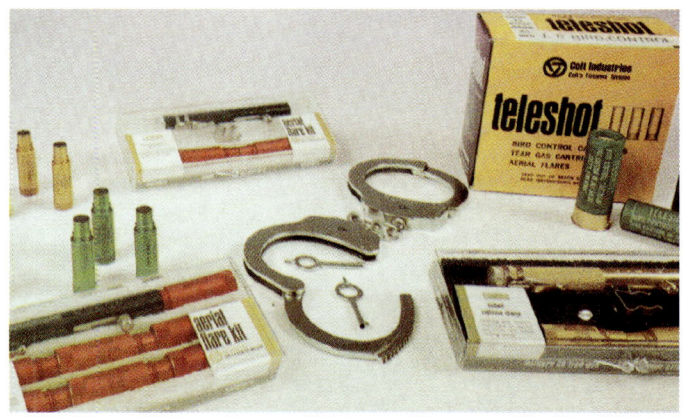

The 1972 catalog offered flare kits, tear gas kits, teleshot and handcuffs.
Prices: flare kit $40, tear gas kit $40, teleshot $40, handcuffs $250

A variation of handcuffs with the horse centered. Courtesy of the Tom Saady collection. **Price: $350**

Handcuffs made for the military. Courtesy of the Tom Saady collection. **Price: $450**

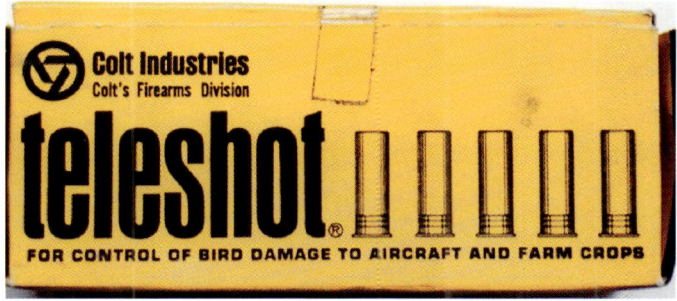

Small box of 10 teleshot bird scare cartridges. **Price: $50-100**

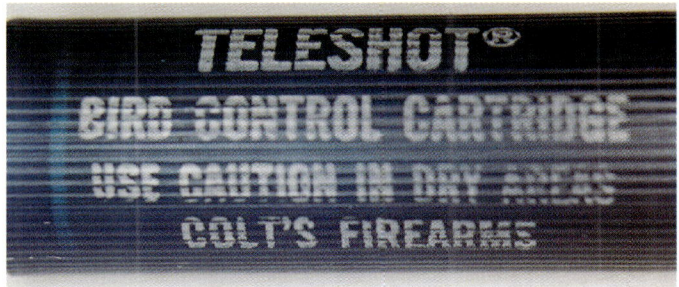

Blue bird scare cartridge made using a Remington commercial case. They were also made in green with the Remington case and a yellow case headstamped "Colt Teleshot." Photo courtesy of the Dick Fraser collection.
Price: $2-5

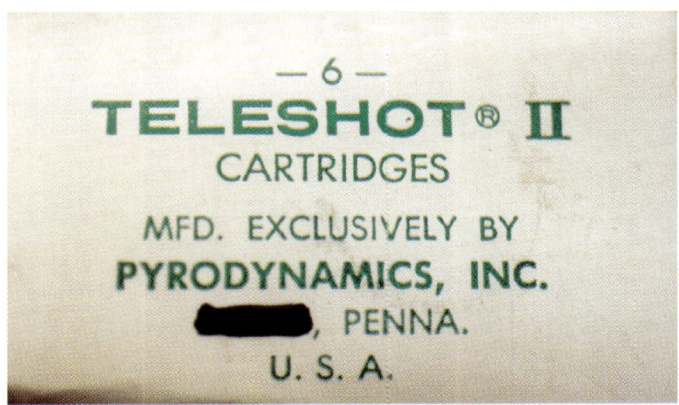

Teleshot II tear gas in 12 gauge cartridge. **Price: $50-100**

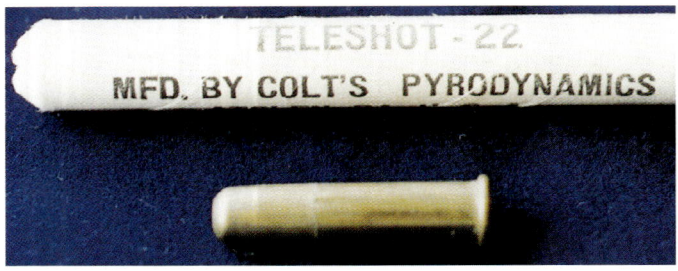

Teleshot in 22 cal. made for the military.
Price: $NEP

SSB cartridges. Courtesy of the Jack Kelley collection.
Value of each item: $5-15

A single paper cartridge. Courtesy of the Mike Poulin collection. **Value of each item: $15-30**

COLLECTOR'S NOTE: With the resurgence of interest in cowboy quick draw shooting in the 1960s Colt again marketed ammunition in the form of red plastic cased pistol ammo loaded with wax bullets. These are found in Colt marked boxes of 50 in .38 Special and .45 Colt.

COLLECTOR'S NOTE: Colt invented the metallic foil cartridge in the 1840s. Despite its marvelous waterproof properties, neither the government nor the general public ever warmed up to the concept and specimens are quite rare today. The then less expensive nitrated paper cartridge, usually sold five or six in a compartmentalized block wrapped with a descriptive label, was a great success in the late 1850s and 60s and are more commonly found. Colt established his own factory, Colt Cartridge Works, in 1857. For the next hundred years, Colt relied on Connecticut's two major ammunition companies, Winchester and Union Metallic Cartridge (merged with Remington around 1910) to develop ammunition for their guns, both commercial and experimental. Some of the latter include the .41 Colt Automatic (1900, UMC), 9.8mm ACP (1910 Win.), .41 Colt Special (1930, Rem., three variations) and the .400 Colt Magnum (1960, Win.).

Other items:

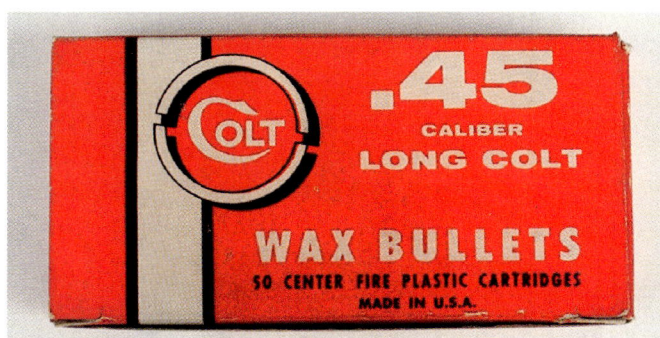

Price: $50

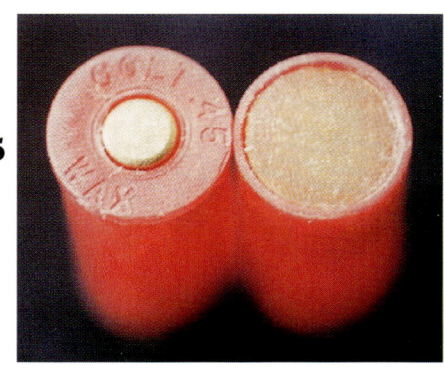

Price: $2-5

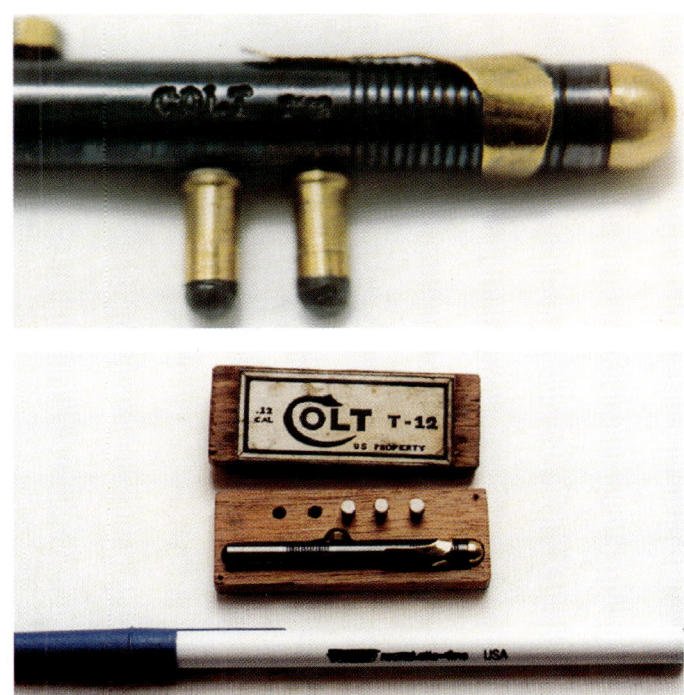

A miniature pen gun developed for the military. Courtesy of the Tom Saady collection. **Price: $750-1,500**

COLLECTOR'S NOTE: Colt has sold holsters from 1957 until 1973. In addition to these brochures, holsters were offered in the 1972 and 1973 retail catalogs. A Plexiglas display case was available for dealers to use for either knives or holsters.

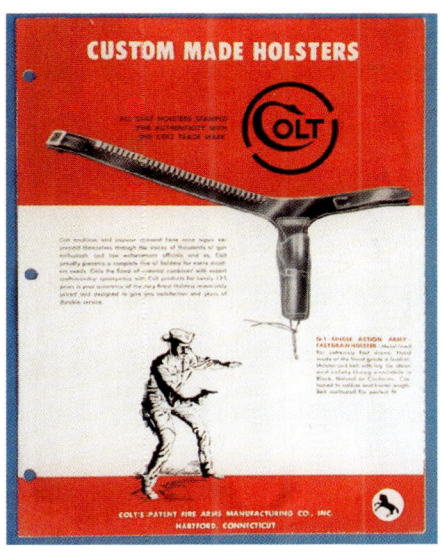

This 1960 brochure (H200) offered sixteen Colt-marked holsters in three different finishes and two colors, for a possible 295 variations. **Price: $10-35**

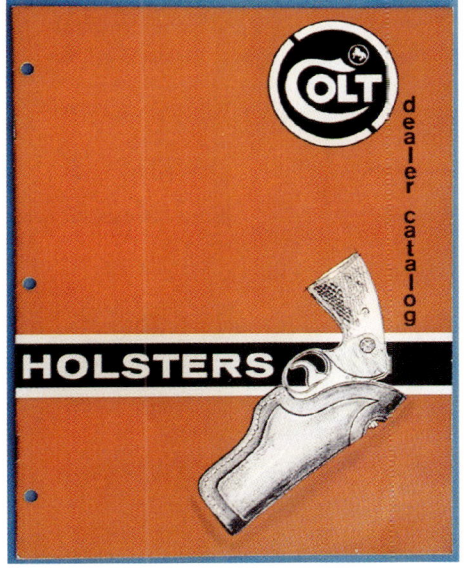

Ninety-one different variations of holsters were offered in this brochure from 1964. **Price: $10-35**

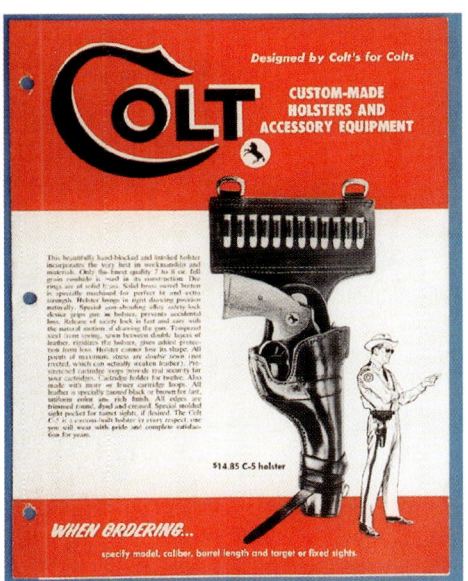

This 1957 brochure (H1000) offered 23 different holsters as well as belts, cuff cases, memo book covers and cartridge holders for police officers. **Price: $10-35**

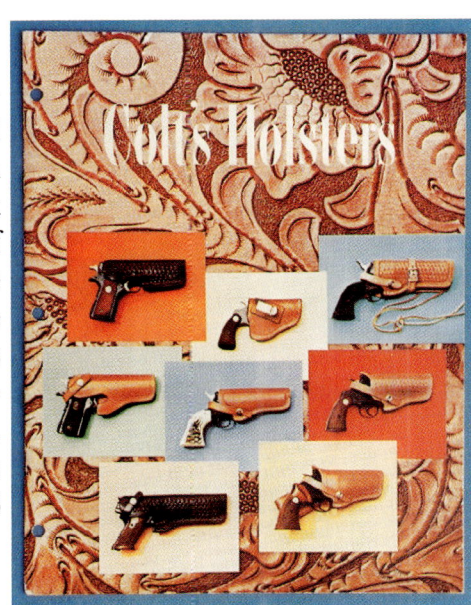

One hundred and fifty-seven different variations of holsters are possible from this 1970 brochure. **Price: $10-35**

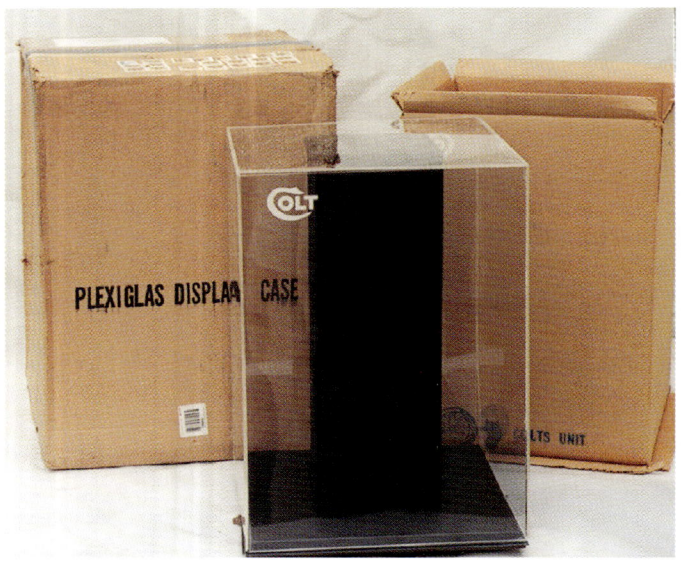

A dealer display case for holsters was shipped in a Colt-marked box.
Price: $75-150

This is the factory display that was used for trade shows by the factory during 1974 and 1975. Photo courtesy of the Doc Palmer collection.
Price: $1,500-2,000

In the late 1960s and 1970s, Colt developed a line of products for police departments including this shield from a bomb disposal kit. Courtesy of the Ron Lough collection. **Price: $300-500**

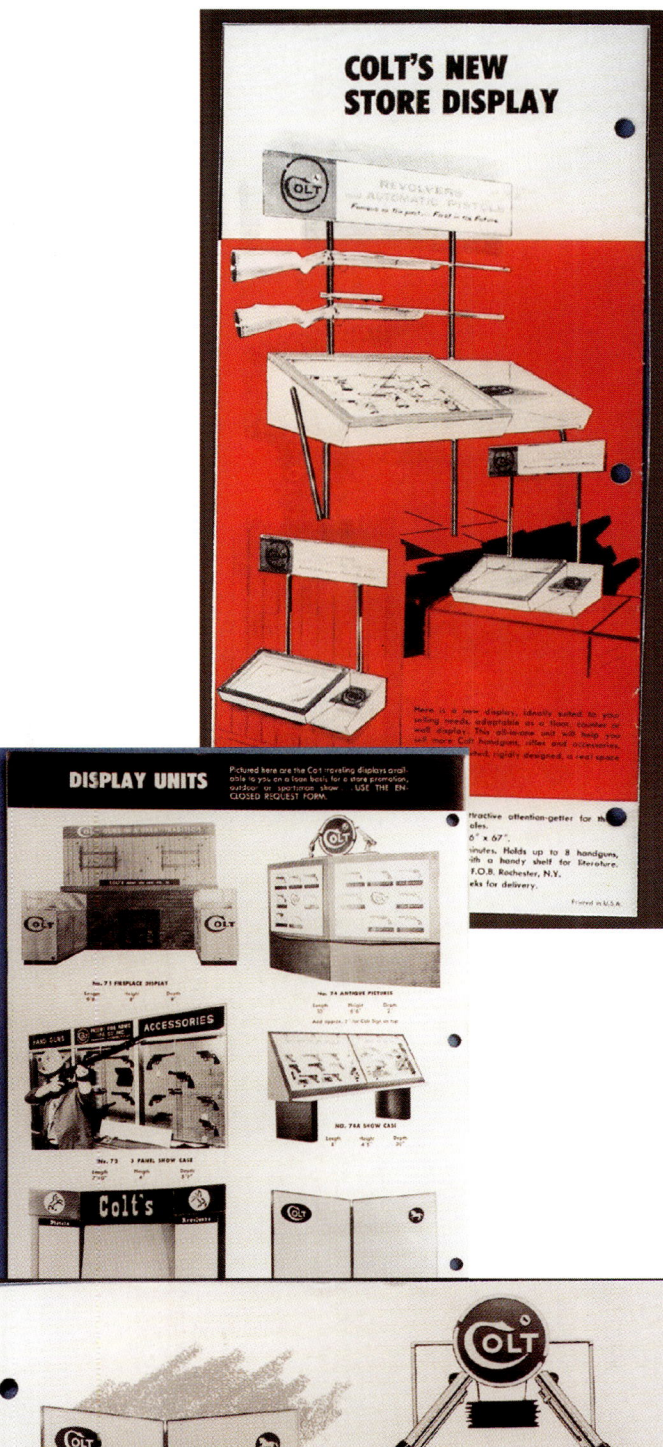

In the late 1960s, Colt also provided display cases for sale or loan to their dealers. No examples are known.
Value for each item shown: $NEP

Chapter 15
GLASSWARE

Colt logo mugs, tumblers and other glassware are not commonly available from dealers. Most dealers of Colt memorabilia are reluctant to buy and sell Colt glassware due to breakage. Glassware also takes up a lot of a dealer's table space that could be devoted to higher priced items. This makes the collection of Colt marked glassware more challenging.

COASTERS

1993 employee safety award. **Price: $50-100**

Produced in 1985. **Price: $25-40**

Produced in 1986. **Price: $25-35**

1989 original made in England. Photo courtesy of the Willard Johnson collection. **Price: $75**

1989 publicly sold variation. **Price: $20**

Stan Newman designed prototype salesman's samples. Five sets of four each were made. Photo courtesy of the Stan Newman collection. **Value of each item: $25-50**

Salesman's samples made for the military division. Courtesy of the Tom Saady collection. **Value of each item: $75**

This ceramic plate came in a matted frame, it may be a coaster, and it may have been produced through the factory.
Price: $20-35

COFFEE MUGS

This coffee mug sold during 1986.
Price: $30-50

Sold from 1989 to 1992.
Price: $25-50

According to Mr. Ron Wagner, this coaster was sold by Colt.
Price: $25-35

1986 oversized prototype. Photo courtesy of the Stan Newman collection.
Price: $35-50

Sold from 1987 to 1992. **Price: $15-25**

A variation without the gold band of what may have been intended as a shaving mug. Photo courtesy of the Willard Johnson collection.
Price: $100

***

COLLECTOR'S NOTE: Mr. Bill Blankenship had these mugs made on the occasion of his retirement from Colt. He did not like the light blue, so he had them remade with the gold lettering. Thirty were given to those employees with whom he had worked at least 10 years.

***

Produced sometime between 1974 and 1981. Photo courtesy of the Stan Newman collection. **Price: $35-50**

Produced sometime between 1974 and 1981. It is not certain if the shaving brush goes with this mug.
Price: $50-100

Price: $50-75

183

Price: $30-50

Photo courtesy of the Willard Johnson collection. **Price: $75**

Photo courtesy of the Stan Newman collection. **Price: $75-100**

Colt gave these mugs out to those people attending the first retirement party of Al DeJohn. **Value of each item: $20-50**

COLLECTOR'S NOTE: The "Made only in the USA" advertising campaign ran during 1989 and 1990. Two sizes of mugs were originally labeled as made in England. Mr. Stan Newman thought that inappropriate, so they were reordered. The mugs were still made in England, however, the gold stripes were added in the U.S. so they could claim to have been "Made in the USA."

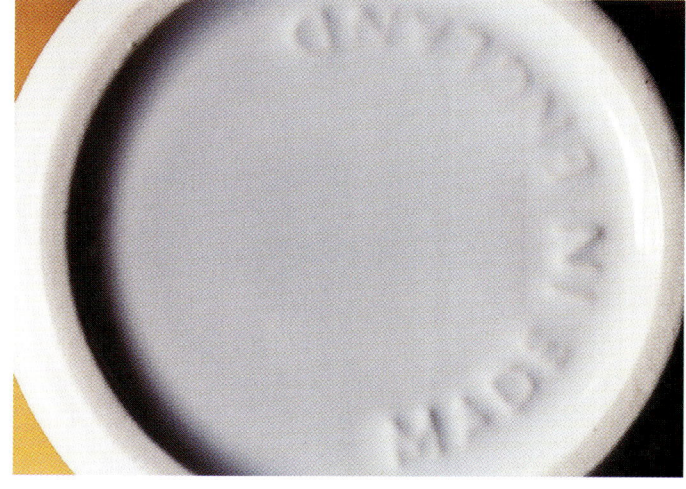

Photo courtesy of the Stan Newman collection. **Price: $35-50**

Price: $15-35

A Stan Newman prototype. A total of five were made.
Price: $50-100

1986 employee safety award.
Price: $10-25

"The Legend Lives" slogan was used during 1991 and 1992. Although offered for sale in the catalog, no mugs are known to have been publicly sold. These are prototype salesman's samples.
Each item is valued at: $50-100

1988 employee safety award.
Price: $10-25

Produced by the Colt Blackpowder Arms Company 1995.
Price: $10-25

Sold during 1996.
Price: $16.95

Sold during 1996.
Price: $16.95

No date known.
Price: $10-15

No date known.
Price: $30-50

Sold during 1997. **Price: $16.95**

Sold during 1995. **Price: $14.95**

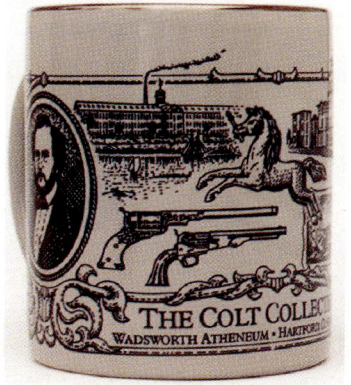

Sold at the Wadsworth Athenaeum in conjunction with the Colt exhibition in 1996 and 1997.
Price: $15.98

BEER MUGS

This pewter tankard made by Leonard in Sheffield, England uses the same emblem as the case for the buckles introduced in 1978. Photo courtesy of the Stan Newman collection. **Price: $75-125**

A 1984 Christmas gift to management club members.
Price: $15-30

This prototype mug may also date from 1978. **Price: $30-75**

This pewter tankard uses the 1985 buckle emblem.
Price: $50-100

Sold during 1986. Photo courtesy of the Stan Newman collection. **Price: $25-35**

1986 prototype samples. Photo courtesy of the Stan Newman Collection.
Each item is valued at: $35-50

1989 prototype sample.
Price: $30-50

Although offered for sale in 1991, none are known to have been publicly released.
Price: $30-50

Sold from 1987 to 1992.
Price: $15-25

Offered for sale in 1995.
Price: $15-20

1986 employee safety award.
Price: $10-20

Offered for sale in 1996.
Price: $10.95

188

A Stan Newman prototype. Five were made.
Price: $50-75

No date known.
Price: $20-50

1991 Prototype.
Price: $50-100

Made by John Hall Plastics and distributed by Silenco.
Value of each item: $5-12

Five prototypes were made. Photo courtesy of the Stan Newman collection.
Price: $50-75

GLASSES

One of the earliest Colt glasses known. Colt operated the Autosan division from 1919 until 1957.
Price: $100-150

Thought to date from the 1960s. **Price: $30-50**

Original box for etched glasses. **Price: $20**

COLLECTOR'S NOTE: Mr. Bill Judd, as sales manager, intentionally created controversy by producing limited numbers of exceptional gifts for his sales force. While attending a European trade show, he learned of a company that produced exceptional etched glass. He had a set of glasses, a decanter and an ice bucket made for his sales staff.

1979 German etched decanter. **Price: $150-300**

1979 German etched glass. At most 12 sets made. **Price: $100**

1980 German etched ice bucket. Courtesy of the Bill Judd collection. **Price: $150-300**

1983 Christmas gift to members of the management club.
Price: $10-25

1989 prototype tumblers.
Value of each item: $30-50

Limited production 150th anniversary wine glass set and decanter developed by Bob Morrison. **Price: $100-250**

1989 prototype "on the rocks" glasses. Photo at left is courtesy of the Willard Johnson collection.
Prices from left: $60, $30-50

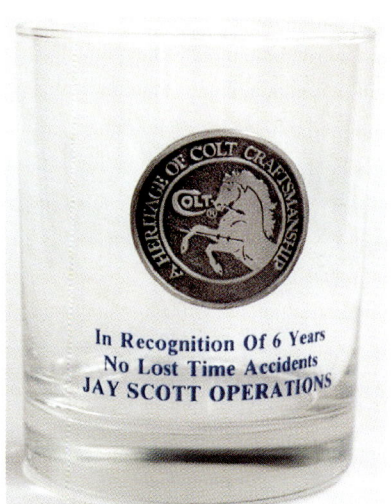

1987 Jay Scott safety award.
Price: $15-30

1989 prototype wine glass.
Price: $30-50

Given to employees attending the 1991 picnic. **Price: $5-15**

No date known. **Price: $20-50**

1992 tumbler. **Price: $5-10**

1995 tumbler. **Price: $20-30**

Two size variations of 1992 "rocks" glasses. **Price: $5-20**

Prototype tumbler and "rocks" glass. Five sets of four each were made. Photo courtesy of the Stan Newman collection. **Value of each item: $35-50**

1991 prototype plastic glasses. One set of four of each known.
Value of each item: $100-150

Sold during 1996. **Price: $49.95**

Prototype plastic patch glasses. **Value of each item: $50**

Plastic patch tumbler sold during 1995. **Price: $30-50**

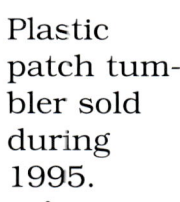

193

Shot glasses sold during 1996. Eleven designs were sold in sets of twelve. **Each set is valued at: $49.95**

Colt-marked huggie. **Price: $5-15**

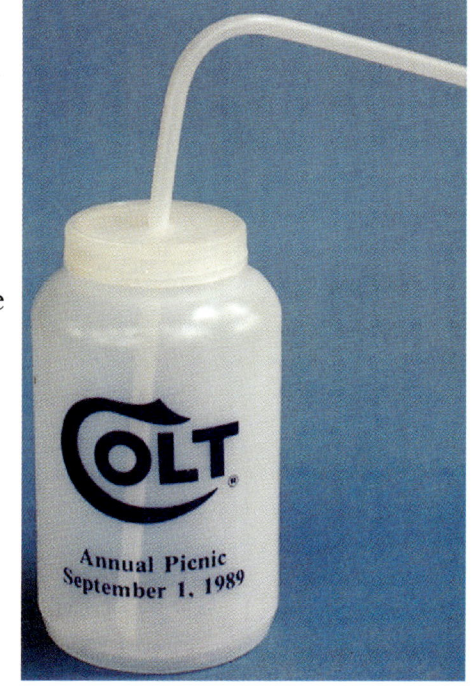

Given to employees attending the 1989 picnic. **Price: $5-15**

Given to everyone attending the 1990 family day open house. **Price: $5-15**

Traveling drink holders from 1994.
Each item is valued at: $10-20

PACIFIC INTERNATIONAL GLASSWARE

The following photos illustrate Pacific International glassware. Pacific International operated as a Colt distributor in California from 1972 until 1991. As a major distributor, Colt allowed them to use the Colt logo. They also became a distributor for an advertising fulfillment company and had a special piece of glassware made every year. This glassware was given to their friends at Colt, and to favored dealers and customers.
Price: $10-25

OTHER GLASSWARE

Large 13-inch diameter plate from 1986.
Price: $150-200

Candy jar sold during 1996.
Price: $16.95

Variation of candy jar sold during 1996.
Price: $16.95

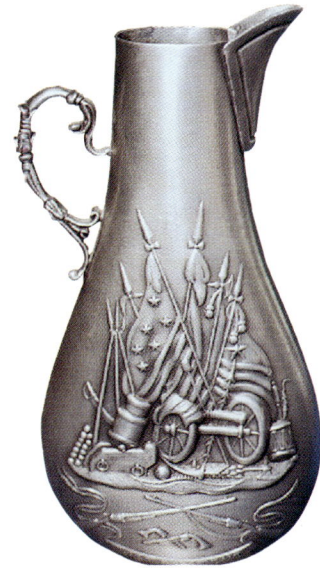

Pitcher made from a powder flask. Photo courtesy of the Willard Johnson collection. **Price: $1500**

The Jaffa crystal dish was made in two sizes to celebrate the 150th anniversary of Colt. **Price: $50-100**

Only 12 of the Jaffa crystal dishes with the plain logo were made. **Price: $NEP**

This canteen was made by the Colt Manufacturing Company of Indianapolis, Indiana. The company, named for its president Alonzo J. Colt, operated until 1945. It made aluminum and steel food and liquid jugs, cream containers in addition to camp, cooking and lunch kits. Photo courtesy of the Tom Saady collection. **Price: $300-1000**

Chapter 16
WATCHES & CLOCKS

Most horologers are probably not aware of the variey of watches and clocks that Colt has had made. Colt generally gives its long term retiring employees a gun instead of a watch. However, Colt had given out clocks and watches to its employees as internal awards, and to friends and dealers of the company. Colt recently offered a line of logo watches for sale to the public.

Thirty of these pocket watches made by Cycle, featuring a hunter scene cover, were given to those attending the sales meeting of 1977. An engraver was present to inscribe the person's name if they so desired. **Price: $500-800**

This watch was given to friends, distributors and major Colt dealers by Jack Kelley. He had 25 made. **Price: $100-150**

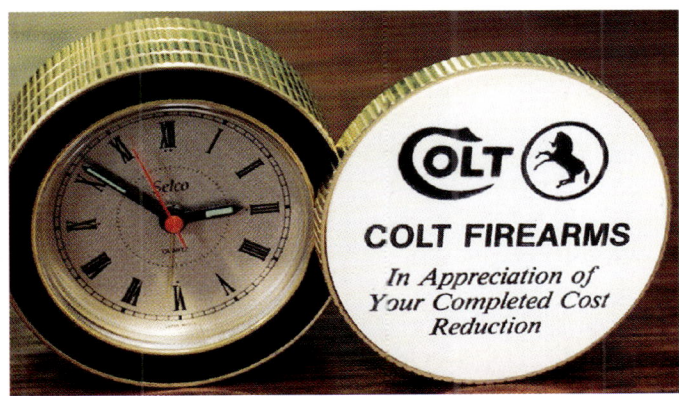

Given to division heads in 1989, in appreciation of their efforts at reducing costs for Colt. **Price: $150-250**

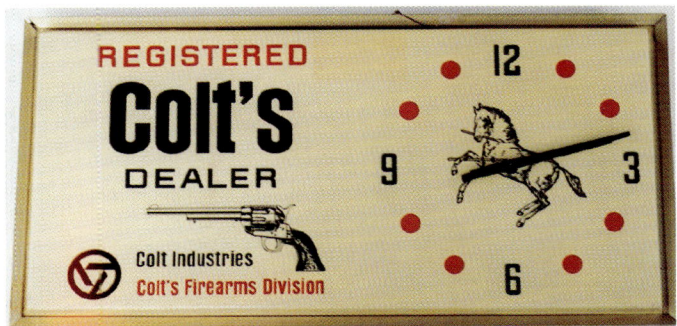

This clock was offered for sale to all Colt dealers from 1968 until 1972. It measures 12x24 inches. **Price: $350**

A gift to those organizing the 1990 family day at Colt. **Price: $250**

A 1992 gift to the 53 members of the Colt Safety Committee. Courtesy of the Dan Chesiak collection. **Price: $250-350**

Men's and ladie's safety award watches of 1986. **Value of each item: $50-100**

A prototype having a black serpentine logo. **Price: $350**

A safety award watch from 1991. **Price: $150**

A 1986 gift to employees and friends of Colt. **Price: $150**

A five-year safety award for the Jay Scott division of Colt. Jay Scott was acquired by Colt in 1974, and employed 35 people. **Price: $300**

Known to have been distributed throughout the factory. Photo of watch at left is courtesy of the Jim Alaimo collection.
Price: $250

Price: $100

CW2 Sahara.
Price: $226

CW4 Cape Hatteras.
Price: $266

CW3 Outback.
Price: $226

CW5 Kenya.
Price: $200

Price: $50

These watches sold through United Cutlery in 1996 are licensed through Colt.

CW1 Monte Carlo.
Price: $307

CW6 Everest.
Price: $200

Dealer display case. Courtesy of the Ron Lough collection
Price: $150-250

This watch, while not distributed through the factory, was given to Marty Huber who wore it for several years. Courtesy of the Marty Huber collection. **Price: $20-40**

A non-factory fantasy pocket watch. A laser copy of the Colt Shooter patch has been reduced and placed over the face of an old pocket watch. **Price: $75-125**

Chapter 17
CARDS & DICE

Cards and Colts are perceived as having a romantic history dating back to the saloons of the wild west. In fact, the first Colt marked cards and dice were given out in 1974. The Colt marked chip reported to have been given in the 1920s may be a fantasy item produced much later. Most of the Colt marked dice are thought to be fantasy items, and there may be only three sets actually issued through the factory.

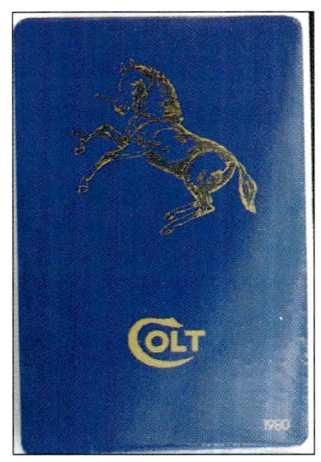 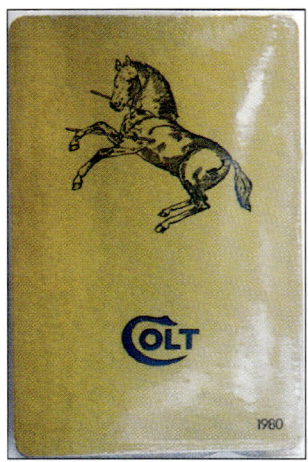

Given out during 1980.
Price of each item: $10-20

Given out during 1981.
Price of each item: $10-20

A 1981 card set. **Price: $25-50**

Front and back of a card set thought to have been given out sometime between 1974 and 1981.
Price: $20-40

Given out during 1986.
Price of each item: $10-25

Two variations of a presentation cased set of 150th anniversary cards.

Photo at right courtesy of the Stan Newman collection.

Prices from top to bottom: $140-150; $150-250

Given to employees as a safety incentive. Courtesy of the Norman Green collection. **Price: $20-50**

Sold during 1898 as a companion to the set of Python revolvers from the Custom Shop known as the "Snake Eyes Limited Edition." **Price: $200-250**

Front and back of a set of cards sold with a special Custom Shop edition, the "Mississippi River Gambler" in 1980.
Price of each item: $20-30

Snake Eyes cards were also available separately.
Price of each item: $5-20

Snake Eyes chips and dice were also available separately. Only ten sets of the square cornered dice were made. Photo courtesy of the Stan Newman collection.
Prices: square dice $50; plain dice $10-20; chips $5-10

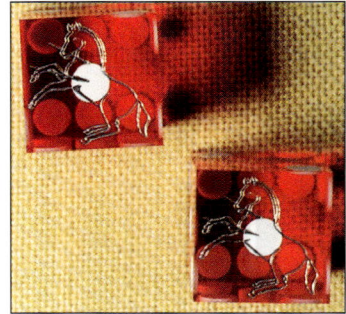

The red dice with the rampant logo were issued with a special Custom Shop edition "Mississippi River Gambler" in 1980.
Price: $20-50

This clay chip was reportedly given out by the factory in the 1920s, along with a black variation. This has not been confirmed or verified.
Price: $20-50

Offered in the 1992 price list, these cards were never publicly sold.
Price of each item: $40-50

This is most likely a fantasy non-factory item. **Price: $10-20**

It has not been established that any of these dice were ever released through the factory. **Price: $10-20**

Chapter 18
OFFICE SUPPLIES

The eclectic collection of items in this chapter have been grouped together under the general heading of items found in an office. Some of the items were actually used in Colt offices, while others were given to employees as gifts or awards. Colt has recently added some of these items to its publicly sold memorabilia.

PENS & PENCILS

In addition to the ColtRock Colt-marked pencil pictured earlier, this is one of the few early Colt advertising pens known. Courtesy of the Tom Saady collection. **Price: $100-250**

An early pencil. **Price: $25-35**

***

COLLECTOR'S NOTE: Mr. Bill Judd is probably responsible for buying the first executive Cross pen and pencil sets with Colt logos as gifts for his sales team sometime in the mid 1970's. Since then, a number of variations have been made. Six different logos are known, with gold, silver and black sets of pen and pencil. Fountain pens are known in gold and silver. It is not known if all combinations of logos in all colors were ever produced. If so, 30 different variations would exist.

***

The first three items are courtesy of the Stan Newman collection.

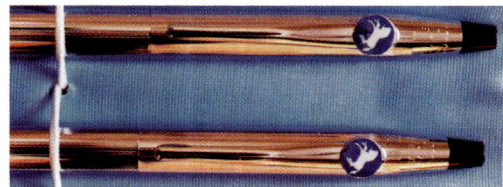

Price: $75-150

Price: $75-150

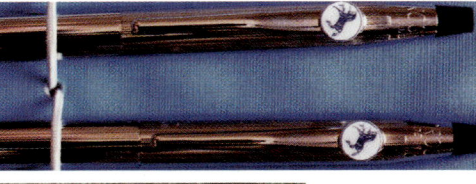

Price: $75-150

Price: $75-150

Price: $75-150

Price: $75-150

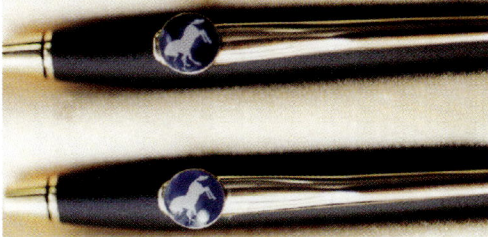

Price: $75-150

Price: $100-250

Price: $100-250

Price: $100-250

Price: $75-150

Mr. Jack Kelley is probably responsible for the first advertising pens in modern time, which he had made for his dealers and distributors. The next five items are examples of these pens.

Pilot pen marked "Selling isn't everything, Selling is the only thing, Plan for sales, SELL COLT BENEFITS, Colt days promote sales."
Price: $10-20

National pen marked "COLT, An American heritage, the standard by which all other guns are measured."
Price: $10-20

Marked "Colt Heirloom, your name is the serial no., write Jack Kelley, 11 Ledgewood Rd., Canton CT. 06019." **Price: $10-20**

Marked "COLT, SG&T of Pennsylvania, your best source for, fine Colt products, SG&T COLT SG&T."
Price: $10-20

Marked "Keep track of your Colt inventory, sell quality sell service sell Colt, call your Colt jobber today."
Price: $10-20

Marked "Colt Firearms, 545 New Park Ave., West Hartford Ct. 06110."
Price: $5-15

National pen marked "Colt, the standard by which all other guns are measured, COLT."
Price: $5-15

Marked "Colt Firearms, Family Day, January 17 1982." **Price: $5-15**

National pen marked "Sam Colt, invented the revolver, finest finish-smoothest action, strongest frame-truest bore, for the man who wants the best, sell quality-sell Colt."
Price: $5-15

National pen marked " Since 1836, An American tradition, call your Colt jobber, for catalogs and prices, or write Colt Firearms, 150 Huyshope Ave., Hartford CT 06102, Colt—An American Heritage—Colt."
Price: $5-15

National pen marked " Trooper-Lawman-Python, sell Colt, S.A.A.-1911-D.S.-Ace."
Price: $5-15

Amsterdam pen marked "Colt Industries Inc., Proteja su hogar, compre un "Colt" AHORA, A.E. Rodriguez, San Juan, P.R. Distributor." **Price: $10-20**

U.S. Pencil Co. marked "Colt Industries, Felices Pascuos Y, Prospero Ano Nuevo, A.E. Rodriguez, San Juan P.R., Distributor for Puerto Rico. **Price: $10-20**

Parker pen marked "Colt M16A1." **Price: $20-35**

Pen marked "We are geared to serve you better, Colt Firearms, 150 Huyshope Ave., Hartford Ct 06102." **Price: $5-15**

Parker pen marked "Colt Industries." **Price: $5-15**

Pen marked "Colt Industries." **Price: $5-15**

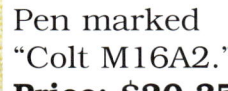

Pen marked "Colt M16A2." **Price: $20-35**

Pen marked "Colt Firearms." **Price: $5-15**

Unipeco marked pen "Colt firearms, Military Operations, Hartford, Conn. U.S.A." **Price: $5-20**

Pen marked "Colt, Military Firearms, Hartford, Conn. U.S.A." **Price: $5-20**

Alexander pen marked "The Legend Lives, Colt's Manufacturing Company Inc." **Price: $10-25**

Alexander pen marked "The Legend Lives."
Price: $10-25

Parker pen marked "The authentic Colt, BLACKPOWDER, Sam Colt."
Price: $10-35

Colt. **Price: $15-25**

Factory giveaway item.
Price: $5-15

Factory giveaway item.
Price: $10-25

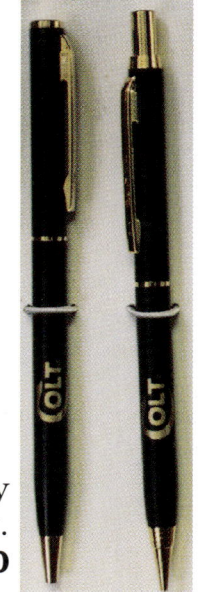

Factory giveaway set.
Price: $35-50

Colt 10mm and Norma
Price: $25-40

A promotional prototype made by Zippo for the president of Colt.
Price: $250

Sold from 1992 to 1996.
Price: $11

Modern pencils given to employees.
Value of each item: $5-10

211

Papermate marked pen "Pratt & Whitney, Colt Industries, Machine Tool Division." **Price: $5-20**

Garland marked pen "Chandler Evans, Control Systems Division, Colt Industries." **Price: $5-20**

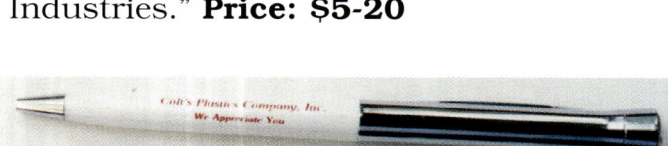

Garland marked pen "Colt's Plastics Company Inc., We Appreciate You." **Price: $10-25**

Prototype desk set. These were too expensive to have made, so Colt never produced them for sale. Four samples are known. **Price: $150-350**

POCKET PROTECTORS

1960s. **Price: $25-50**

1986 150th anniversary. **Price: $25-50**

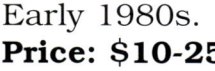
Early 1980s. **Price: $10-25**

A Cross desk set presented to C.E. Warner, president of Colt from 1976 to 1981. **Price: $350**

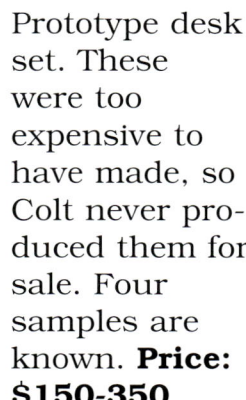
Desk set. **Price: $75-150**

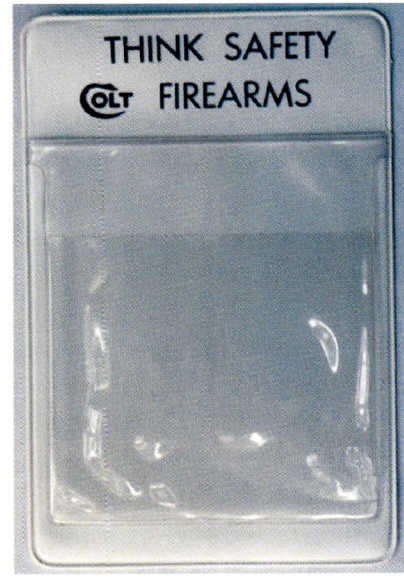

1985 employee safety incentive.
Price: $5-15

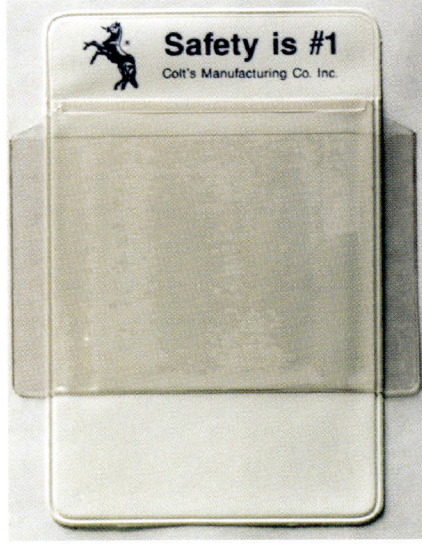

1991 employee safety incentive.
Price: $5-15

SAFTEY AWARDS

COLLECTOR'S NOTE: In late 1985, Colt created a committee to oversee safety. There were separate committees of 25 employees for both the Knudson and Hartford facilities, a head of safety for both facilities and a committee chairman for a total of 53 members. Chester Marsh was the first to head the new safety committee. He began the policy of providing prizes to employees and safety committee members. Prizes were awarded based on quarters worked with no time lost due to an accident. Different prizes were awarded for each of the four quarters of the year successfully completed with no accidents.

In an attempt to make the awards more equitable, different types of employees would be grouped together. Employees working at jobs for which safety is a high concern would be grouped with executives, for example. In addition, incentive awards were occasionally given to those employees who attended a particular safety lecture. Hourly employees were rewarded for safety through drawings for awards.

Gifts were either taken from memorabilia inventory intended for public sale or were ordered specially made from a variety of companies. All items were marked with Colt logos and many were identified as safety awards. Some items are dated.

Today (1995) employees accumulate points which can be traded for merchandise from the Wares Catalog. In addition to glassware, bags, clocks and watches issued as safety awards and presented in previous chapters the following items were awarded to employees as safety awards.

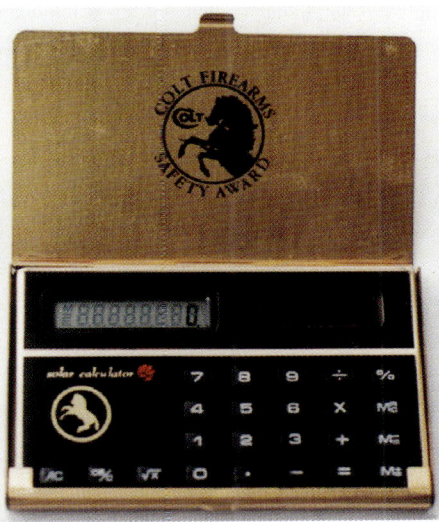

1986 calculator.
Price: $50-100

1987 magnet. **Price: $5-15**

1988 wallet. **Price: $15-25**

1988 door alarm. **Price: $25**

1988 poncho. **Price: $25-40**

1988 gold desk calendar set. Courtesy of the Tom Saady collection. **Price: $75-150**

1988 blued desk calendar set. **Price: $75-125**

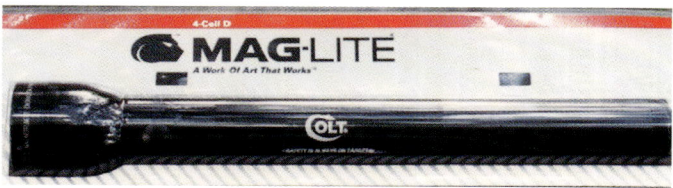
1988 Mag-Lite flashlight. **Price: $50**

1988 fire alarm. **Price: $30**

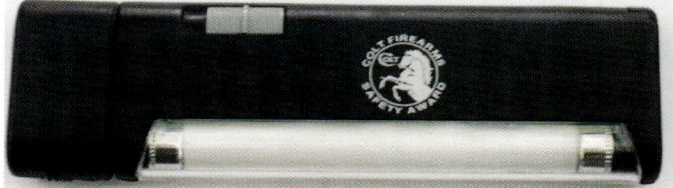
1989 flashlight. **Price: $30-50**

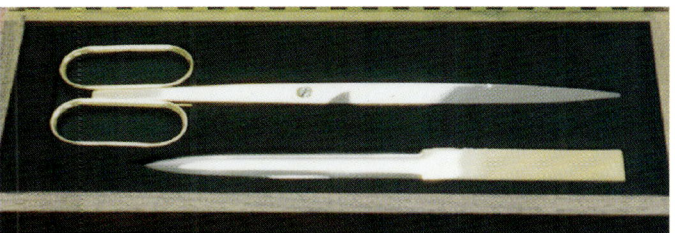

1989 library desk set. **Price: $150-250**

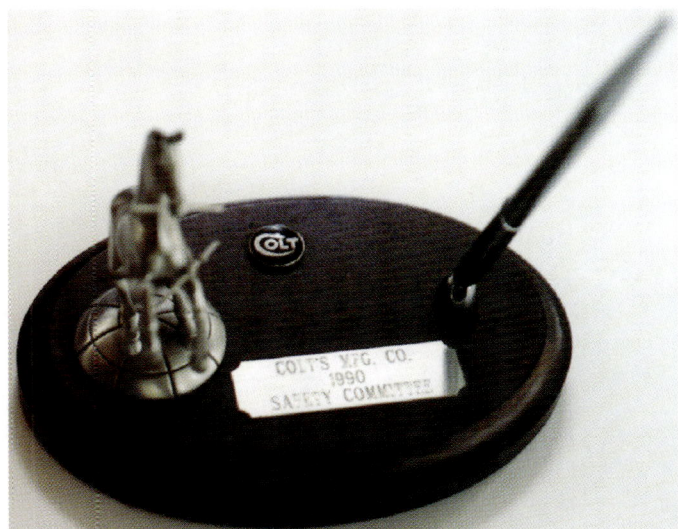

1990 desk set. **Price: $100-150**

1994 Christmas ornament. **Price: $40**

M16 RELATED

COLLECTOR'S NOTE:
The Colt M16 A2 rifle was dedicated on April 12, 1984 with a ceremony at the Colt factory in Hartford. A number of items were made to be given away for that ceremony or sold later.

A Lucite embedment of the brass M16A2 pin. **Price: $35-50**

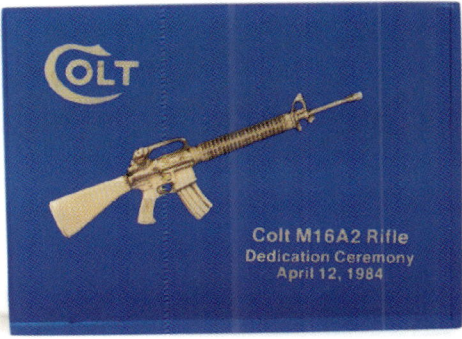

The wrong pin was embedded in this Lucite paperweight. **Price: $35-50**

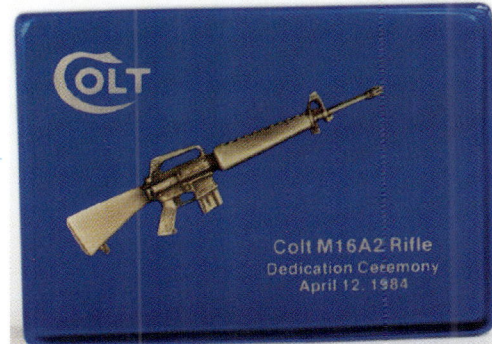

A generic M16 Lucite paperweight. **Price: $35-50**

215

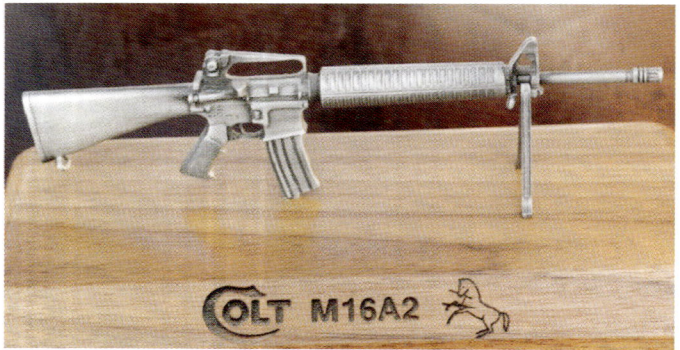

This desk set was sold from 1989 until 1992. **Price: $50-100**

Black based variation. **Price: $50-125**

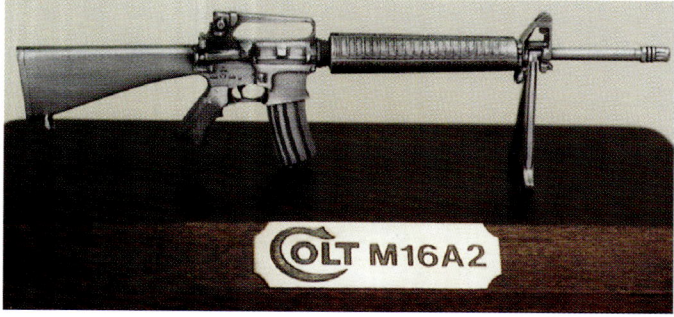

A different variation of the desk set. **Price: $35-150**

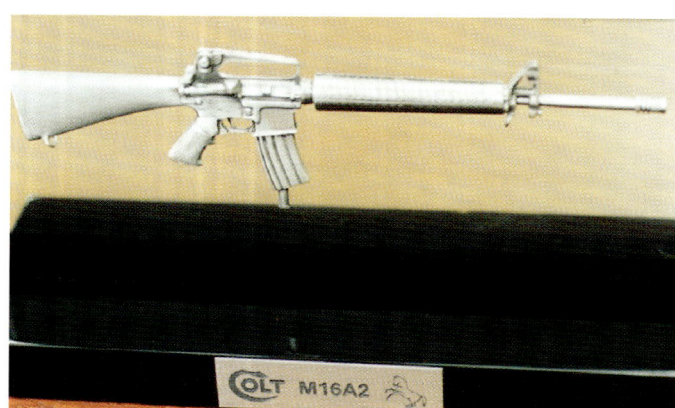

Lucite embedment in a desk set. **Price: $100-150**

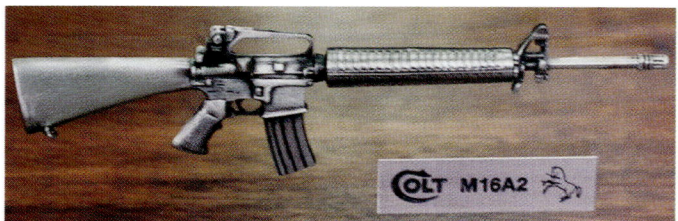

Lucite embedment in a paperweight. **Price: $100-150**

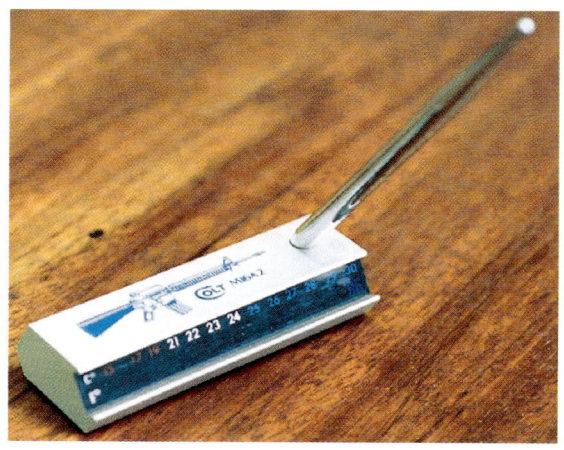

Combination desk set. **Price: $50-75**

Calculator. **Price: $35-50**

Ruler, clock, calculator combination. **Price: $45-75**

M16 on marble.
Price: $25-50

Zippo pocket knife.
Price: $25

AR15 on marble.
Price: $25-50

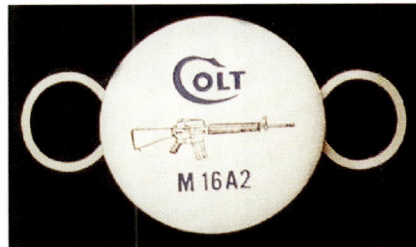
Zippo key ring.
Price: $30

Rubber jar opener.
Price: $5-10

This desk set of the AR15 was made as a gift when Colt was attempting to build a plant in Korea during the late 1960s.
Price: $100-250

Magnet. **Price: $2-5**

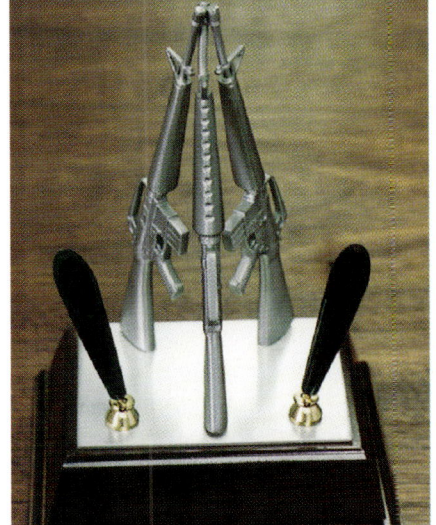
It is not certain if this desk set was released through the factory.
Price: $150

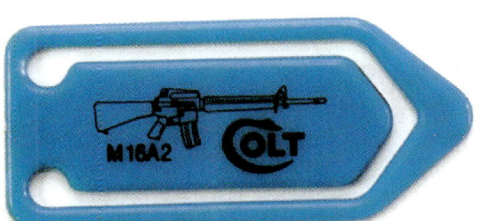
Paper clip.
Price: $5

217

OTHER ITEMS

An award from the Colt Pistol and Revolver Club, date unknown. Courtesy of the Ron Lough collection. **Price: $150-200**

This rubber jar opener was a gift to those employees attending the 1982 Family Day. **Price: $2-5**

Bookends featuring either a pair of deactivated derringers or a rampant Colt statue were offered for sale in 1971. They remain scarce and the rampant Colt bookends were not available to photograph. **Price: $350-500**

Several of these chairs were auctioned at the 1992 Colt Collectors Association show. They were used by Colt at trade shows in the 1970s. **Price: $100-250**

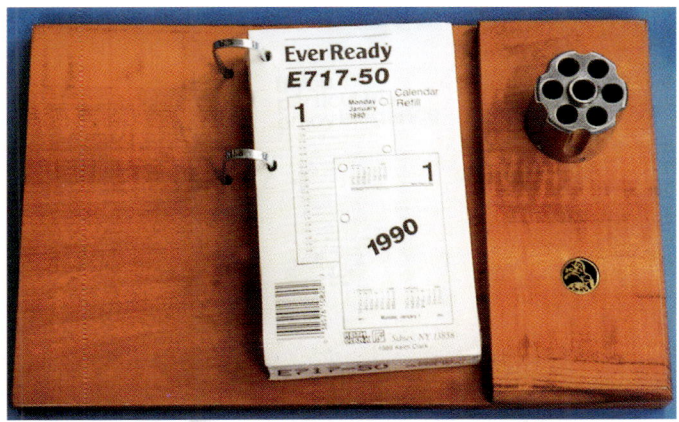

This desk calendar set with nickeled cylinder is the variation that was sold in the 1989 accessories catalog. **Price: $50-75**

Letter box from the desk of Mr. Rob Roy. **Price: $50**

Name plate from the desk of Mr. Messemer. **Price: $150**

Employee calculator. **Price: $45**

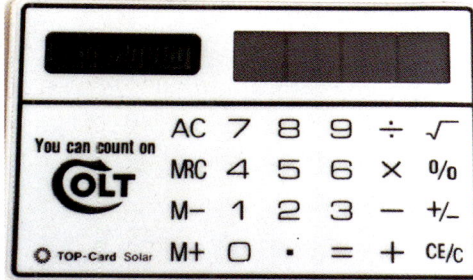

Giveaway calculator. **Price: $25-35**

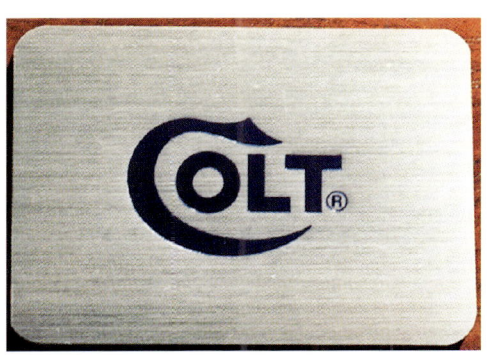

An address book given out in 1990. **Price: $5-20**

1981 Lucite embedment of a rusty nail from the armorer's residences. These were also included with the special edition guns. **Price: $35-50**

1981 Blackpowder. **Price: $50-150**

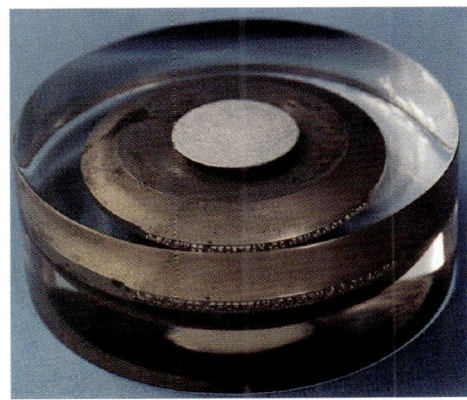

Lucite embedment of roll dies from the factory were offered for sale at the 1984 Colt Collectors Association meeting. **Price: $50-100**

Given to investors at the March 22, 1990 meeting where Colt Industries became Colt's Manufacturing Company, Inc. **Price: $250**

Prototype Lucite embedments. Photo courtesy of the Stan Newman collection.

Price: $75-100

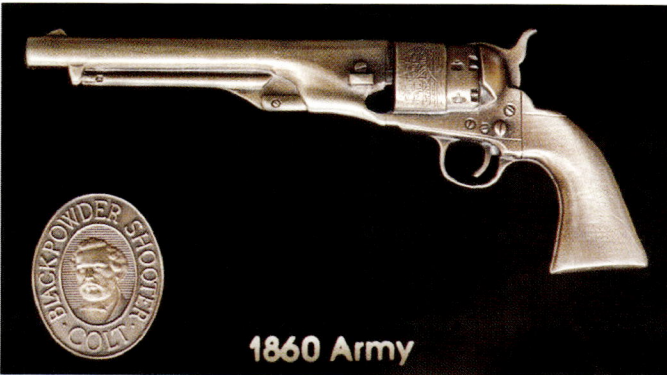
Price: $75-100

Price: $100-150

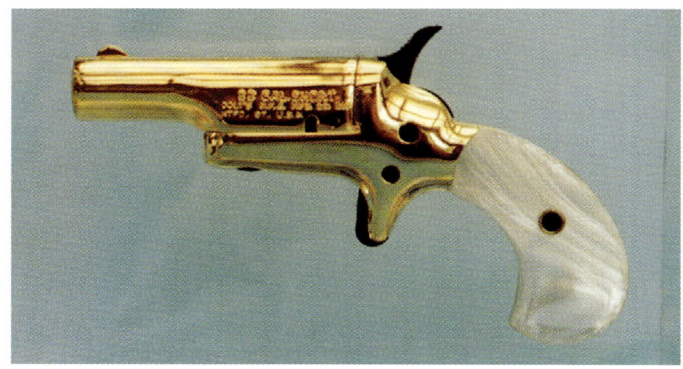
Prototype Lucite embedment of derringer. Courtesy of the Tom Saady collection. **Price: $100-300**

Paperweight sold in the 1995 accessories catalog. **Price: $30.95**

A brick from the original factory in Hartford was sold from 1994 to 1996 to commemorate the move out of the building on May 31, 1994. Only 500 were offered for sale. **Price: $150**

This replica being sold as a paperweight was actually part of a WWII commemorative desk set from 1995. Courtesy of the Tom Saady collection.

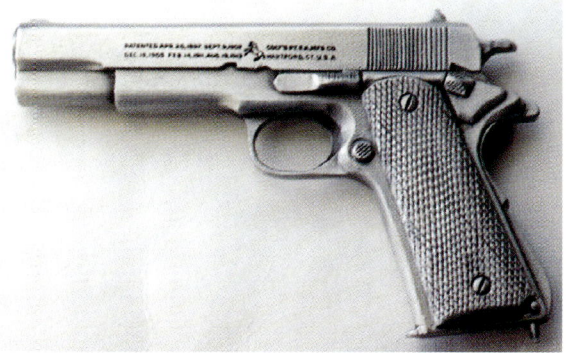

Price: $25-35

Price: $35-50

This 24kt. gold-plated medallion was included in the 1984 Winchester-Colt commemorative set. The set was numbered and limited to 4,440.
Price: $50-100

Medallion issued in 1914 by Colt to honor Sam's 100th birthday. Three hundred eighty-eight bronze were made. In addition, 10 were made in 10kt. gold. Courtesy of the Dan Chesiak collection.
Price: $1,000-1,500

Medallion issued in 1964 by Colt to honor Sam Colt's 150th birthday; 5,300 were made. Courtesy of the Dan Chesiak collection.
Price: $75-200

Medallion issued by Colt from 1976 to 1978. An original 1,500 were struck but 1,000 were later melted down.
Price: $100-150

Given to members of the Colt Commemorative Gun Collectors Association in 1969. **Price: $35-50**

***

COLLECTOR'S NOTE: Another one of the special gifts Bill Judd had made for his troop of salesmen was a walking stick. There were 24 reportedly made in 1981 with the rounded head and ivory insert. Most were engraved with the individual's name. An additional 36 were made with a flattened head and serpentine logo to be given to those who complained about not getting one of the engraved sticks.

To show his appreciation, Mr. Jack Kelley had a swagger stick made to give to Bill Judd. A minimum order of 12 swagger sticks were made. Most, including Bill Judd's carried the individuals crest of the Armed Services under which they had served. Only four were engraved with the Rampant Colt.

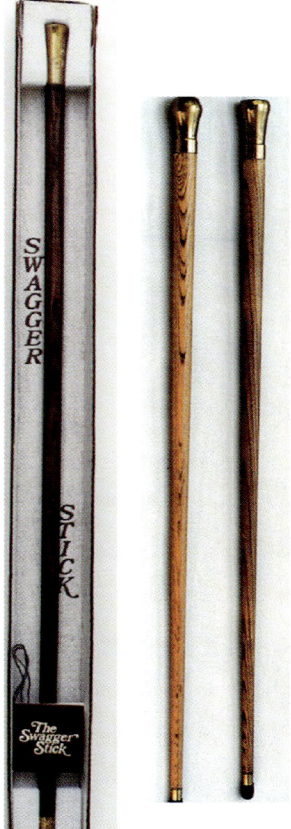

The first two items are from the Bill Judd collection. The final item is from the Jack Kelley collection. **Prices: brass $200-400, ivory $250-500; $250-500**

An early note pad. Courtesy of the Tom Saady collection.
Price: $50-75

An early note pad. Courtesy of the Tom Saady collection. **Price: $50-75**

1991 calendar. **Price: $10-25**

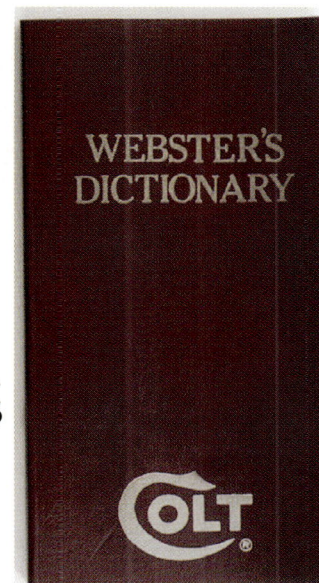

Office dictionary. **Price: $10-25**

1987 calendar. **Value of each item: $15-30**

1995 organizer given to senior personnel. **Price: $25-35**

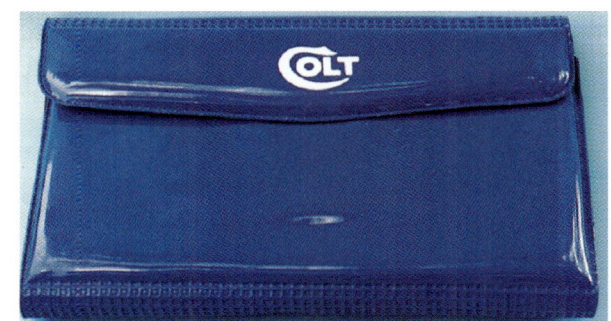

Calendar. **Price: $15-30**

Prototype business card holder from early 1990s. **Price: $25-50**

Leather business card holder sold in 1995. **Price: $17**

Ceramic magnets sold in 1996. **Price: $4**

Daily planner sold in 1995. **Price: $38**

Travel organizer sold in 1995. **Price: $40**

Seat cushion given to employees in 1987. **Price: $25-50**

Money clip sold in 1995. **Price: $16**

Ice scraper given to employees attending the 1990 Family Day. **Price: $5-20**
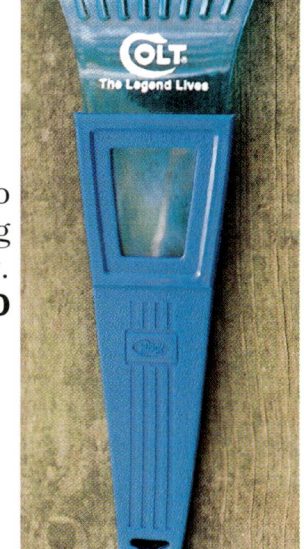

Zipper pull sold in 1996. **Price: $4**

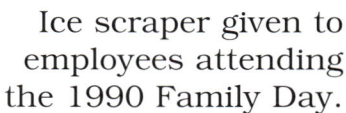

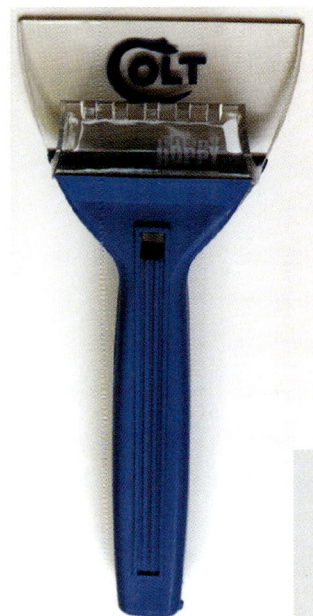
Ice scraper. **Price: $10-20**

Work gloves given out in 1989. **Price: $10-35**

A miniature brick measuring two inches that was given to Custom Shop employees in 1994. As few as ten may have been made. Photo courtesy of the Tom Saady collection. **Price: $15-50**

Christmas ornament given to employees in 1988. Courtesy of the Ron Lough collection. **Price: $50-100**

Another Custom Shop Christmas ornament made of wood. Photo courtesy of the Tom Saady collection. **Price: $15-50**

Eyeglass case. Date not known.
Price: $25-50

Trade show display flags, 1989.
Price: $10-30

A metal plate given to division heads in appreciation for reducing costs. Photo courtesy of the Doc Palmer collection.
Price: $50-75

Trade show display flags, 1991.
Price: $50-100

The factory prototype plate used to promote the Custom Shop engraving program. this plate appears on the back cover of the 1992 Custom Shop Catalog. Courtesy of the Ron Lough collection.
Price: $1500

This brass plate is drilled to be hung on a wall and reportedly dates from the turn of the century. Photo courtesy of the Tom Saady collection. **Price: $NEP**

Bookmark sold at the Wadsworth Athenaeum in conjunction with a Colt display in 1996 and 1997. **Price: $5.95**

These fantasy items are known to be non-released through the factory.

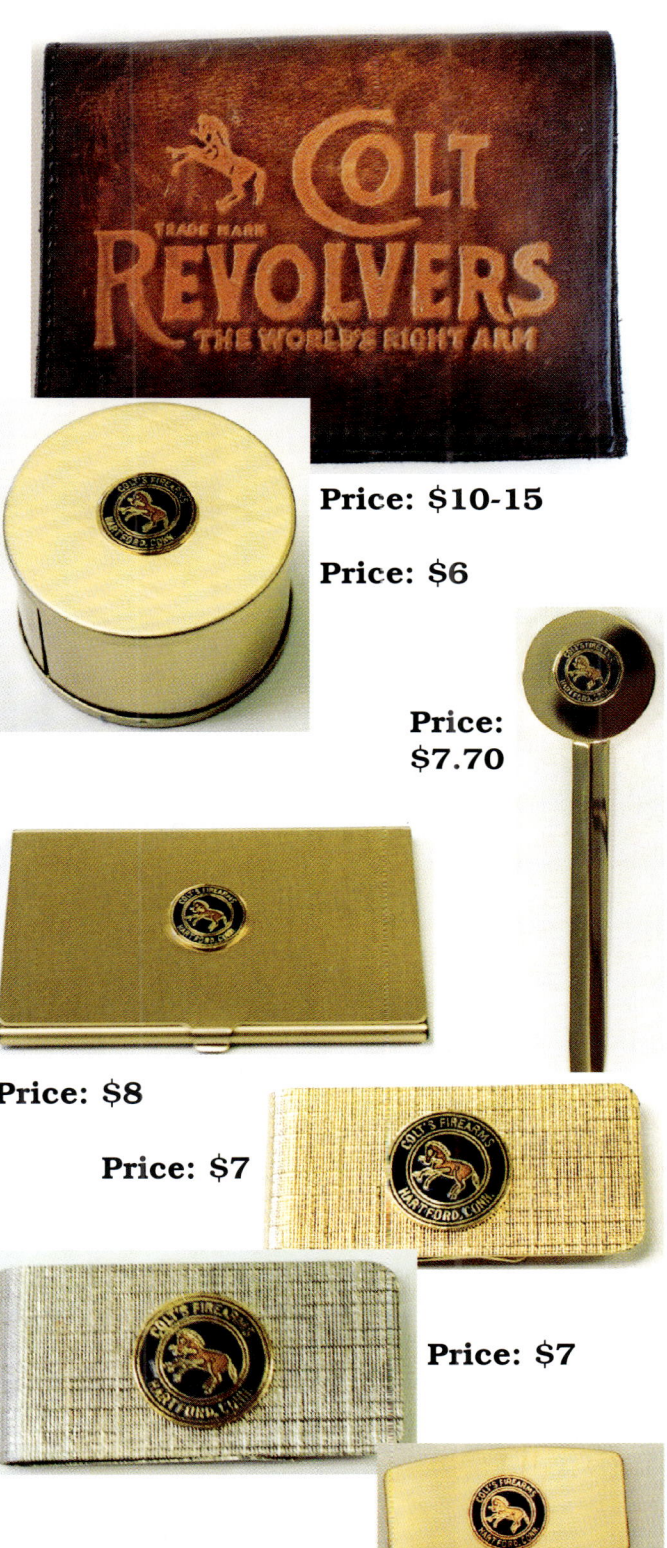

Price: $10-15

Price: $6

Price: $7.70

Price: $8

Price: $7

Price: $7

Price: $3.50

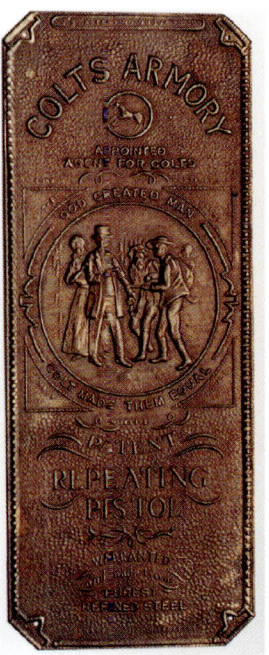 

These door push plates are most likely a fantasy item. **Price: $15-25**

Chapter 19
ASHTRAYS, LIGHTERS AND ZIPPO

Surprisingly few Colt marked smoking items are known to collectors. The plastic ColtRock tobacco accessories from the 1930s which are pictured in Chapter 3 are the most common. Modern Colt marked smoking accessories are rare. Even with the popularity of Zippo lighters as a collectible, it was not until 1996 that a set of Colt marked Zippo lighters were licensed for sale to the public.

Ashtrays

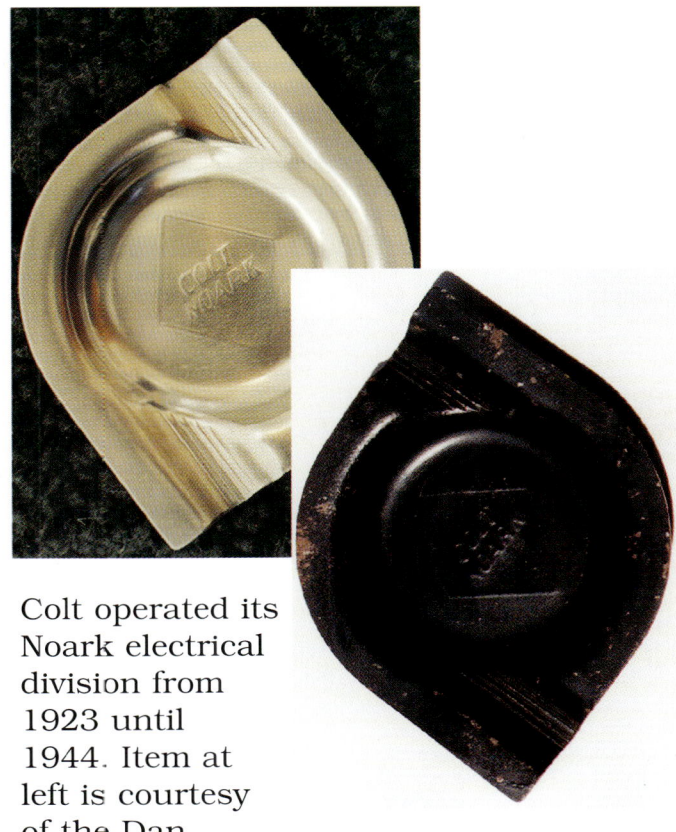

Colt operated its Noark electrical division from 1923 until 1944. Item at left is courtesy of the Dan Chesiak collection. Item at right appears courtesy of the Mike Poulin collection.
Value of each item: $350

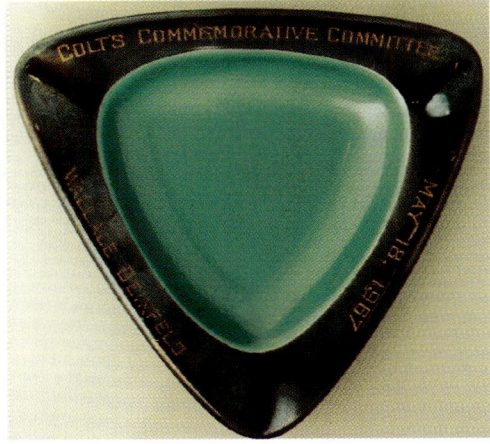

Colt organized a committee of independent dealers to advise them on the production of commemorative guns. The Colt Commemorative Advisory Committee operated from 1965 until 1976 with about five members. This sterling silver ashtray made by Reed and Barton was given to the members in 1967.
Price: $300-500

No date known. **Price: $50-100**

A Colt Industries parking sticker was used to create this ashtray known to have come from the factory.
Price: $20-50

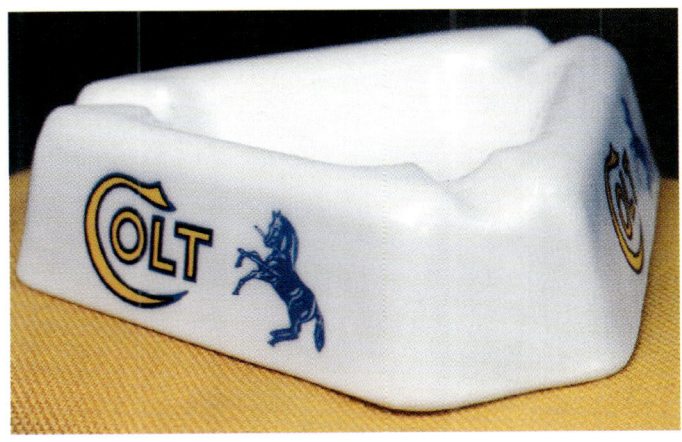

This is one of five Stan Newman prototypes. Photograph courtesy of the Stan Newman collection. **Price: $250-350**

These are fantasy non-factory ashtrays. Courtesy of the Tom Saady collection.

Lighters

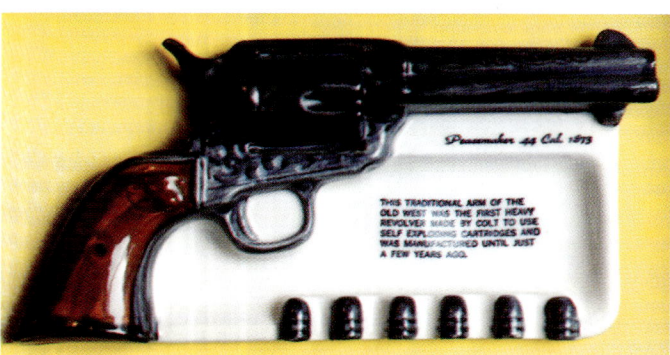

Price: $125

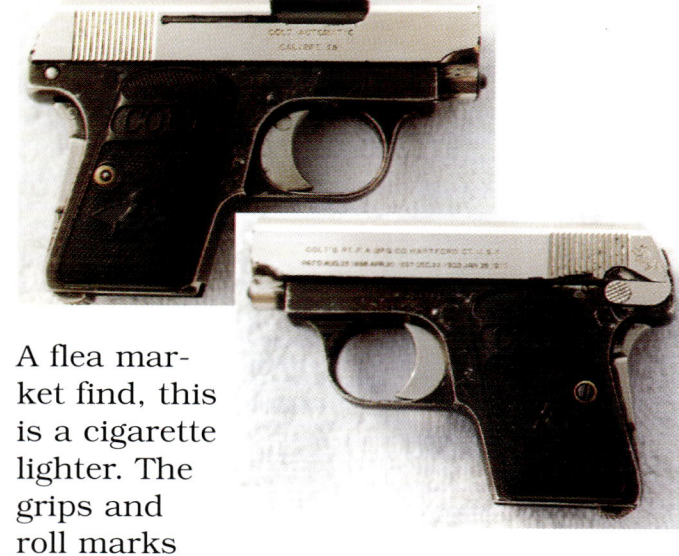

A flea market find, this is a cigarette lighter. The grips and roll marks are Colt and the serial number would indicate a possible 1914 date of manufacture. Photo courtesy of the Tom Saady collection. **Price: $100-300**

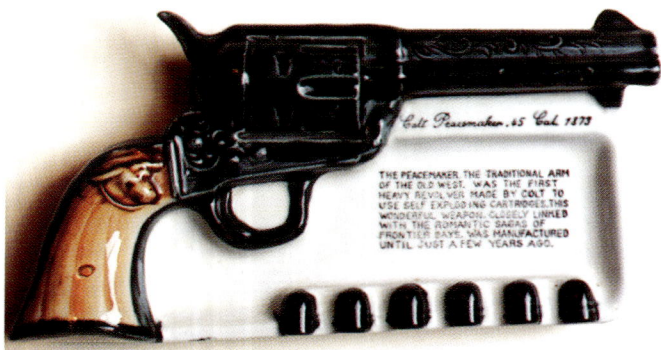

Price: $30-60

1980 Zippo. Photo courtesy of the of Stan Newman collection.
Price: $100-150

Price: $75-150

1982 Zippo.
Price: $150-350

1982 Zippo.
Price: $150-250

Set of licensed lighters sold by Zippo in 1996. **Price: $198.60**

One of five Stan Newman prototypes. Photo courtesy of the Stan Newman collection.
Price: $150-250

Matches.
Price: $10-25

Prototype gas lighter. Photo courtesy of the Willard Johnson collection.
Price: $400

Most likely a fantasy item. **Price: $5-15**

Zippo Products

These Zippo lighters have had non-factory emblems applied. **Value of each item: $20**

Non-factory lighters. Courtesy of the Ron Lough collection. **Price: $125-150**

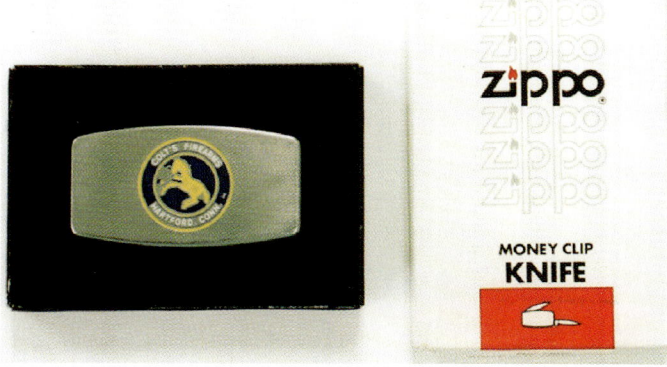

1980 money clip. **Price: $30**

1980 magnifier. **Price: $30**

1984 pocket knife. **Price: $30**

1984 golf marker and keeper. **Price: $30**

Chapter 20
STATUES

The Rampant Colt has come to symbolize Colt and is a registered trademark of the company. Sir Thomas Colte of Essex was granted his title for participating in a battle during which three horses died beneath him. This was represented in the Colte coat of arms by three running horses. Sam Colt adopted that coat of arms, and it is used even today by the Colt Custom Shop.

Early uses of a logo by Sam Colt to mark his products portrayed four horse heads, or a single running horse. How the running horse logo came to be portrayed as rampant, and who decided to add the broken spear is unclear. When Sam built his factory and his home in Hartford, a Rampant Colt appeared on top of the dome, and one was placed in a pond on the grounds of his home. The fire of 1864 destroyed the Colt on top of the factory dome. When the factory was rebuilt, a Rampant Colt, thought to be the one from the pond, reappeared on top of the dome.

Colt produced a highly detailed statue of the Rampant Colt in 1986. The pewter version was a limited edition of 5,000 signed by the sculptor Dr. Brian Rodden. Those statues are still available today in the 1996 accessories catalog. **Price: $200**

A cold-cast bronze variation was more fragile. It was difficult for Colt to ship them without damage and undamaged ones are difficult to find today. Courtesy of the Albert Brichaux collection. **Price: $350**

A gold-plated version was also produced. It was not widely distributed. It was offered for sale in the 1992 price list, but none are known to have been sold. Instead, they were used as incentive awards to those who donated $2,500 or more to the preservation fund for the original factory statue in 1993. **Price: $350-500**

A silver-plated version was produced and is known to have been used internally by Colt for awards. **Price: $250**

A black variation on marble base. Courtesy of the Albert Brichaux collection. **Price: $350-500**

A sterling silver smaller variation about which nothing is known. Courtesy of the Mike Poulin collection. **Price: $250-350**

A factory-marked horse about which nothing is known. Courtesy of the Tom Saady collection. **Price: $NEP**

The present location of this horse in unknown. It was made to replace the original horse when it was removed from atop the factory in 1990. **Price: $NEP**

Several individuals have had statues of the Rampant Colt made by various artists.

Alvin White made 50 of these horses in 1972. Two were made in sterling silver. Courtesy of the Tom Saady collection. **Price: $2,000-3,500**

Bryson Gwinnell made 14 of these horses for Philip LoPiccalo in 1993. Photo Courtesy of the Bryson Gwinnell collection. **Price: $6,000**

Leonard Francolini made this horse in 1990. **Price: $500**

John Guest had 30 of these horses made in 1994. Courtesy of the Ron Lough collection. **Price: $750**

A sterling silver variation of the Francolini horse. Photo courtesy of the Tom Saady collection. **Price: $500-800**

The CCA has three of these horses made every year as display awards for their annual show. **Price: $NEP**

Tommy Haas had one hundred of these horses made in 1969 using a mold found at the factory. Photo courtesy of the Ron Lough collection. **Price: $2,500-3,500**

A horse of unknown heritage. Courtesy of the Ron Lough collection. **Price: $NEP**

Chapter 21
TOYS

Toy cap pistols made by Hubley have now been documented as having been licensed by Colt in 1959. This makes them fair game for those collectors of Colt. A variety of other Colt marked cap pistols are still considered to be non-factory fantasy items. Company picnics and an open house have produced a few additional items that are included here under the general heading of toys.

Given out at the 1990 Family Day.

Price: $10-15

Price: $10-15

Price: $10-15

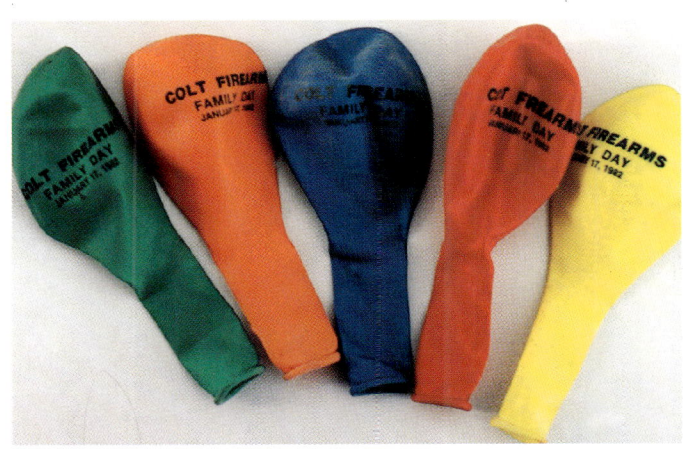

Given out at the 1982 Family Day.
Price: $5-15

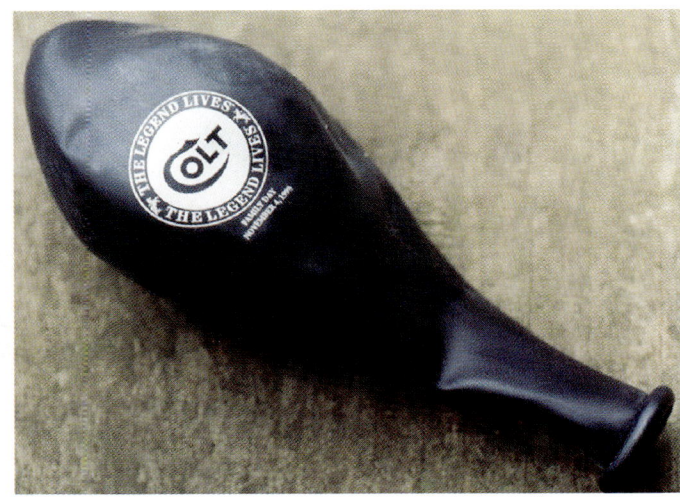

Price: $5-10

1989 picnic gift. **Price: $20**

Colt Frisbee. **Price: $20**

Price: $350-800

Price: $350-800

Colt beach ball. **Price: $20**

A marble thought to have been released through the factory.
Price: $5-10

Colt worked with a tennis pro to develop a line of rackets. As many as a dozen may have been made. Courtesy of the Ron Lough collection.

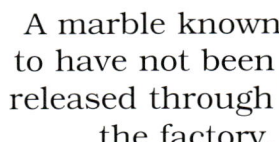

A marble known to have not been released through the factory.
Price: $2-5

Price: $180-350

A mylar balloon of unknown origin.
Price: $5-20

COLLECTOR'S NOTE: Hubley made several cap pistols in the 1940's that had a rampant Colt represented on the grip. It was not until 1959 that Colt actually licensed Hubley to produce cap pistols through a company called "Colt Firearms Toy Company" located in California. The Colt 45 Model 1860, a Detective Special and a 1911 automatic were produced. The Colt 45 Model 1860 came boxed alone, boxed with the Detective Special or a pair boxed with holsters. It was also produced as the Colt 44. The Detective Special came boxed alone or on a card that can only be considered politically incorrect today.

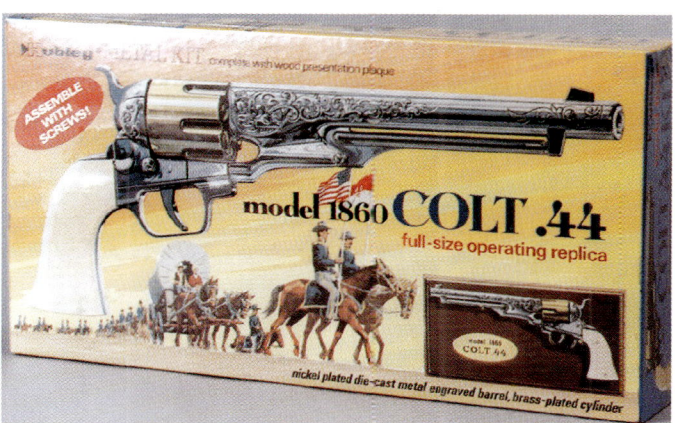

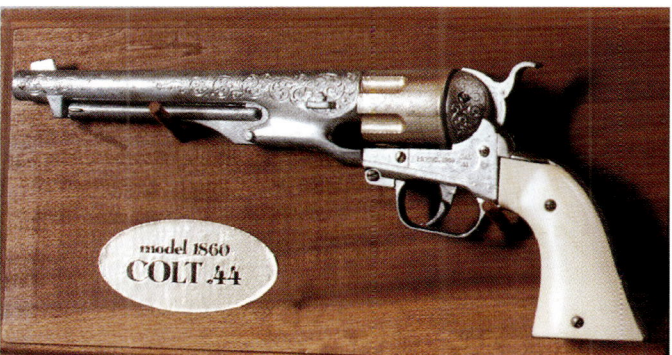

Hubley Colt 44. Courtesy of the Ron Lough collection. **Price: $200-250**

Hubley Colt 45 Model 1860. **Price: $100-250**

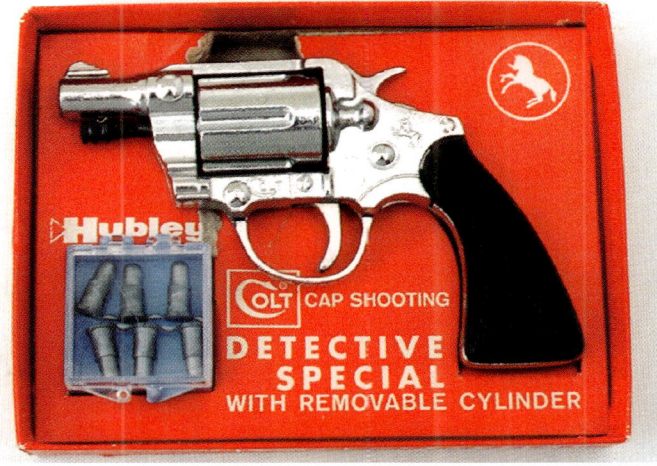

Hubley Colt Detective Special in box with bullets. **Price: $100-150**

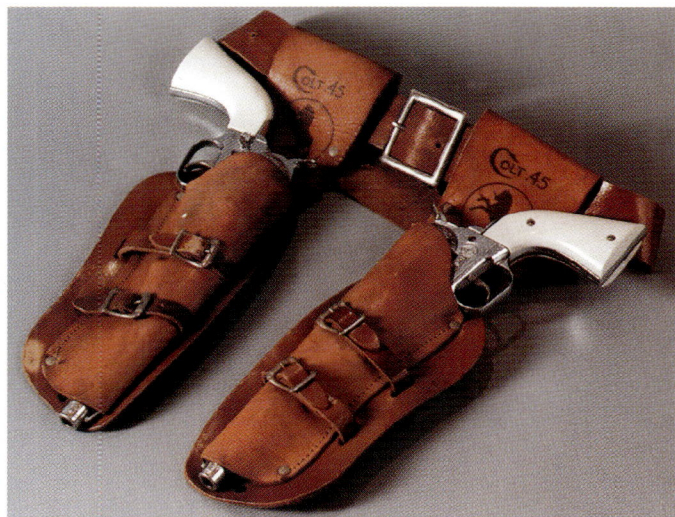

Hubley Colt 45's with Colt marked holsters. Courtesy of the Ron Lough collection. **Price: $450-500**

Hubley Colt 1911 automatic cap pistol. **Price: $80-100**

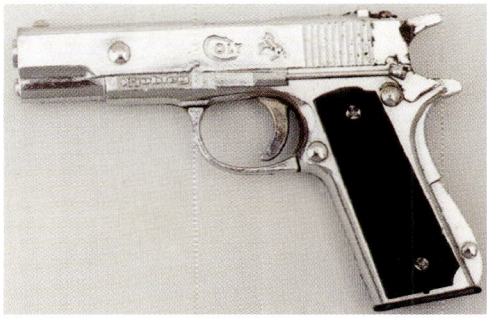

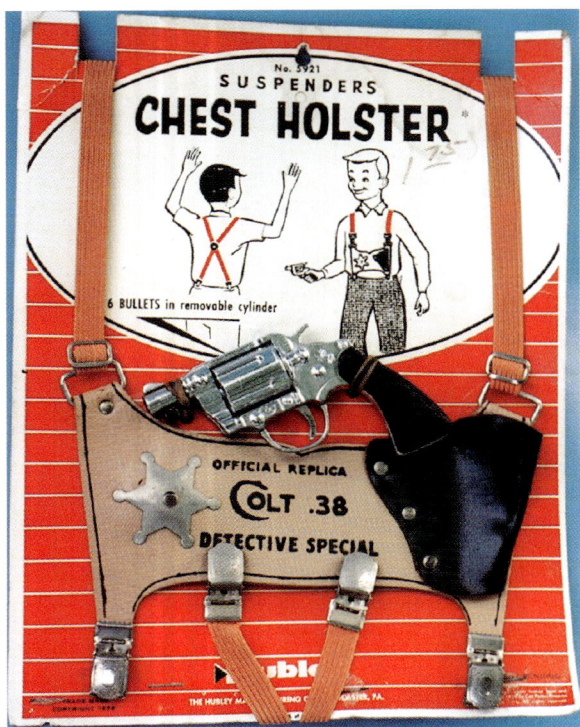

Hubley Colt Detective Special on card. Courtesy of the Tom Saady collection.
Price: $150-300

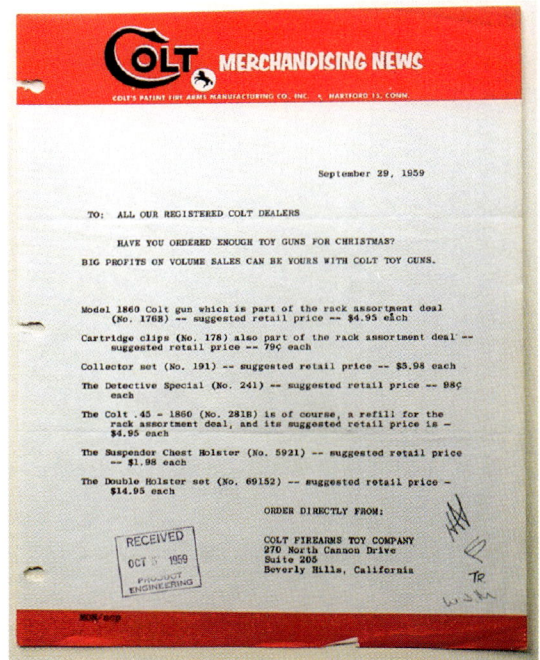

If any doubts exist, this dealer newsletter proves that Colt did indeed sell Hubley-made and Colt-marked cap pistols.
Price: $100

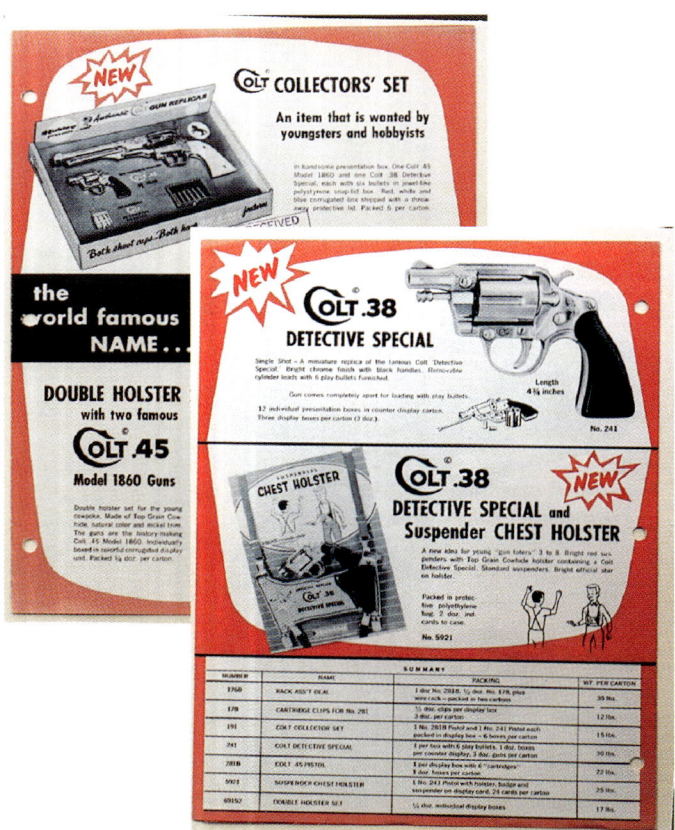

Rare brochure documenting the authenticity of the Colt licensed Hubley's.
Price: $250

Colt-marked cap and water pistols most likely having no relationship to the Colt company. Courtesy of the Ron Lough collection. **top $200-250, middle $80-150, bottom $40-50**

Price: $100-150

Price: $100-150

Price: $50-75

Another non-Colt toy pistol. Courtesy of the Wayne Becicka collection. **Price: $100-150**

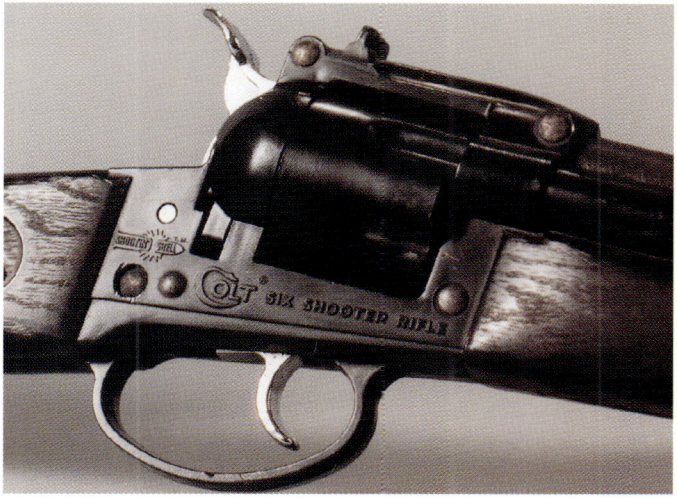

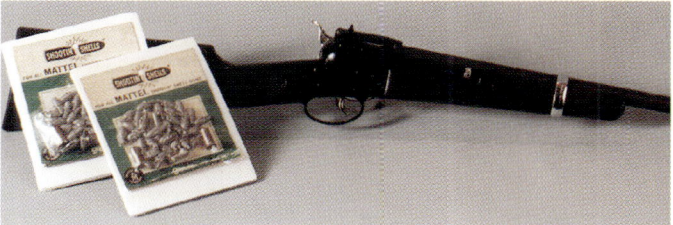

A Colt marked toy rifle made by Mattel with no known official connection to the Colt company. Courtesy of the Ron Lough collection. **Price: $175-200**

Another unofficial Colt-marked toy. Courtesy of the Ron Lough collection. **Price: $50-100**

Plastic model kits that have to be assembled. Courtesy of the Ron Lough collection.

Price: $50-100

Price: $100-150

Cap pistol patented in 1890 and marked "Colt." Courtesy of the Ron Lough collection. **Price: $80-150**

Made by Hubley in 1940. Courtesy of the Ron Lough collection. **Price: $75-100**

A Colt-marked toy dart pistol. Courtesy of the Ron Lough collection. **Price: $25-50**

A solid prop pistol or toy. **Price: $35-50**

In 1995, a number of Korean-made die cast replicas of the Colt military rifles were sold.

M60 L.M.G. toy replica. **Price: $40**

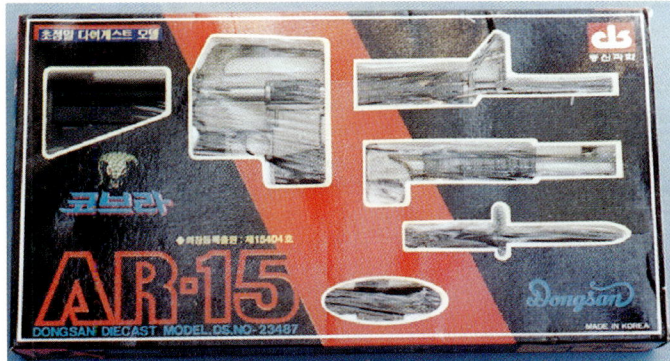

AR-15 toy replica. **Price: $25**

M203 toy replica. **Price: $25**

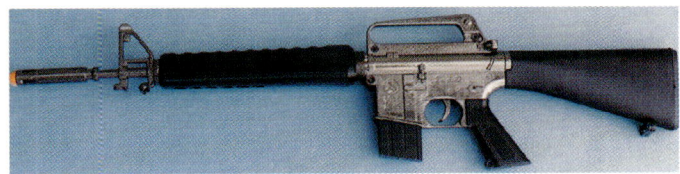

M16A1 toy replica. **Price: $20**

Chapter 22
BANNERS

Colt collectors generally aspire to own a factory banner until they realize they are too big to display. The smaller banners are, therefore, more highly prized. Banners are known to have been used at the factory during WWII and possibly as early as the 1920s.

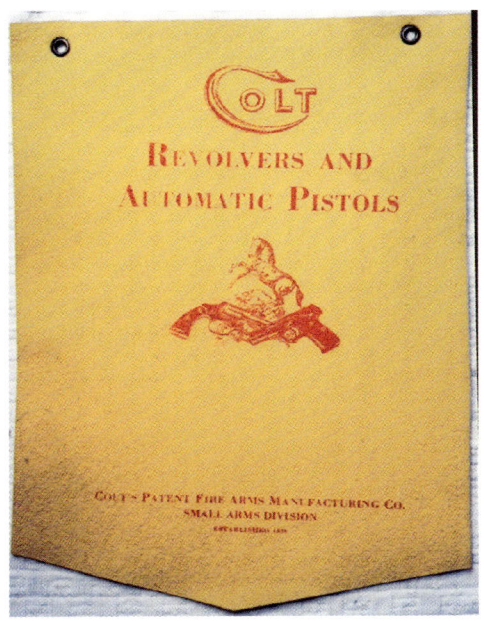

An early felt banner. The logo was used on catalogs from 1922 to 1928. Courtesy of the Tom Saady collectioon.
Price: $100-250

Most likely from the 1960s.
Price:$150- 250

Most likely from the 1970s.
Price: $150-200

From 1984 and 1985. **Price: $100-150**

From 1989 and 1990. **Price: $100-150**

From 1991 and 1992. **Price: $100-150**

From 1992. **Price: $250-350**

From 1996. **Price: $100-150**

Cimarron. **Price: $50-150**

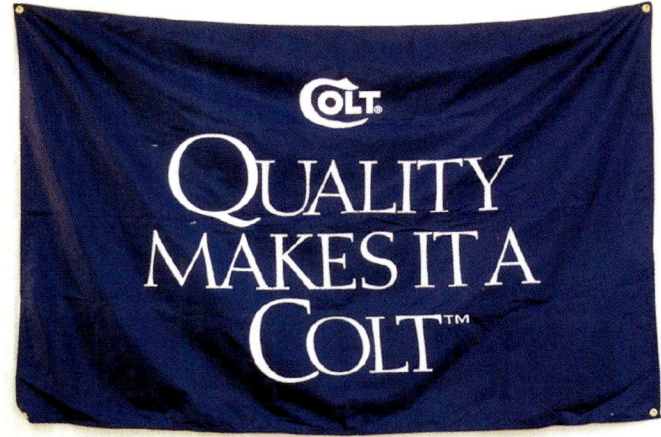
From 1993 to 1996. **Price: $100-150**

1995 and 1996. **Price: $100-150**

1995. One of two made. **Price: $250**

1995. One of two made. **Price: $250**

From 1990s. **Price: $75-150**

Chapter 23
ARCHERY

Colt operated an archery division from 1958 until 1967. Colt, under the advisement of champions, developed a line of archery products. Employees at Colt set up an indoor range at the factory. It was a popular winter activity when the outdoor pistol range was covered with snow. Colt sponsored two indoor archery championships, the first in 1965 in Las Vegas and the second in Connecticut in 1966.

The archery patches, pictured previously, are the most desired of Colt archery memorabilia. The most common collectibles are the bows, arrows, quivers, gloves and bow strings. A total of 15 different bows and as many as 15 different arrows were made. A dealer fletching kit and notching points are also known.

Less common and harder to find are paper items such as catalogs, price lists, and a 1961 press kit. Colt released 20 different advertisements featuring its archery line, yet, copies and broadsheets are scarce. One counter card is known.

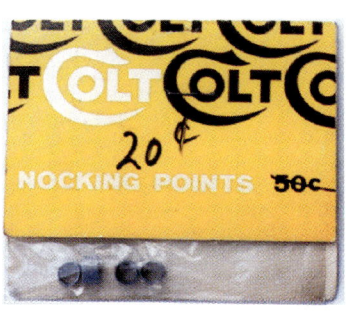

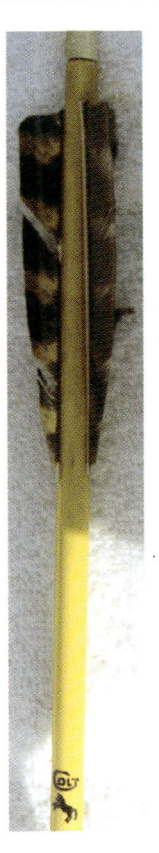

Archery advertisements. **Price: $20-30**

1961 archery press kit. Courtesy of the Tom Saady collection. **Price: $100-200**

Bow strings. **Price: $15-30**

Archery price list. **Price: $10-20**

Nocking points. **Price: $15-25**

Archery counter card. **Price: $25-50**

Quiver. Photo courtesy of the Tom Saady collection. **Price: $75-125**

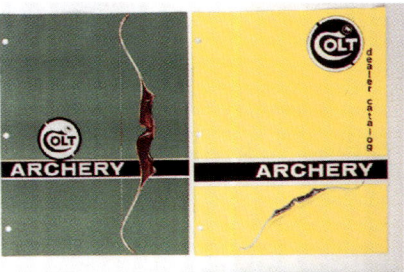

Archery catalogs. **Price: $25-50**

Double logo marked arrow. Photo courtesy of the Tom Saady Collection. **Price: $40**

Other archery products. Photo courtesy of the Tom Saady Collection. **Price: $10-40**

Archery products. Courtesy of the Ron Lough collection.
Price: bows $200-300; arrows $40 each; quiver $75-125

Chapter 24
OTHER COLT COMPANIES

There are a number of companies having the name Colt that are not related to the company that Sam Colt founded. A beer company and a football team are rarely confused with our Colt. Nameplates from the car, however, have been seen at gun shows. More confusing are those companies that may have been founded or are owned by a Colt. Sam was the great, great, great, grandson of the John Colt who immigrated to the United States in 1633. There are currently in the U.S just over 400 families with the name Colt. Many, if not all, can probably trace their ancestry back to that first John Colt.

Any company or product of a company owned by such a Colt could claim to be related to Sam by virtue of common ancestry. The most confusing of all these companies is that of J.B. Colt & Company Manufacturers and J.B. Colt Co. This company manufactured acetylene gas generators and lamps.

James Bennett Colt, born in 1842, was Sam Colt's fifth cousin once removed. He died in 1906. He started a business selling "notions" in 1873. In 1884, he incorporated as J.B. Colt & Co. Manufacturers and in 1885 he began selling "Magic Lanterns." In 1892, it was discovered that calcium carbide when placed in water would provide a cheap source of acetylene gas. Acetylene gas burned cleaner and brighter than coal gas, kerosene or tallow candles. Electricity was new and not widely available. In 1893, J.B. Colt began manufacturing and distributing the Criterion brand of whole house acetylene gas generators and lamps. The company incorporated as J.B. Colt Co. with Charles Goodyear as president in 1900. J.B. Colt was no longer listed as part of the company.

The company continued until it was bought out by Air Linde Products Co., which produced items under that trademark until 1945. The trademark of the J.B. Colt Company, a distinctive round-headed and banner-tailed representation of Colt, easily allows the identification of items produced by this company. The most common collectibles are gas lamps and a trivet. The trivet is actually a base for an acetylene gas heated iron sold by the company. The Colt firearms company, incorrectly thinking they were reproducing a piece of their history, issued a "reproduction" of the trivet. Thus the "reproduction" is a true "Colt" collectible and the originals are not.

Sales notebook showing the distinctive J.B. Colt logo. Courtesy of the Tom Saady collection.
Price: $250

J.B. Colt catalog. Courtesy of the Tom Saady collection.

Price: $150

Price: $50-100

Price: $50-100

J.B. Colt sign photographed in a restaurant somewhere in Houston. Photo courtesy of Anne-Marie Green. **Price: $NEP**

J.B. Colt lighting and cooking. Courtesy of the Ron Lough collection.
Price: $250-350

A J.B. Colt pipe case. Courtesy of the Ron Lough collection. **Price: $1,500**

Colt gas lamp. Courtesy of the Ron Lough collection. **Price: $800**

J. B. Colt logo on a gas lamp. Courtesy of the Ron Lough collection. **Price: $350-700**

Original J.B. Colt trivet. Courtesy of the Ron Lough collection. **Price: $10-50**

1982 Colt firearms trivet. Courtesy of the Dan Chesiak collection. **Price: $20-50**

J.B. Colt acetylene gas generator. Photos courtesy of the Ron Lough collection. **Price: $2,500**

An acetylene gas iron. Courtesy of the Wayne Becicka collection. **Price: $300-400**

COLLECTOR'S NOTE: The Colt Clamp Company has operated in Batavia, NY, since 1881, making clamps and car jacks. Originally known as the Batavia Clamp Co., the company manufactured a clamp based upon the patent of Alva M. Colt. In 1973, they took the name Colt Clamp Co., even though many of their early products were labeled as Colt.

It is not known if this hatchet was used at the Colt factory or was made by some company with the name Colt. Courtesy of the Ron Lough collection. **Price: $200-300**

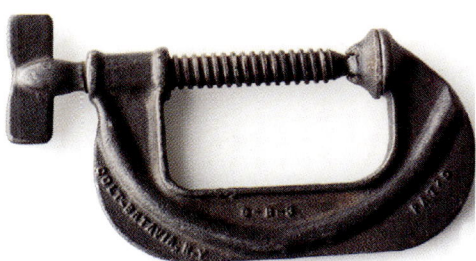

Courtesy of the Ron Lough collection. **Price: $10-30**

Lighter for J.B. Colt gas lamps. Courtesy of the Ron Lough collection. **Price: $50-250**

A variety of fire nozzles are known bearing the word Colt.

The Colt Co. of Nashville, TN, starting making candy in 1984. The company was started by Mackenzie Colt, the stage name for one of the Hee-Haw Honeys. Courtesy of the Ron Lough collection. **Price: $1**

They are known to be present on a 1938 fire truck, however, the relationship to Sam Colt's company has not been established. Courtesy of the Ron Lough collection. **Price: $250-300**

Jeff Faintaich had this chocolate made as a Christmas gift for his friends. **Price: $NEP**

Logo of the car called Colt. **Price: $5-15**

From top to bottom one never knows where the word Colt will show up. The two bottom items are courtesy of the Ron Lough collection.
Price: $15

Nothing is known about this box. Courtesy of the Ron Lough collection.
Price: $50-100

Price: $15

Some other Colt-marked products that have no connection to the company that Sam Colt started. Courtesy of the Ron Lough collection.

Price: $150

Price: $150

Price: $250-300

Price: $25-50

Until recently, there was no connection between the NFL football team and the arms maker of the same name. However, in 1996, the Southeastern regional sales manager, Mr. David Ridley promoted a 30-day "first and ten" sales program. Colt sponsored football celebrities to autograph sessions at participating Colt dealers. The individual selling the most guns during the 30 day period was awarded a helmet autographed by Jim Harbaugh, number 4 of the Indianapolis Colts. Colt also sponsored Greg Blanche of the Colts to sign autographs at the 1997 Shot Show.
Price: $NEP

Price: $25